T0341105

Leadership Strategies
in the Age of Big Data,
Algorithms, and Analytics

Leadership Strategies in the Age of Big Data, Algorithms, and Analytics

NORTON PALEY

CRC Press
Taylor & Francis Group
Boca Raton London New York

CRC Press is an imprint of the
Taylor & Francis Group, an **informa** business

A PRODUCTIVITY PRESS BOOK

CRC Press
Taylor & Francis Group
6000 Broken Sound Parkway NW, Suite 300
Boca Raton, FL 33487-2742

© 2017 by Norton Paley
CRC Press is an imprint of Taylor & Francis Group, an Informa business

No claim to original U.S. Government works

Printed on acid-free paper
Version Date: 20170127

International Standard Book Number-13: 978-1-4987-6414-8 (Hardback)

This book contains information obtained from authentic and highly regarded sources. Reasonable efforts have been made to publish reliable data and information, but the author and publisher cannot assume responsibility for the validity of all materials or the consequences of their use. The authors and publishers have attempted to trace the copyright holders of all material reproduced in this publication and apologize to copyright holders if permission to publish in this form has not been obtained. If any copyright material has not been acknowledged please write and let us know so we may rectify in any future reprint.

Except as permitted under U.S. Copyright Law, no part of this book may be reprinted, reproduced, transmitted, or utilized in any form by any electronic, mechanical, or other means, now known or hereafter invented, including photocopying, microfilming, and recording, or in any information storage or retrieval system, without written permission from the publishers.

For permission to photocopy or use material electronically from this work, please access www.copyright .com (http://www.copyright.com/) or contact the Copyright Clearance Center, Inc. (CCC), 222 Rosewood Drive, Danvers, MA 01923, 978-750-8400. CCC is a not-for-profit organization that provides licenses and registration for a variety of users. For organizations that have been granted a photocopy license by the CCC, a separate system of payment has been arranged.

Trademark Notice: Product or corporate names may be trademarks or registered trademarks, and are used only for identification and explanation without intent to infringe.

Library of Congress Cataloging-in-Publication Data

Names: Paley, Norton, author.
Title: Leadership strategies in the age of big data, algorithms, and analytics / Norton Paley.
Description: Boca Raton, FL : CRC Press, 2017.
Identifiers: LCCN 2016035603 | ISBN 9781498764148 (hardback : alk. paper)
Subjects: LCSH: Strategic planning. | Leadership. | Management--Statistical methods. | Big data.
Classification: LCC HD30.28 .P2853 2017 | DDC 658.4/092--dc23
LC record available at https://lccn.loc.gov/2016035603

Visit the Taylor & Francis Web site at
http://www.taylorandfrancis.com

and the CRC Press Web site at
http://www.crcpress.com

To the next generation:

Zeke, Natalia, Isaiah

Contents

Introduction xv

SECTION I   Digital Technology

Chapter 1   Developing Effective Leadership: The Human
Interface with Big Data, Algorithms, and Analytics 3

Leading Your Staff and Organization for the Digital Age 7
Digital Technology 7
Competitive Strategy 9
Corporate Culture 10
Organizational Structure 11
Physical 11
Psychological 13
Strategic Business Plan 15
Characteristics of a Successful Leader 17
Levels of Leadership 18
Direct Leadership 18
Organizational Leadership 19
Strategic Leadership 19

Chapter 2   Integrating Business Intelligence and Security
with Competitive Strategy 23

Managing Business Intelligence 24
Managing Data Security 26
The People Part of Intelligence 28
Unintentional Agents 29
Competitors' Agents 30
Double Agents 30
Broadcasting Agents 31
Credible Agents 31

Where Your Data Resides 32

Customers 33

Intermediaries 34

Competitors 34

Government/Environment 35

Internal Sources 36

Where Your Data Applies 36

Internal Planning 37

Organizational Procedures and Processes 38

Competitive Strategy 39

Competitive Problems 39

Competitor's Performance 40

Your Company's Performance 40

Chapter 3   Neutralizing a Competitor and Creating
a Competitive Advantage 43

Neutralizing a Competitor 49

Weaken the Rival 49

Prepare Successive Campaigns 51

Reduce the Competitor's Effectiveness 52

Make the Campaign Costlier for the Rival 54

Wear Down the Competitor 54

Neutralization Plan 57

SECTION II   Competitive Strategy

Chapter 4   Apply Analytics to Concentrate at Decisive Points 63

Origins of Strategy 64

Strategy Applications 68

Concentration 68

Guidelines to Developing and Monitoring
Concentration 70

What Lessons Emerge from the Alibaba Case? 72

Strategy Applications for the Small and Midsize
Organizations 73

Step 1: Establish a Vision 74

Step 2: Select, Monitor, and Concentrate 75

Step 3: Sustain Innovation 75
Step 4: Deliver Growth 80

Chapter 5 Initiate Speed to Maintain a Digital Advantage 83

Market, Competitive, and Corporate Conditions
Related to Speed 85
Implementing Speed 88
Align Big Data with the Corporate Culture.................... 88
Require Managers at All Levels to Submit Proposals
Based on Data Analytics...89
Reduce the Chain of Command and Increase
the Speed of Communications..89
Maintain Reliable Market Intelligence 90
Uphold Your Indispensable Role as a Leader.................... 90
Barriers to Speed...91
No Confidence by Employees in Their Leader's
Ability to Make Accurate Decisions 93
Ineffectual Support from Senior Management.................94
Confrontations among Line Managers
about Objectives, Priorities, and Strategies......................94
A Highly Conservative and Plodding Corporate
Culture Places a Drag on Speed 95
Lack of Urgency in Developing New Products
to Deal with Short Product Life Cycles..............................95
Fear of Hardline Competitors Can Damage Morale
and Suspend Plans 96
Millennials of the Digital Age.. 96
Maslow's Hierarchy of Needs...97
Herzberg's Motivation-Hygiene Theory 98
McGregor's XY Theory...98
Speed: A Core Rule of Strategy 101

Chapter 6 Activate Indirect Maneuver to Create Surprise 103

Emotions...107
Anxiety...109
Frustration 109
Stress 110
Fear 110

Activating an Indirect Maneuver 112
  Thinking Strategically 112
  Destabilizing the Competitor 116

SECTION III   Corporate Culture

Chapter 7 Align Big Data with the Corporate Culture 125

Defining Corporate Culture 126
Attributes of a Healthy Corporate Culture 128
  Beliefs and Values 128
  Employee Treatment and Expectations 129
Developing a Cultural Profile 133
Aligning Big Data with the Corporate Culture 136

Chapter 8 Apply Offensive and Defensive Strategies 143

Advantages and Disadvantages of Defense 145
Relationship between Offense and Defense 147
Applying Offensive and Defensive Strategies 149
  Waiting 150
  Blocking 152
  Moving to the Offensive 153
How Offensive Campaigns Can Fail 156

SECTION IV   Organizational Structure

Chapter 9 Evolution of the Modern Organization 161

Evolution of the Modern Organization 163
  Frederick Taylor 163
  Human Relations School 164
Giants of Industry 165
  John D. Rockefeller 166
  Henry Ford 166
  Alfred P. Sloan 167
Organizational Thinkings and Strategists 168
  The Business–Military Connection 169

Organizations: A Panoramic Overview 171
    The 1950s...171
    The 1960s...172
    The 1970s...172
    The 1980s...174
    The 1990s...175
    The 2000s 176
The Age of the Digital Organization...................................177

Chapter 10 Activate an Agile Organization.................................... 179

Agility Links to Preparedness...180
Agility Leads to Effective Performance 183
    Quick to Mobilize 183
    Nimble...184
    Collaborative 184
    Easy to Get Things Done 185
    Responsive...187
    Free Flow of Information......................................187
    Quick Decision Making..188
    Empowered to Act 189
    Resilient...190
    Learning from Failures 190

SECTION V Strategic Business Planning

Chapter 11 Leadership and the Strategic Business Plan................. 197

Components of a Strategic Business Plan 199
Level 1: Strategic 200
    Strategic Direction or Vision................................200
    Objectives..204
    Strategies 207
    Portfolio of Products and Services 208
Level 2: Tactical...211
    Situation Analysis 212
        Historic Performance 212
        Competitor Analysis.......................................213
        Market Background...213

Market Opportunities 214
    Present Markets 214
    Targets of Opportunity 215
Objectives 215
    Assumptions 215
    Primary Objectives 216
    Functional Objectives 216
Strategies and Tactics 218
Financial Controls and Budgets 219

Chapter 12 Using Segmentation to Engage Customers
    and Neutralize Competitors 223

Utilizing the Energy of Digital Marketing 224
    Understand Customers 224
    Apply Technology 225
    Monitor Systems 226
    Measure Success 226
Buyer Behavior 227
Employing the Power of Segmentation 229
    What Does a Decisive Point or Segment Look Like? 230
Advanced Techniques for Selecting a Market Segment 231
    Natural Markets 232
    Leading-Edge Markets 233
    Key Markets 233
    Linked Markets 234
    Central Markets 235
    Challenging Markets 235
    Difficult Markets 236
    Encircled Markets 236
Summary 237

Chapter 13 Leadership at the Culminating Point
    of a Competitive Campaign 239

Culminating Point: Applications 241
Building Morale 247
    Morale Interfaces with Innovation 249
    Relationship of Morale with Digital Technology 251
Summary 254

Appendix: A Model Program for an Internal Communications
Network... 257

References.. 269

Index.. 271

About the Author... 283

Introduction

If you went to bed last night as an industrial company, you're going to wake up this morning as a software and analytics company.

Jeffrey Immelt
Chairman and CEO, General Electric Co.

That transformative comment translates to such marketable capabilities as GE offering customers predictive maintenance services for Internet-connected industrial equipment, ranging from medical equipment to jet engines. GE's sensors collect and analyze essential data. As problems are detected, a robot sends a report to an individual wearing smart eyeglasses where step-by-step repair instructions are downloaded from a cloud database.

The endpoint: Big data, sophisticated analytics, and creative algorithms help GE's customers perform predictive maintenance to reduce downtime, assist in developing additional user applications, and drive overall higher operational efficiencies, all of which contribute to GE maintaining a leading-edge competitive advantage.

IBM is also immersed in data analytics, and more specifically in the Internet of things. It provides services to aid companies in such specialized areas as retailing by providing weather data to guide business decisions for adjusting store merchandising based on forecasts over a specific 48-hour period. Its technology applications also apply to a variety of industries, for instance, auto insurance and energy companies, to target new markets for growth.

The endpoint: Big data allows for more accurate segmentation of customer markets, which results in more precisely tailored products and services.

Caterpillar, along with its partner Uptake, utilizes predictive diagnostic tools to organize the enormous quantities of data spewing from sensors implanted in its bulldozers and hydraulic shovels. In turn, the data becomes meaningful information that its customers use to detect potential maintenance issues before breakdowns occur. As a result, downtime is minimized, efficiency is improved, productivity increases, and profitability soars.

The endpoint: The data analytics generated from these efforts lead to more productive joint projects that create closer relationships with Caterpillar's product users. In turn, these ventures strengthen its competitive strategy.

Then, there are such high-profile firms as Burberry, Home Depot, Uber, Zipcar, Capital One Bank, Nordstrom, Walmart, and Walgreens that also use algorithms and analytics to combine transaction data across a number of businesses or channels. Doing so allows them to accurately document how consumers engage with websites or decide between shopping online or in stores.

The endpoint: Observing such patterns of behavior sharpens managers' abilities to fine-tune promotional offers, optimize inventory levels by channel, and redirect spending across types of media—all of which become a basis for successfully engaging competition and fostering growth for each of those firms.

These companies made significant commitments to the digital age, or were in the process of making the transition. Other companies fed the transition as well with a variety of products and programs, such as PayPal, Square, Stripe, and Cisco Systems.

Within that maelstrom of activity, other far-thinking organizations, including Google, Facebook, and Amazon, which pioneered digitally mined businesses, continue their innovative approaches by making day-by-day progress as they explore machine-to-machine communications, improved platforms for employing big data using artificial intelligence, and advances in the Internet of things with its ever-growing capability to take on complex tasks.*

Yet within these highly publicized and fast-moving developments not all organizations fully internalized the necessity for shifting into the digital age. Instead, they often gave the procrastinating comment of "It's something we'll have to look into." At times, that approach turned into knee-jerk actions that resulted in too little, too late.

However, if not too late, those surviving companies were often pushed into change when jolted by a collapse in sales or fallen market share, or more noticeably, when obscure start-ups appeared from nowhere and began taking away key customers. Examined more closely, these new competitors

---

* A McKinsey & Co. report indicates that the Internet of things could have up to an $11 trillion impact on the global economy by 2025. That enormous number expands the definition of Internet of things to mean everything and everybody connected to everything and everybody else, and generating massive quantities of data in the process.

were relying on big data and algorithms to understand who buys what, when, and why. Guided by data analytics, they confidently moved rapidly with the appropriate strategies to decisively attack key market segments.

In reality, many of the digital processes consuming the attention of executives have been around for more than a decade, but several of the original Internet innovators suffered with the dot-com crash. Now the urgency is more pronounced as the digital technologies move forward with greater speed, refinement, and accuracy. And as never before, huge amounts of data are readily accessible from internal and external sources to feed the systems.

Internal data flows in the course of doing everyday business from such areas as call center recordings, meeting memos, reports, and client notes. That includes data from security cameras, traffic monitoring, and other electronic devices.

External sources of additional data come from various touch points along the supply chain or from government sources. And then there are the voluminous quantities of data from the Internet, customer tweets, social network postings, YouTube, and numerous photo sites.

As a way for you to internalize the full scope of data as a remarkable resource of knowledge to be perpetuated, mined, and disseminated, the following two categories provide organization and structure: *explicit knowledge* and *tacit knowledge*.

EXPLICIT KNOWLEDGE

This category forms your internal databases, which include records, manuals, documents, and the raw numbers in spreadsheets. Then, there is the output from sophisticated analytics that incorporates data from a variety of the above-cited customer touch points, proprietary big data, and public sources of open data.

TACIT KNOWLEDGE

This more subtle area of knowledge generally resides in the minds of individuals who have accumulated it through discovery, experience, intuition, or numerous interactions with others. Since tacit knowledge tends to be less structured, it cannot always be put on paper. Instead, it is transferred indirectly through conversation, anecdotes, observation, or other types of informal interchanges.

Tacit knowledge can originate in a variety of patterns, such as the impressions, feelings, and insights of a sales rep returning from a visit with a key customer. Or it can start with an engineer making an offhand comment about a gestating idea to an associate in a casual setting over lunch.

For many organizations, explicit knowledge is tangible and available on a widespread basis, or minimally, it is accessible to several layers of personnel. On the other hand, tacit knowledge is somewhat unbounded and tends to be used by individuals who need to protect what they know as a personal defense or a power barrier. It is this form of knowledge that is often lost to others, if not captured, organized, and available.

Yet if both categories of knowledge were blended into a disciplined business system built around big data, algorithms, and analytics, it would function as a balanced, multidisciplinary framework for capturing, sharing, and spewing forth immensely valuable intelligence with the result of making more accurate decisions.

To break through the barriers that could prevent aligning such a system with the culture of your firm means establishing a level of trust up and down the organization. It also means instilling a spirit of teamwork to make the digital tools work to the full benefit of the organization.

You would then be in a far more advantageous position to justify (or recommend to a management committee) allocating funds for rolling out a new product or service, adopting a cutting-edge technology, or probing an evolving market segment. Perhaps too, in the context of this book, you would further hone your leadership skills to sustain a competitive edge.

The responsibility for big data can reside with any number of individuals, depending on the size of your company and the level of priority given to the project. The range of titles includes company librarian, information technology (IT) manager, market research manager, chief information officer, and the evolving duties of the data scientist who creates or manages systems to connect employees with the knowledge they need.

In parallel with any of those titles, however, your central responsibility is to make tangible use of the immense fund of knowledge flowing from big data. That, in part, is what living in the digital age is all about. It is anchored to the most fundamental requirements for all decision making when developing competitive strategies: obtain accurate information and refine it into usable intelligence.*

Expressed another way, the aim is to make better-informed decisions, discover hidden insights about customers' and competitors' behaviors, and develop winning strategies. That need has always been paramount. Now, better tools are available to handle the task.

Thus, armed with organized and integrated intelligence, the uncertain variable is your *readiness* to apply the mass of knowledge to market advantage. Readiness in this context incorporates such vital attributes as your personality and experience. These include the deeply embedded human qualities of ambition, courage, tenacity, and determination, which are essential to taking meaningful action.

Thus, the paradox!

What if the straightforward facts generated by data analytics across digital networks defy what your experience, intuition, and gut feel tell you as you look at market conditions through your own eyes? Now, you face the proverbial horns of a dilemma about deciding which path to take.

Part of that quandary is determining how the selected pathway would impact your day-to-day operations, what effect it would have on employee morale and behavior, and would it align with your corporate culture? As one C-suite executive succinctly remarked, "Remember the human interface or all this data means nothing."

The following company example illustrates the impact of such a dilemma and the influence of the human interface as one leader dealt with digital age technology.

Indra Nooyi, CEO of PepsiCo, faced monumental, and at times confusing, challenges in managing the variety of its product lines, its markets, and diversity of its customers she oversees. The company's formidable market research revealed an inconsistency: consumers wanted healthier fare. Yet at the same time, they were devouring such products as its Lay's chips, which was contributing mightily to PepsiCo's high-growth snacks division. Then, there was its hugely successful big soda brand, Mountain Dew, a highly sugary and acidic drink that was raking in record sales and also adding substantially to PepsiCo's overall performance.

---

* The ancient Chinese strategist Sun Tzu summed up the purpose of accurate intelligence more than 2500 years ago (simply substitute *enemy* with *competitor*): "Know the enemy and know yourself; in a hundred battles you will never be in peril. When you are ignorant of the enemy, but know yourself, your chances of winning or losing are equal. If ignorant both of your enemy and of yourself, you are certain in every battle to be in peril."

With big data documenting the trends and eating preferences, and sales metrics revealing a different story, how might these discrepancies be resolved? How should decisions be made about committing resources where data analytics and sophisticated algorithms produce outcomes contrary to actual results? In other words, where do experience, intuitive-based human judgment, and the personality traits listed above interconnect with the machine-generated facts?

Nooyi took several decisive steps: First, she took a bold strategic viewpoint that helped drive her actions by declaring that Pepsi must address "one of the world's biggest public health challenges, a challenge fundamentally linked to our industry: obesity." Subsequently, she put resources behind her proclamation by shifting from junk foods to healthier alternatives. At the same time, Nooyi vowed to improve the healthiness of Pepsi's core products by reducing the sugar content while maintaining the traditional taste experience.

Product developers experimented with new drinks that included healthy versions of old ones, such as Mountain Dew Kickstart, a fruit-flavored, lower-calorie drink, and a super-crunchy potato chip developed first on a three-dimensional printer. The company reports removing 400,000 tons of sugar from its drinks since 2006, and reducing the salt and saturated fat in Lay's and Ruffles chips.

To more readily manage change, Nooyi moved to alter Pepsi's culture. Historically, the company was a decentralized place where local managers operated without much central interference. She restructured the organization into a leaner, top-down design. As Nooyi points out, "The top needs to know all the pieces. And the top better really get into the details … to know what questions to ask." With that shift in orientation, she was able to more readily take action to develop new, healthier products and initiate change with existing products by altering their ingredients, all while providing customers with the same taste satisfaction of the original products.

In a like manner, what can you do in such a paradox? What action can you take where actual behavior is incompatible with digitally generated data? What thought processes are needed to think and act as a strategist? What are your leadership responsibilities to prepare you and your organization or group for the digital age?

The chapters in this book present ideas, processes, and techniques that you can use as operating guidelines to cope with a variety of competitive situations. These are organized around major forces that would affect your ability to successfully lead in a work environment where big data, algorithms, and analytics dominate managerial practices.

As illustrated in the following diagram, the forces of leadership shaped by digital technology consist of five sections: *digital technology, competitive strategy, corporate culture, organizational structure,* and *strategic business planning*. In turn, each section is comprised of supporting chapters.

The Five Forces of Leadership Shaped by the Digital Age

■ Digital technology

■ Competitive strategy

■ Corporate culture

■ Organizational structure

■ Strategic business planning

The Five Forces of Leadership Shaped by the Digital Age

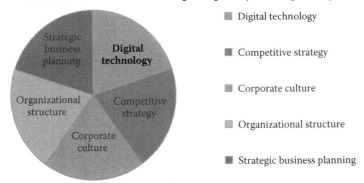

Section I

Digital Technology

There's no algorithm or formula that says technology will do X, so Y is sure to happen. Technology doesn't work on its own. It's just a tool. You are the ones who harness its power.

Eric Schmidt
*Executive chairman, Google Inc.**

---

* Excerpt from Eric Schmidt's commencement speech to students at Virginia Tech, May 2015.

1

Developing Effective Leadership: The Human Interface with Big Data, Algorithms, and Analytics

To harness the enormous power of technology is one of the key measures of your effectiveness as a leader, especially in the active environment of disruptive technologies and intense competition. Your leadership determines how successful you will be in mobilizing your staff and preparing your organization, or business unit, to operate competitively in the digital age.

As Schmidt points out, technology is just a tool and does not work on its own. From that viewpoint, your leadership (within the parameters of your responsibilities) means giving prime-time attention to the following key areas:

1. Developing a strategic business plan and committing to its overall direction, objectives, and strategies, which include dedicating a portion of the plan to opportunities and threats resulting from the output of big data

2. Encouraging your staff, through training and orientation, to think like strategists and apply the vast potential of digital technologies to the long-term growth of the enterprise

3. Aligning your corporate culture to the disruptive changes of operating in the digital age

4. Designing a responsive organizational structure that utilizes total communications to encourage speed of reaction

5. Coaching the staff in the art of strategy and honing their skills in developing defensive and offensive plans

Leading an organization, business unit, or product line can be a daunting challenge even when equipped with the seemingly convincing evidence being touted about the infallibility of big data, algorithms, and analytics. Yet, how trustworthy are these people-made algorithms?

Do they contain built-in biases that can lead to inconsistent outcomes? Is the raw data stored in your system still valid? Are the extrapolations made about customer behavior reliable enough that you can make major new product commitments? Are the outputs explicit enough to make confident decisions?

Thus far, there is sufficient proof to accept the undeniable power, sophistication, and future potential of digital technologies. Analytics can see what you cannot. You can dig beneath the surface of your data to uncover hidden possibilities. You thereby have the potential to create highly interactive relationships with your customers beyond what was previously possible.

What, then, are the issues that should concern you and which can impact your ability to lead in a digital world? Two considerations arise: First, the intimidating fact is that vigilant competitors are equally fortified with similar or superior algorithms. They may even do a better job of tracking and predicting consumer preferences with available software, such as being able to analyze millions of transactions from thousands of customers to predict trends months or years in advance.

That said, rival managers could have the edge in deploying resources to meet changing demands more rapidly than you. Further, they even may be better prepared to keep track of all of the touch points of a user or buyer in real time.

There is also the undeniable fact that the enormous potential of algorithms and analytical software is moving ahead at turbo speed, which means that alert competitors can maintain a lead in such areas as forecasting, market behavior, resource allocation, product modification, innovation, and new product development.

Second, even where technology in many situations can be the tipping point in deciding who wins the competitive race, it is more likely that effective leadership most often remains the pivotal factor. It is leadership that develops the strategies and sees that they are successfully implemented. It is leadership that harnesses the human elements of courage, decisiveness, responsibility, and accountability that are essential to achieving objectives.

Where those attributes of leadership are ingrained, you can then inspire your people to action. Then it is possible to reach new heights of performance through innovative tactics that respond to market and competitive uncertainty with speed and accuracy. Overall, those meaningful outcomes may be viewed as effective where leaders act to win: to win customers, to win market share, and to win a long-term profitable position in a marketplace—and do so before a rival can do excessive harm. If leadership fails, organizations suffer. In the broader sense, the surrounding communities in which the company operates feel the pain.

To function as a leader, then, means influencing people by providing purpose, direction, and motivation, while improving the viability of the organization. Therefore, anyone responsible for supervising people or accomplishing an organizational objective that involves committing resources is a leader. Taking this a step further, anyone who influences and motivates people to action or affects their thinking and decision making is a leader. Leadership is not only a function of position but also a function of an individual's role in the organization. The following example illustrates these points.

A. G. Lafley, CEO of Procter & Gamble, retired from the company in 2010 after an illustrious career helping to build the world's largest consumer product company. He more than doubled the company's portfolio of brands and helped turn such products as Pampers and Crest into global winners. All told, P&G's sales surged and profits quadrupled during Lafley's nine-year tenure.

However, the good times at P&G did not last after Lafley left the company. In 2013, he was persuaded to return and deal with a different kind of problem: scores of its brands were forecast to have dreary growth prospects. In part, the obstacles were due to the recession, cheaper competing brands, changing buying patterns, and an overall corporate condition whereby P&G had become too large to compete effectively in all markets. Lafley reached a culminating point where his previous strong expansive moves reverted to defending existing businesses.

To remake the company into a more competitive and profitable entity, Lafley had to shrink what he assiduously built. The plan called for dropping as many as 100 product lines, which left P&G with a more manageable portfolio of 65 leading brands, including Tide, Bounty, and Gillette, which account for almost 85% of the company's sales.

Lafley's actions of compressing his lines of products is opposite of P&G's culture. Historically, the company was bent on expanding and aggressively marketing new products that were carefully developed and thoroughly tested through a long and expensive process.

Lafley represents the flexible role of leadership, which displays the discipline expected of a CEO. His movements also demonstrate discipline and agility to pivot on events as he shifted from offense to defense, a role that is contrary to the typical mindsets of most executives. Yet Lafley knew he had to redirect P&G into an organization to fit a changing competitive battleground where rapid-moving, nimble competitors armed with algorithms and data analytics can track trends that redefine market segments as a means to secure firm footholds for revenue growth.*

Thus, in a market-driven, technology-driven, and highly competitive environment such as in the case of P&G, it is essential to work at developing a flexible managerial style. This is especially important if you expect your staff to support the objectives and strategies set out in your business plan. Anything else will come across to personnel as rigid with an inability to adapt to a changing marketplace, especially where there is an influx of offshore competitors and a torrent of changing technologies.

Consequently, if you rely on only one leadership style, you suffer the consequences of appearing unyielding. Such situations occur where projects are complex and require different leadership skills at each stage of development. For instance, products in the early phases of design, where patient testing for performance and quality dominate, require a far different leadership style of dealing with scientists, engineers, and product designers, from that of pumping up a sales force for a new product launch. Similarly, products at various stages of their life cycles—introduction, growth, maturity, decline, and phase-out—involve diverse leadership styles to correspond with the varying market and competitive conditions at each juncture.

Whole Foods, for example, built a wildly successful niche for itself by establishing a position of selling organic groceries to the masses, which brought fast growth and high profit margins to the grocery chain. Here, too, in circumstances similar to those of P&G, Whole Foods' big success did not go unnoticed by savvy competitors, notably Kroger, Costco, and Walmart. Those rivals were hungry enough to relish cashing in on the trend. The effect was that Whole Foods' growth during its high-growth day of averaging more than 20% annually from 2000 to 2008 fell to below 10% by 2014.

Cofounder of Whole Foods John Mackey found himself shifting to a high combative mode of leadership by developing plans to fend off equally

---

* Lafley retired for a second time in 2015.

aggressive competitors. One of his turnaround strategies to revive growth was to target millennials with a smaller, lower-priced chain focused on value, convenience, and technology. The question, then, was, after big data analytics clearly indicated competitive trends and slowing sales growth, did Mackey wait too long to prevent what he viewed as his company's firmly entrenched position in organic foods being upended by competitor inroads?

The essential points: Given the nuances of managing in a planning and working environment driven by algorithms and big data, how should a leader cope with the powerful forces of competition, changing customer behavioral patterns, and technology disruptions? Add to those the need to react with speed, flexibility, and bold action. These questions are addressed in the following sections as you lead for the digital age.

LEADING YOUR STAFF AND ORGANIZATION FOR THE DIGITAL AGE

Five primary forces impact your leadership role in mobilizing your staff, organization, or business unit for the digital age. These consist of digital technology, competitive strategy, corporate culture, organizational structure, and the strategic business plan. (See the five forces diagram on the chapter's opening page.)

Digital Technology

Referring again to Schmidt's comment that technology is "just a tool … you are the ones who harness its power," this first force requires you to prioritize training that informs and excites the staff to all of the tremendous possibilities existing and evolving with big data, algorithms, and analytics.

For instance, big data allows ever-narrower segmentation of markets and improves the accuracy of tailoring products and services to fit customer needs. As such, digital is a more effective way of engaging them and being able to concentrate marketing efforts with greater precision and economy.

Algorithms can track the behavior of competitors and predict with some measure of accuracy how they will respond, for example, to competitive attacks built around price, promotion, product, or new service introductions. Data analytics also aids in pinpointing competitors' vulnerabilities in ways that were not previously seen through conventional analysis. Doing so creates opportunities to move more rapidly and gain footholds for market expansion. In effect, digitization often lowers entry barriers.

As for communications and strengthening relationships in and out of the organization, the interactions among customers, suppliers, stakeholders, and employees are enhanced through digital channels, which makes content universally accessible by creative applications of graphics and video, tailoring messages for exactness, and adding social connectivity.

Thus, in your role as a leader, regardless of your level in the organization, digital technology is the game changer in leading a business in a fast-moving marketplace against start-ups that seem to come from nowhere and hit the market with major impact with a few clicks or finger swipes from sophisticated software. As such, they place increasing pressure on price and margins by reducing transaction and labor costs, all of which create an open field for other competitors to cross borders with amazing swiftness.

One organization, Sears, found a solid footing in one area of its business by using big data to become a leader as a repairer of home appliances in the United States. The venerable, and in recent years vulnerable, department store is the single largest seller of those services. Its technology center in Seattle mines data gleaned from the tens of millions of visits that Sears technicians have made to American homes over decades, so that a more effective diagnosis of an air-conditioning unit or refrigerator problem can be made before a service technician actually calls.

The system collects data on a wide variety of brands, including its own Kenmore line, so that its diagnostic technology can calculate the complexity of a repair, as well as prepare a cost and time estimate. Result: A reduction in the number of times Sears must dispatch technicians, saving the retailer time and money, creating a more favorable customer experience, and maintaining a meaningful advantage over competing repair services.

As important, from a strategic viewpoint, is that the digital advantage gives Sears a quantum leap forward in the emerging market for smart home tech and services, which fits into the organization's overall strategy to revive and reinvent itself into a technology company.

Competitive Strategy

The second force to impact your leadership role in the digital age is the application of competitive strategies. When looked at as a set of rules or principles, they are shown as *speed, concentration at a decisive point, maneuver by indirect approach*, and *bold action and shifting to the offensive*. These are covered in detail in the following chapters, but are condensed as follows:

Speed. This application is consistent with the pace of operations where big data analytics highlight opportunities that require rapid response. Unless used as a deliberate strategy of watchful waiting, rarely has an overlong, dragged-out campaign proved successful. It is exhaustion through the prolonged draining of resources that damages more companies than almost any other factor.

Concentration at a decisive point. With the huge capability of analytics to pinpoint segments of opportunity with impressive accuracy, being able to concentrate at decisive points permits targeting and deploying resources where you can gain superiority in selected areas. You thereby emerge stronger than your competitor in key segments of your choosing.

Maneuver by indirect approach. As an enduring rule, an indirect approach stands out as one of the consistently successful components of strategy. If skillfully implemented, the maneuver applies strength against a competitor's weakness, resolves customer problems with solutions that outperform those of your rivals, and achieves a psychological advantage by creating an unbalancing effect in the mind of the opposing manager.

Bold action and shifting to the offensive. All of the output of big data, algorithms, and analytics is aimed at permitting you to go forward with speed and confidence to protect existing businesses against the inroads of competitors, and to gain a foothold by expanding with fresh market opportunities. Boldness complements the above strategy principles.

There is one additional dimension to strategy: Success in most competitive situations is not the result of winning or losing in one decisive event. Rather, most encounters consist of numerous engagements, large and small, simultaneous or consecutive. Each has a specific purpose that links to the whole.

Expressed another way, in a competitive battle the outcome of a single event is never to be regarded as final. It is part of a total picture. Thus, should one campaign or competitive encounter fail, it should be considered a transient event for which a possible solution can be found at a later date through some innovative strategy, an alliance with a technology-rich organization, or some other potential breakthrough. Then, there is the realistic possibility that your rival has made an error, or has become complacent with a false sense of security, and opens a fresh new opportunity for you.

Corporate Culture

The third force impacting leadership in the digital age is corporate culture. While organizations invested in digital capabilities such as big data, analytics, and digital content management, they found it necessary to sustain a strong and flexible culture that could adapt to the psychological and physical changes needed for a successful transition. Doing so would mean that managers could then make data-empowered decisions more rapidly in responding to changing market conditions.

In contrast, a staid and unresponsive organization would tend to miss the shifts to digital technologies. If it vacillates over the competitive impact of big data, or focuses only on building market share in existing markets, then it does not have a working environment where individuals can push the boundaries into new markets with innovative products and services.

The essential point: If an organization's management shows a conscious disregard for making its culture compatible with a fast-moving digital marketplace, the company loses its competitive edge. Complacency spreads, customer focus declines, and originality dries up, all of which are extremely difficult to reverse.

A vibrant example of a spirited and robust digital culture is Google. The company describes its culture as "incredibly scrappy," which is anchored to being totally data driven. In practice, that means all proposals must be supported with finite data and less hyperbole. Another characteristic of *scrappy* is being agile, which reflects on its leaders, employees, and overall way of doing things. Thus, as the operating system and nerve center of the organization, its dynamic and adaptive culture shapes how employees think and how they react under a variety of conditions.

Another key element of Google's culture is to actively think about technology applications as a way for the company to fundamentally transform an industry. In turn, that entails clearly defining a market, inspiring people to think big about the goals of the company, and uncovering ways to change the overall direction of an industry. In effect, the process defines Google's culture to include innovation and autonomy, forward thinking, and teamwork. All of these components are viewed as essential to the DNA of Google's technology culture.

Agility also translates to being able to conduct thousands of tests and experiments a year while using only a small 1% test with each core product. Managers are able to determine if the experiment can be scaled up or quickly eliminated. They view the process as part of their test-and-learn culture.

Another famous practice that supports Google's culture is its 20% feature: employees can use 20% of their time to work on a product idea of their choosing. Originally, it was somewhat free flowing, which permitted them to think in all way-out directions. It is now somewhat modified to require employees to focus their creative time on something that would complement a core product. In turn, this effort would pyramid into a team effort when championed by an individual who "sold" the idea for others to participate.

Consequently, a positive, supportive corporate culture drives ambitious business decisions, generates customer loyalty, and ignites employee involvement in a robust work environment utilizing digital technologies. It is the cement that binds together all of the qualities and gives an organization a unique personality. Expressed another way, corporate culture combines qualities that give solidarity to the organization and forms the underpinnings for collaborative efforts. In effect, it becomes the human interface with big data, algorithms, and analytics.

Organizational Structure

The aim of an organization's structure is to create an agile and innovative work climate, which consists of two dimensions: physical and psychological.

Physical

Establishing a "lean and mean" organization has been an overriding organizational goal over the past few decades. The notion was to eliminate the layers of management and any barriers that suggested a bureaucratic format, which would impede the free flow of upward and downward information. Therefore, the intent was to deal with the timeliness of market and competitive moves that required quick responses. Those needs are still present. But it is now supported through the instantaneous forms of communication made possible by big data and reinforced by data analytics.

Thus, it is still important to realize that the primary rationale for developing an organizational structure for the digital age is to create a work climate that invites creativity and innovation that is free of cumbersome, inflexible systems and procedures. That is the reason for the current approach by organizations to establish a start-up climate.

A prime example of such an approach is Dow Chemical. Continually transforming its work climate is evidenced by how the company attempts to reinvent itself by fostering a culture that takes on the character of a start-up. Dow shifted from a traditional orientation of developing a portfolio of products to assembling a portfolio of value-added markets. That orientation is also expressed by how the organization has evolved from an inorganic chemical company, to an organic company, to a petrochemical company, to a plastics company.

From a leader's viewpoint, CEO Andrew Liveris has skillfully maneuvered the company to be at the nexus of where evolving markets and technologies intersect. And he sees his primary job as directing the thinking of his staff to seek targets of opportunity where there is the likelihood of achieving substantial breakthroughs.

In the world of digitization, Liveris has embraced the whole information technology (IT) world and challenged Dow not only as a data provider, but also as a knowledge provider. One of his big concerns is not drowning in the voluminous quantities of data. Rather, his interest is in molding the information into a usable model, so that it is not just raw IT, but knowledge.

In all, Liveris refers to the role of leadership as going through a series of reinventions, which require switching priorities as the company goes through changes. He views change as overlapping circles: Circle 1 is strategy and operations. Overlapping circle 1 is the more important one: the company's reputation, where everything that a company does is scrutinized through the world of social media. Therefore, according to Liveris, it is necessary to pivot with the constituency that wants to know more about the enterprise.

In some instances, to develop the desired climate, an organization relocates groups to remote locations that are removed from the formality and structure of the parent and gives them the freedom to start up operations as they see fit. Similarly, there is the instance of the above-mentioned Google and its approach to creating a climate for innovative thinking.

In these examples, establishing a climate means recognizing and appreciating the inherent dignity and worth of people. And even where some individuals' ideas will not succeed, their efforts are still recognized and respected. This is especially relevant when working with culturally diverse personnel with a wide range of ethnic backgrounds.

In those instances, leaders must stand aside and empower their people, give them overall direction based on the strategic business plan, delegate the necessary authority, and let them do their work.

Therefore, central to the job of leading an organization is helping subordinates grow and succeed by communicating a forward-looking strategic outlook, encouraging collaboration to cope with disruptive change, and providing counseling and training to get the staff to "create a customer"* and acquire the art of strategy to successfully compete against rivals.

Psychological

The psychological phase of leading a digital organization leans heavily on the interaction between you and your staff. It encompasses such all-embracing factors as morale and motivation, as well as courage, determination, and persistence. Here is how one leader is described by a member of his staff: "He was a very outstanding leader with calmness, consideration of all possibilities, and the courage to carry out his decision. He certainly set the example that had the respect of every individual in the group."

Likewise, those you manage want a self-confident leader who can accurately assess internal and market conditions and motivate the staff to take decisive action. This capability is becoming increasingly more precise with the availability of big data analytics and the quantum leaps being made in that technology almost daily.

Underlying that confidence is your judgment when looking at various options and making choices, especially when it concerns the amount of risk your organization can tolerate. As important is determining if your personnel are properly trained, motivated, and up to carrying out their tasks.

---

* This phrase is attributed to Peter Drucker's famous definition of the purpose of business.

Then, there is the task of actually taking action. That is where you need to show self-confidence to tackle tough problems with calmness and consideration of all possibilities. Yet, a reality does exist: How many individuals can maintain such a psychological state under all circumstances? The likelihood is that only a few can sustain such a herculean mental effort under all competitive conditions.

For example, data analytics may reveal that a rival is superior to you in key areas. Such a realization could realistically cause a collapse of all hopes and break down self-confidence. In turn, that mindset has a way of spreading to others on your staff and creating demoralizing fear that dissolves into a climate of hopelessness and defeatism.

Consequently, your leadership role is to forcefully maintain a view of the big picture, which should be shaped by your strategic business plan. In turn, that picture would take the form of opportunities that should be convincingly communicated with supporting data, along with a tactical action plan, to your staff. This point is lucidly expressed by CEO Jim Smith of Thomson Reuters:

> We've done a lot of work around shared purpose, around values, and about the behaviors that we have to exhibit if we're going to live those values. It's about creating a team that's capable of morphing and changing as opportunities arise, and redirecting throughout the year as opportunities arise.

Thus, from a leader's perspective, decisiveness, persistence, and determination beat out overly cautious and indecisive behavior. You can be more proactive by taking a few positive steps: First, in your plan, establish primary and secondary objectives so that if your main objectives cannot be achieved, you have a fallback position. Then, develop corresponding strategies and tactics for each of your objectives, which include setting metrics to measure performance or red-flag problems. Doing so permits you to manage unexpected situations. Also, prepare contingency plans, which include an exit plan should you need to salvage an untenable situation.

Second, create a working climate within your group that relates to your staff's perceptions and attitudes. You should be concerned with their day-to-day functioning and interactions with other groups in the organization. The aim is to interface with digital technology to develop and implement strategies and tactics in an organizational structure that supports speed, concentration, and boldness.

The whole notion is to be proactive in creating a working environment of trust and understanding whereby your staff is encouraged to seize the initiative and act with a sense of direction and purpose, which also serves to strengthen loyalty. For employees, it is no giant leap from thinking their leader is confident and firmly in control to thinking their leader is insecure and vacillating.

Third, you can achieve excellence as a leader when your people are disciplined and committed to the organization's cultural values. Excellence in leadership, however, does not mean perfection. On the contrary, an excellent leader creates a climate that allows subordinates room to learn from their mistakes, as well as from their successes. In such a positive climate, people work to improve and take the risks necessary to learn. A leader who sets a standard of "zero defects, no mistakes" is also saying, "Do not take any chances. Do not try anything you cannot already do perfectly, and do not try anything new."

Strategic Business Plan

The strategic business plan serves as the focal point for inputting, sorting, and disseminating the data from all contact points. As such, it serves to organize ideas into actionable objectives and strategies.

The planning structure permits prioritizing the various functions and activities needed to mobilize for the digital age.* By clearly defining the firm's strategic direction, objectives, and strategies, one can make sense of incoming data and give context to securing existing, as well as pursuing entirely new, businesses.

Included within the plan should be details associated with market segments, products, and services. Making use of the seemingly limitless potential inherent within big data analytics and algorithms, the plan should contain strategies to reach customers in geographically and culturally dispersed markets.

Thus, the plan is the juncture where experience, skill, and insight converge to envision the future. It is the point to highlight objectives; shape imaginative strategies; deploy people, material, and financial resources for maximum impact; assign levels of authority and responsibility; and train individuals who can skillfully implement the plan.

---

* A detailed outline for a strategic business plan is given in Chapter 11.

Therefore, the principal reason to focus on developing a plan as the initial mobilizing force is to create a cohesive and managerial whole from which to make sense of the organization and its interplay with the marketplace. Its aim is to create order out of what can easily deteriorate into disorder.

This is where effective leadership provides a human face to planning, which is expressed as energizing the morale of the rank and file to push forward in an increasingly competitive environment. Often, it is the singular factor in deciding the success or failure of the business plan.

The following guidelines help provide such an interface:

- Develop and communicate a clear statement of a vision and strategic direction for your firm or business unit that embraces digital technologies.
- Involve your staff in navigating the future with clearly stated priorities and objectives that incorporate the findings of data analytics.
- Install a system of recognition and rewards for individuals who identify data-related opportunities for growth and expansion.
- Allow individuals reporting to you to make decisions, supported by data analytics, that are consistent with the plan's overall objectives.
- Maintain a leadership style that is consistent with your company's values and that reflects a working climate of trust.
- Act on signs of tensions among your staff, or where there are clues of damaging infighting within the organization, or where there are instances of other managers projecting negative role models.

A pragmatic example of where some of these issues apply is the precarious situation faced by Cisco Systems during the time it encountered disruptive consumer and competitive changes. Even after declaring he was ready to retire as CEO of Cisco in 2015, John Chambers envisioned vibrant new growth in networking technology and Internet-connected appliances that would set Cisco on an entirely new pathway of growth.

Chambers, along with his successor Chuck Robbins, had to overcome one challenging trend: hardware was becoming less expensive and thereby gave cloud service providers such as Amazon and Google an open advantage to offer Cisco's customers an alternative to buying its costly data center equipment. In response, Cisco made changes to its traditional business plan. It shifted strategy to sell more cloud services and position its software separately from its hardware for special applications.

The key point: Chambers's and Robbins's leadership faced up to the continuing transformations taking place in their markets. Yet they meticulously sustained a forward-thinking and confident work climate within Cisco.

In another instance, once-fierce rivals Apple and Samsung consented to tone down their costly and damaging patent lawsuits and instead collaborate on technology research and manufacturing. Samsung agreed to make the main chip for the next iPhone. And it committed to investing multibillions of dollars for new plants and equipment to make chips for other Apple products.

From a strategic view of the alliance, Apple gained by associating with one of the biggest, most sophisticated chip manufacturing operations in the world. As for Samsung, it obtained much-needed new chip orders to help make up for stagnating mobile phone profits. They both achieved their objectives of retaining their respective leadership positions in the industry.

CHARACTERISTICS OF A SUCCESSFUL LEADER

What type of leader can manage within the framework of the above five forces of leadership? In general, it is the inquiring rather than creative mind, the comprehensive rather than specialized approach, the calm rather than excitable head, the flexible rather than stubborn attitude, and the determined rather than indecisive personality that can sustain self-confidence and lead.

Specifically, however, you have to connect with your personnel, all of whom come with a set of values, developed and nurtured from childhood through lifetime experiences. In varying degrees, these values are expressed as loyalty, duty, respect, and integrity.

However, they can also be empty ideals and may not fully surface if your personal behavior does not mesh with your organization's values, ethics, rules, and culture. Where an interconnect does occur and there is a lack of unity, you, through words, deeds, and everyday practices, must be able to communicate purpose, provide direction, instill motivation, hone skills, and deliver action.

As for employees, what characteristics are they looking for in a leader? First and foremost, and as indicated above, they want a self-confident individual who can accurately assess internal conditions that could impact the smooth running of the company or business unit. That leader should have the foresight and skill to utilize big data and convert it into smart data to evaluate the market and competitive scene with a sense of clarity of what needs to be done and the capability to organize resources and motivate the staff to take action. For instance,

Direction means prioritizing tasks, assigning responsibility for completing them, and making sure personnel understand the goals. The aim is also to deploy resources for the best outcome.

Motivation inspires personnel to act on their own initiative when they see something that needs to be done—that is, within the overall guidelines of business objectives.

Skills relate to technical competence to use required tools and techniques. Skills also pertain to understanding how to work within the new frontiers of technology and their known and yet to be discovered applications.

Action means assessing the market and competitive situation, looking for opportunities, developing strategies and tactical plans, and implementing them. Part of such action requires setting key performance indicators (KPIs), thereby allowing personnel to discover for themselves what happened, why something happened, and how to sustain strengths and improve weaknesses.

Levels of Leadership

Leadership exists at three levels: direct, organizational, and strategic.

Direct Leadership

This level is face-to-face and highly interactive. It takes place when subordinates are used to seeing their manager frequently. Of course, this point varies by how much intervention is needed in managing various job levels, from scientists to assembly-line workers. Then, there is the issue of a manager's individual managing style. The legendary former CEO of General Electric, Jack Welch, was known to devote more than half his time to direct leadership with people. By way of his informal leadership style, he gained the steadfast respect of his employees. He acted as if each employee with whom he interacted was a friend.

Welch often wandered the factory floor checking products and starting conversations with workers by using his informal "Call me Jack." His favorite practice was to bypass corporate protocol by sending handwritten notes to those he had direct contact with during his walking-around practice. Those notes presented a lasting and, in some cases, emotional impression. All those actions were intended to lead, guide, and influence the behavior of individuals throughout GE's complex organization.

Organizational Leadership

This level influences larger and more diverse groups. Executives lead indirectly, generally through more levels of subordinates than do direct leaders. The additional levels, however, can make it more difficult to see actual results. For the most part, organizational leaders deal with more complexity, more disruptive forces, and more unintended consequences.

This is especially so where an increasing number of companies are becoming virtual, globally distributed corporations, where many services and functions from call centers, to R&D, to manufacturing, to back-office operations are outsourced. This increasingly prevailing business model means adding a new dimension to organizational leadership, from managing the few to the many, regardless of location.

Leaders at this level find themselves influencing people more through policy making and systems integration than through face-to-face contact. They focus on strategic planning and global competition over the longer term.

Yet developing meaningful collaborations, sharing goals, and applying the principles described above remain steadfast leadership rules as they learn to leverage global talent. And, as practiced by Jack Welch, getting out of the office at regular intervals and visiting outlying sectors of the organization where the daily work takes place is still especially important.

Strategic Leadership

This type of leadership is prevalent in larger organizations among senior executives. These C-suite leaders establish organizational structure, allocate resources, communicate strategic vision, and prepare business units for their future roles in a digitally driven and competitive environment.

They apply many of the same leadership skills and actions they mastered as direct and organizational leaders. They process information quickly, assess alternatives based on big data analytics, make decisions, and generate support.

Their decisions affect more people, commit more resources, and have wider-ranging consequences in both space and time than do decisions of organizational and direct leaders. In smaller organizations, or in business units of larger ones, all levels of leadership are usually focused with the owner or general manager.

In a more specialized application where authority and responsibility are delegated to the lower echelons, field sales managers, for instance, take on the additional roles of organizational and strategic leadership for their respective sales territories.

In addition to their direct leadership role of motivating, training, and coaching salespeople reporting to them, these managers get involved in shaping a strategic vision for their respective territories, developing long- and short-term objectives, designing action strategies and tactics, and providing useful feedback to developers for future products and services.

As leaders, they think through their specific problem and act with the initiative of a self-starter. That is, they move when there are no clear instructions, act when unexpected opportunities appear, react when the competitive situation changes, and maintain flexibility when the original business plans fall apart.

This is done within the framework of those leaders understanding the organization's overall strategic plan. As important, they do not just give orders. They are careful to communicate clearly the intent of the specific objectives to be achieved. All this effort is anchored to the leaders' *discipline*, *character*, and *ambition*.

Such characteristics do not just appear. They must be developed, practiced, and honed within the leader and among subordinates. Examples of such characteristics include the following.

Discipline

This characteristic comprises order, self-control, restraint, obedience, and deference for authority, as well as a sense of duty. It is through discipline that you shape a united effort, which is then fortified through training. The one reality you have to face is that in day-to-day competitive encounters, your personnel are enveloped by the instinct of self-preservation that takes hold over all other emotions.

The aim of discipline, therefore, is to control that instinct. In even the most pressured situation, the individual tends to lose his reasoning power and becomes instinctive. This is especially critical where the presumably infallible big data metrics would steer you in a precise direction that is contrary to what you intuitively feel and your experience indicates.

Only with discipline is there good order and a feeling of collaboration realized through teamwork and pride. Collaboration, in this context, exists among individuals working as a team who know each other well and who share the company spirit. Many companies talk about seeking collaboration through team effort. However, few reach that level according to one major business publication that cited the following major organizations as having mastered such an achievement: Nike, Lockheed Martin, Kohl's, Starbucks, and Johnson & Johnson.

Even with those standouts, it is altogether too common in many organizations that only the numbers are seen and not the underlying events governing them. The individual as an intrinsic part of any corporate effort often disappears, or is taken for granted, rather than viewed as valued for his or her intellectual capability, experience, and inherent skills. Yet for anything significant to happen, it is the mind and quality of the individual, the unity of team effort anchored to discipline, and organizational support that produce any meaningful effect.

Character

This quality represents an individual's inner strengths. It helps the individual know what is right. More than that, it triggers the courage to do what is correct regardless of the circumstances or the consequences. It is character that influences an individual's behavior, as it links intuitive insight into action.

However, to hold to a consistent course is difficult. The steady stream of erratic impressions eating at an individual's convictions never seems to cease. Even the greatest stability and determination cannot completely protect the wanderings of the mind. Negative impressions are strong and vivid and can affect the mind almost unconsciously. It takes strong feelings and strength of character to overcome them.

At critical times, however, successful leaders are able to master their feelings and keep their determination. Deep as their feelings are, they maintain their poise and equilibrium. Thus, individuals with strong feelings, great strength of character, and a solid dose of good sense are outstanding leaders. These qualities make it possible to see the critical issues in any event.

Stubbornness, on the other hand, distorts determination. It borders on vanity, but goes deeper and is displayed as a narrowness of mind, which views giving in on one's own ideas as a sign of weakness.

Ambition

This trait is one of the essential qualities of a leader. There never was an outstanding leader without ambition. Ambition is the mainspring of all actions. But for pragmatic meaning, ambition must be worthy of the organization's mission and its culture and not a pathway to solitary power.

Ambition is difficult to separate from courage. In analyzing great leaders, it is generally impossible to decide which of their actions in the face of severe problems bore the mark of boldness or that of ambition. Both are characteristics of the truly outstanding ones.

It is constructive ambition and the intense desire to excel that stimulate ambition in others. The magic of winning always arouses ambition, which gives momentum to the organization. Therefore, nurturing constructive ambition is another prime duty of the leader.

Yet the unwelcome reality exists that unrestrained personal ambition does live, with all its excesses and potentially harmful outcomes— as shown by the highly publicized debacles of the earlier recession. It is through uncontrolled raw ambition that similar scandals have destroyed employees' careers and the economic livelihoods of communities in which the organizations operated.

Finally, embedded throughout any enterprise is the deep-rooted and monumental influence of organizational culture. It functions as the backbone that supports discipline, highlights character, and encourages positive ambition. With its long-lasting and more complex set of beliefs, customs, values, and practices, culture is expressed in a corporate climate of how people currently feel about their organization.

Further, if you seek competence as a leader in the age of big data, algorithms, and analytics, understand the five forces that impact your role in mobilizing your staff and organization: digital technology, competitive strategy, corporate culture, organizational structure, and strategic business planning. Add to those the leadership and sensitivities of interfacing with technology, regardless of your operating levels.

2

Integrating Business Intelligence and Security with Competitive Strategy

We don't think of security as being a separate piece of technology. It has to be core to the operational systems that you use, where your data resides, where your most critical applications usage is.

Satya Nadella
CEO, Microsoft Corp.

Nadella's comments are open to several interpretations: First, security involves protecting all that represents a company's secrets and plans. To that end, the dominant issue and key challenge for Microsoft—as well as for your organization—is cybersecurity. The threats and potential vulnerabilities extend to the public sector, as well as to national and local governments globally. It has stretched to such heights of concern that international summits are addressing the dangers. By any measure, then, cybersecurity is one of the biggest common threats organizations face.

Second, with an increasing number of businesses adjusting their operations to the digital age, leaders are broadening their view of security to include protecting the continuous flow of data from every conceivable source. Moreover, that inflow of data accelerates with the speed and availability of cheaper computer power, sensors, and mobile communications.

Thus, as technology-advanced companies hone their digital skills and experiment with data generated across a base of thousands or even millions of transactions, they are able to test new products, services, pricing, and marketing approaches with remarkable speed by using the readily available analytics software. With the quick feedback, they determine which products and strategies produce higher revenues or greater customer engagement. In this manner, every digital-engaged business operates as a big data business with security as an integral part.

Third, Nadella's comments that "[security] has to be core to the operational systems that you use" and "where your most critical applications usage is" can be legitimately understood to include Microsoft's strategic business planning process, with its output of competitive strategies. As such, Nadella's remarks would include such leadership tasks as (1) create and retain customers, (2) secure Microsoft against competitors interfering with its plans, and (3) develop defensive and offensive strategies.

Whereas the complex issues surrounding cybersecurity have yet to be resolved, it remains a problem with which you and all leaders must stay involved. However, there are manageable aspects of business intelligence and security that do fit into your immediate role. And these will be the focus of the balance of this chapter.

MANAGING BUSINESS INTELLIGENCE

"You cannot deny what may be happening in the marketplace because it doesn't feel good for your portfolio," declared Chuck Robbins, CEO, Cisco Systems. Robbins's comment is of vast importance for business intelligence and managing in the digital age. Specifically, as his remarks relate to a competitive situation, data analytics can help you understand what "may be happening in [your] marketplace" when it comes to identifying your competitor's operating patterns.

Armed with such intelligence, you can then deploy your personnel and determine where the competitor's strength is formidable and where it is weak, which gives you lead time to take counteractions. In turn, that information serves as reliable data for constructing a budget and determining the types of resources required for the situation.

What better way to establish your personal credibility as a leader than being able to demonstrate to your staff that you can handle potential threats and take positive actions on opportunities? Therefore, business intelligence with the embedded use of big data and analytics can be "core to the operational systems that you use." It affects all operating parts of a business either directly or indirectly.

In another instance, John Deere & Co., a leading agricultural machinery maker, faced a market of soft crop commodity prices that weakened demand for farming equipment, and intense competition from equally strong competitors, which caused Deere's revenue to tumble. Deere responded by turning to a new source of revenues: software services that deliver information and advice to farmers in the field. With embedded technologies in its equipment, the data helps farmers manage their fields from their mobile devices.

Those organizations faced common issues built around developing strategies within two zones of activities: First, as stated above for Microsoft, is creating and retaining customers with the longer-term view of contributing to the long-term growth of the market, whether it is through disruptive technologies or by means of innovative products, logistics, and enhanced services. Second is preventing competitors from interfering with their business plans through security and effective counterstrategies.

Should ongoing competitive threats prevent those organizations from carrying out those two fundamental activities, they can totally unbalance any organization—and in the extreme, imperil an organization's survival. Within that context, a leader's initial task is to organize his or her staff to observe and analyze rivals' activities in real time and prepare counterstrategies. The object would be to secure existing market positions and frustrate competitors' efforts.

As for your leadership, given the scope of information required to develop competent strategies, it is especially important to look at a competitor with a 360° view. That is, use a circular approach by utilizing big data to open your eyes to a changing marketplace of evolving technologies, environmental trends, and shifting buying patterns among your customers.

In this panoramic scene, seeking information to sharpen your insights can impact your decisions when selecting markets, launching new products, and searching for competitive advantages. In turn, you will improve your chances for establishing a formidable defense in those segments that represent your core business.

Business intelligence, then, functions as the centerpiece of all offensive and defensive actions by exposing strengths and weaknesses in your situation, as well as in those of your competitors.

The intelligence function serves as a core component for developing strategies and tactics. For that reason, if utilized with the same care you would give to a delicate instrument, the system can signal subtle changes in the marketplace. For instance, it can help you preempt and outmaneuver competitors, preserve financial expenditures for the most expeditious timing, and even protect your corporate secrets from inquisitive onlookers.

Therefore, look carefully and thoughtfully at incoming data and be sure to evaluate the reliability of each source. Doing so permits you to validate or disprove reports, especially from questionable sources. After you have assembled reliable intelligence and carefully deliberated on all that is meaningful, develop and implement your strategy with speed. You can then feel confident that the intelligence you have assembled and screened, and the analytics you have received, will produce the best results, as well as red-flag questionable actions.

Moreover, even in the penetrating light of reality, should you discover that some intelligence is contradictory, false, or doubtful, you have little recourse but to lean heavily on your judgment and move on. It would be a far greater error to wait for a situation to clear up entirely. The reality of working in a dynamic digitally driven marketplace is that rapid decisions are required—even in the fog of uncertainty.

That also means depending on your knowledge of the industry, trusting your years of experience, showing confidence in those key individuals with whom you work, recognizing the value of your formal and informal training, and relying on the richness of your intuition. Taking it a step further, should pangs of doubt still persist, yet intuitively you know that rapid action is called for if you are to prevent a potentially bad situation from deteriorating further, tell yourself that little is accomplished without shifting to the offensive.

MANAGING DATA SECURITY

Beyond the persistent stories in the media of hackers aggressively attacking corporate databases with regularity and seeming impunity, there are less publicized cases of electronic bugging of company offices. Add to that the blatant situations where employees steal secrets and sell them to competitors for pure monetary gain. Still other individuals pass on confidential information about new products through prearranged agreements with rival companies.

The most flagrant illegal examples over the last few years include the following:

> *Apple Computer*: A global supply manager at Apple was caught sending drawings, pricing information, and projected sales figures on various Apple products to suppliers in China, South Korea, Taiwan, and

Singapore. Suppliers paid kickbacks to the individual, which totaled more than $1 million.

Dow Chemical: A research scientist who worked at Dow for 27 years stole trade secrets for making chlorinated polyethylene and sold them to Chinese companies.

DuPont: A research chemist working on organic light-emitting technology secretly downloaded files to an external drive. He then covertly took a job with Peking University, which was working on the same technology. He went on to make personal presentations about commercializing the research.

Ford Motor: A product engineer, before leaving Ford, copied 4,000 documents, including design specs. As he was about to leave the United States on a one-way ticket, the data turned up on his laptop when confiscated at an airport.

Goodyear Tire & Rubber: Two engineers at a Goodyear supplier were convicted of entering a Goodyear plant, photographing a device used to wrap cable for a tire's inner thread, and transmitting the photos to a rival company.

Motorola: An engineer was charged with economic espionage by stealing trade secrets to benefit a foreign government. The individual was caught at a U.S. airport with 1,000 Motorola documents and a one-way ticket to China. Among the papers were confidential documents relating to Motorola's mobile phone technology.

Boeing/Rockwell: An engineer was caught with 300,000 pages at his home, including technical information on a U.S. space shuttle, F-15 fighter, B-52 bomber, and Chinook helicopter.

Other victims of espionage include Google, Lockheed Martin, Chicago Mercantile Exchange, American Superconductor, and Dow AgroSciences.

What implications do these cases of deception have on security and competitive strategy? From a macroviewpoint, stealing a company's technology, seizing advance research, and accessing any other area that converts data to a product or service advantage can seriously jeopardize a manager's strategy options and ability to compete effectively. At the microlevel, such outrageous acts explicitly place a manager in a high-risk situation by blocking him or her from building strong defensive barriers to protect an existing market position.

From your viewpoint, similar situations can realistically gut your efforts for developing expansion strategies by stripping away at the uniqueness of your product or service advantage. Thus, maintaining security means guarding against rivals stealing your competitive advantage and turning it around to their benefit and against you.

Therefore, where individuals driven by assorted motivations embezzle secrets, it is appropriate to discuss the *people* part of intelligence gathering. In turn, that leads to the use of specific types of people who, consciously or not, act as agents to acquire and disseminate information.

Engaging in such stealth activities is usually contrary to the type of practices most leaders care to undertake. Yet, within ethical and legal bounds and in a highly competitive world, clever deceptions and distractions are legitimate weapons. And individuals are essential components of the business intelligence process.

These individuals serve a highly credible role in interpreting industry events, organizing stray pieces of competitive information into coherent intelligence, and flushing out information about a competitor's plans. They also contribute to disseminating deceptive information so that the competitor sees only what they want seen, which could encourage perceptions of strengths as weaknesses and weaknesses as strengths. Consequently, it is to your best interest to use the following guidelines when employing such individuals as agents.

THE PEOPLE PART OF INTELLIGENCE

Notwithstanding all the sophisticated software to extract intelligence from big data, there is still the effect of "boots on the ground" to gather firsthand intelligence at conferences, trade shows, and even at your competitor's locations. Most often, again thinking of them as agents, they go beyond the analytics, charts, surveys, benchmarking, and other intelligence-gathering techniques. In other situations, such observations can verify and support the digital findings.

They explore the human side of competitor intelligence by reporting on the behaviors and personalities of key individuals. Their primary tool is personal interaction and observation. They screen and interpret events and news and validate or dismiss information gathered by other means.

Before moving forward and employing such agents, however, observe a few general cautions: First and foremost, make certain that you are not violating ethical and legal guidelines, as cited in the above examples. Check, too, that your use of agents agrees with your company's policies.

Second, assess prospective agents' motivations, personality traits, and talents. Then, you can determine in what capacity to employ them. For instance, some individuals' primary pursuit is money, with minor interest in obtaining accurate information about the competitor. In such cases, question their integrity and use great care in employing them.

Third, develop a clear idea about the information you seek. Then make certain these agents understand what you want.

The following categories represent the people part of intelligence, along with suggestions on how to use them.

Unintentional Agents

These individuals are not solicited as agents. They are people with whom you would normally interact during professional gatherings. They tend to volunteer their company's information freely to satisfy their personal interests, make new contacts, and advance their careers. Often, they are somewhat uncaring about their respective company's security. Or they were not cautioned about the dangers of revealing company secrets.

You will find them in a variety of places. Trade shows serve as fertile venues for gathering intelligence from those individuals. This is also a place where they reveal extensive information about their products, usually through elaborate demonstrations. Then, they freely distribute literature overflowing with facts about pricing, backup services, logistics, and product specifications.

In addition, if some are key executives, they often present papers at open meetings that detail sensitive information about upcoming products, services, and even market entry plans. Then there is the question-and-answer period where they try to further impress an audience by impulsively and unwittingly pouring out classified information.

Another prime area for intelligence gathering is the familiar hospitality suite at trade shows and professional meetings where alcohol and talk flow freely. It is a site where security is often lax and everyone's guard is down.

College classrooms represent another source of information, particularly where part-time instructors are also executives and use their respective companies as case examples. In addition, at management seminars, participants often reveal data about their companies through formal presentations or after-hours casual conversations.

Competitors' Agents

These individuals work for competitors or are former employees. In many cases, they may have been bypassed for promotion. They may feel underpaid and underappreciated, relegated to an insignificant job, and generally pushed aside in a variety of power struggles within the organization. They feel abused and see their careers languishing unless they make some bold move. They may also find themselves surrendering to financial pressures to keep family and self whole. And their attitude may be "now or never."

You need to assess such individuals carefully for their stability and determine how to use them judiciously. Obviously, you want their information, but only within the bounds of ethical and legal guidelines.

Beyond personal observations, you would employ those agents for their expertise to sort out meaningful information from scientific and professional journals, industry studies, or innovative projects described in articles and professional papers written by the competitors' employees. Product literature and product specification sheets, readily available at trade shows and meetings, are packed with tremendous detail. Your agents should be able to interpret the data for meaningful intelligence.

In-house company newsletters and news releases contain a fountain of information about individuals who left a competitor's employment and may have moved to the consulting circuit. If approached, these former employees may be willing to reveal information—unless specific contractual restrictions apply.

Press releases may include new employee announcements, along with job descriptions, contracts and awards received, training programs available, and office or factory openings or closures. You may also find specific news items that reveal competitors' current plans.

Here, again, such agents could handily provide useful analyses. Beyond the above listing, there is the continuing flow of rumors from customers and suppliers that these individuals can sort out and verify. Additionally, there are local sources worth tapping, such as banks, local trucking companies, and real estate offices.

Double Agents

These agents, in turn, may try to extract intelligence about your company. Stay alert to their intentions. Once identified, you could attempt to turn them around and get them working on your behalf.

If successful, they could serve your purposes. In this situation, assume double agents may show personality traits and motivations similar to those of competitors' agents. However, it is in your best interest to exercise caution. That is, determine the sincerity of these individuals, consider the reliability of their information, and estimate how long you can expect them to remain loyal to your cause. Once again, make certain you are not violating ethical, legal, or policy guidelines.

Broadcasting Agents

This type of agent has a special purpose: deliberately disseminate wrong information to distract competitors into making wrong decisions. Such contrived leaks take many forms, for example, broadcasting fabricated information about new product features through sales reps that come in contact with competitors' reps. Or it could be a product manager revealing false dates about a product launch that would disrupt a competitor's plans.

In spite of your possible discomfort when undertaking such activities, look at the situation from strictly a strategist's viewpoint. Disinformation for the purpose of deception needs distribution to divert competitors from directly opposing your moves and consuming resources that you cannot replace. You thereby preserve your company's hard-won market position, control needless expenditures of financial and human resources fighting unnecessary market battles, and avoid upending your strategies.

Credible Agents

These individuals usually provide the most credible information. They are generally experienced and talented individuals who can gain access to, and become intimate with, individuals in key positions. They are in a position to learn their plans and observe movements. These individuals are your eyes and ears, as they often enjoy the closest and most confidential relationships.

Perhaps the one unsettling issue to cope with is the notion that one of your employees, knowingly or inadvertently, passes your company's sensitive information to competitors. Where possible, make every effort to find out the perpetrators and obtain clues about what motivated their behavior. It may be comforting to know that many of those individuals are often exposed—ideally, before too much damage has been done.

The list below provides general questions for guiding you to use the most intelligent people as agents. You may wish to add your own specific questions as they relate to your business and industry.

Employing Agents for Business Intelligence.

Questions you should ask agents include the following:

- What are the competitor's overall business strategies, particularly ones that would impact your business?
- What is the competitor's financial picture, including breakdowns of costs and sales by product lines?
- What new products or services are under development?
- What markets could be targeted for expansion?
- How are the competitor's business units staffed and organized, especially in marketing and product development?
- What is the caliber of the competitor's leadership?
- What market positions or market shares do key competitors hold within each product segment? Are there plans to increase, maintain, or reduce their respective positions?
- Where are the competitor's vulnerabilities, which could represent a decisive point for a concentrated effort, e.g., product depth, product quality, customer service, price, distribution, marketing, or reputation?
- How advanced are the competitor's capabilities in the use of big data, algorithms, and analytics?

WHERE YOUR DATA RESIDES

Intelligence gathering begins by completely grasping what Nadella terms "where your data resides." The following five primary categories provide a systematic approach for you to see all sides of your internal and external operating arena: *customers, intermediaries, competitors, governmental/ environmental*, and *internal sources*.

It is unlikely that you can develop expertise in all categories and the numerous subcategories that comprise business intelligence. However, they do provide you with a tableau of inquiry in which all types of valuable data reside. With this macro look at your market, you can challenge your subordinates to immerse themselves in gathering, interpreting, and utilizing intelligence.

Thus, the following review will enhance their understanding of the possibilities, probabilities, and subtle nuances that make up the marketplace. Internalizing data in this way adds an additional layer of knowledge to their conscious thinking, as it nourishes their intuition when viewing the reports generated by the digital systems.

Customers

For your company, as well as for Nadella's organization, as much knowledge as possible is required to understand who are your ultimate users. That means knowing about the primary physical and psychological influences that guide their buying decisions. That is where analytics can help profile buyers by behavioral factors. It is all part of understanding their attitudes, values, and habits.

For instance, you can determine when they shop, where they consume your product, and with what frequency they purchase. As important, you want the system to feed data on what needs your products or services satisfy. That is all part of knowing how your buyers perceive your product or service in their minds. In turn, that feedback would give you clues about the direction of your branding and marketing campaigns.

As an example of behavioral factors, one start-up, Kreditech, has carved out a segment that targets individuals who do not have bank accounts, a credit score, or a financial identity, which means no ability to borrow money. That emerging market comprises 2 billion people internationally who fit such a profile and are potential customers for borrowing money. That is the market where Kreditech aims to become a market leader.

The German company's algorithms generate as many as 20,000 data points from online shopping histories, geolocation data from mobile phone calls, and similar information by which they qualify an individual for a loan. As of 2015, Kreditech had evaluated more than 2 million applicants, had approved 15% of them, and has an acceptable loan loss rate of 15%.

In other approaches, data benchmarks how well a company's offerings satisfy compared with similar ones offered by competitors. Applied on a segment-by-segment approach, the information yields how to allocate resources effectively for better targeting based on the economic outlook over the near and far term. (See advanced segmentation techniques in Chapter 12.)

Intermediaries

In this category, the central idea is knowing if you should continue with intermediaries, such as distributors or retailers. If so, you want to know how influential they are in selling and servicing the end-use customer. Also within that framework, you want to know how you can support their needs, and what special areas would help solidify relationships. These areas could include financial assistance, improved training, sharing of market data, improved product information, or specialized technical assistance to close a sale.

Here, too, you want to know how much data about end-use customers resides exclusively with them, which ideally includes answers to questions about what motivations drive the end-use customers' buying decisions. That includes knowing what significant changes have influenced sales over the past 12 months, such as the impact of social media on overall sales. Likewise, you want data analytics about possible changes over the next 12 months.

Then, there is information about such areas as significant movement in the intermediaries' locations relative to the end users, types of noncompeting products they carry, what competing product lines they handle, and what percentage of total revenue does each competing product line represent compared with yours. What follows are details about how much support they give your product. That all leads to how you can motivate them to work harder for you—beyond the typical response of wanting more money.

What follows, then, are major strategic questions, such as, Do you need intermediaries in light of advances in digital technologies? Do they need you? That is all part of your discussion on the use of multiple channels, including e-commerce. And would you be better off setting up your own distribution system? Alternatively, should you go directly to the end-use customer?

Competitors

The above two categories concern your customers. This part deals with competitors. Exactly who are your competitors and what is the extent of their influence? Wells Fargo CEO John Stumpf says, "The people who influence us the most are outsider industries—the IBMs, the Apples, the Amazons."

In all probability, you have a good deal of intelligence about your traditional rivals. Nevertheless, in the context of Stumpf's comment, this digital world spawns companies from outside your industry, as well as the fresh-on-the-scene start-ups that suddenly appear and turn out to be more adept than your organization at utilizing big data, algorithms, and analytics.

In addition, they even use the technology with greater skill and innovative agility. In effect, they open you to a completely new path of inquiries about where data resides. Can you afford to disregard how they enter, what market niches they fill, and what competitive advantages they use in their strategies?

Along with the above information, you will need data to understand if their participation in the market is growing or declining, why your traditional customers are leaving you, and to whom they are attracted. If possible, you want clues about what new directions, if any, they are pursuing.

For both established and new rivals, such data provides you with valuable insights about their strengths and weaknesses, overall size, and where they are located relative to your key customers. As for specifics about products and service offerings, data should reveal information about their product mix and any gaps in their mix that would create an opportunity for you.

If fortunate, you can gain details of the competitors' strategies as they relate to markets, products, pricing, marketing, supply chain, technologies, and leadership. Such data will also give you a handle on how threatening they are, and which competitive strategies and tactics appear particularly successful or unsuccessful.

If successful, you will also gain a keen awareness about the types of competitors you will have to confront and what strategies you will have to use, if you want to maintain a viable market position.

Government/Environment

Here, your interest should be in assembling data about the legal and environmental constraints affecting your marketing efforts over the immediate and long term. That means knowing the extent to which government regulations could restrict your flexibility at various levels of business activity. The most visible example is Uber's travails in both domestic and foreign markets as it navigates through extensive interactions with national and municipal governments.

In China, for instance, local governments periodically summon Uber and its competitors to "rectify certain problems." Uber claims that it is in close communication with local officials and is "on par with other Chinese companies in the industry, meeting all potential required qualifications."

Within that monitored environment, there are further issues that go deep into Uber's everyday operations, such as its use of data analytics to figure out where next to send drivers. In still another instance, Airbnb and others in the short-term rental business are obligated to cooperate with city governments challenging them over zoning and tax issues.

Thus, data resides in those segments of your market that feel the presence of governmental and environmental regulations and scrutiny. As such, you have to determine how to maneuver as ongoing flows of data reveal demographic and geographic shifts and buying behavior swings. Then, there are the social and "green" issues that can further influence your business.

Therefore, what data do you need to comply with regulations? What political or legal developments are looming that will improve or worsen your situation?

Internal Sources

In this category, data resides in your internal market research function, through outside resources, and with the data supplied by the agents referred to earlier. Data also exists in the minds of your people—the human and intellectual capital of the organization—and in the vast written and oral histories that are core to the organization's culture.* Their value depends on the efficacy of those sources, the expertise of the people operating the system, and the sophistication of the software utilized.

――――――――――

WHERE YOUR DATA APPLIES

Beyond where data resides, Nadella then talks about "where your most critical applications usage is." One essential application is how data affects the development of your business plans and strategies. For instance, accurate data applies to assessing competitors' strengths and weaknesses,

---

* See discussion on *explicit* knowledge and *tacit* knowledge in the introduction.

pinpointing a decisive point through which to enter a market, and determining how to budget resources. It also provides some degree of accuracy about which strategies are likely to succeed and then rejects those with minimal chances of success.

In a parallel move, precise data applies to preserving your market position against rivals that are looking to aggressively attack your customer base. You are then in a better position to concentrate your efforts and thereby improve your chances of establishing a formidable defense in the segments that represent your core business.

The primary areas where data applies include

- Internal planning
- Organizational procedures and processes
- Competitive strategy
- Competitor's performance
- Your company's performance

The commentary that follows illustrates the pervasiveness of each of these areas to business intelligence and its effect on overall business performance.

Internal Planning

Where a formalized planning procedure exists to provide direction and purpose to your organization, it also functions as a repository for assembling, digesting, and applying data for particular applications. That includes acting as a collaborative force for harnessing the diverse and creative energies of dispersed groups in the organization. In addition to gaining the input of various points of view, it often leads to higher levels of morale and results in greater buy-in to implement the plan.

Specifically, by reviewing the plan's strategic direction and long- and short-term objectives, there is an opportunity to determine to what extent the data applies to those areas of the plan. Should there be little or no alignment, then those responsible for developing data retrieval specifications would make the appropriate adjustments.

Doing so adds precision to the plan and helps prioritize objectives to avoid internal conflicts among other business units. Adding credibility to the usefulness of data reaffirms that the objectives are realistic, achievable, and measurable. In turn, they assist in setting up key performance indicators (KPIs.)

Thus, applying data analytics into the planning process provides a more accurate way to

- Integrate what-if scenarios to the process by highlighting known and unknown competitive challenges and threats to your business
- Examine diversification or joint venture possibilities and relate them to such areas as determining decisive points through which to enter a new market segment
- Improve budgeting by determining if resources are optimally allocated to the major elements of your market mix
- Estimate the amount of available resources remaining in reserve and under what conditions they would be released

Organizational Procedures and Processes

The essential idea is to organize the intelligence function into efficient procedures and processes so that disseminating market and competitor intelligence reaches all appropriate units of the organization. The overall expectation is that analytics activities have a positive impact on company revenues, margins, and organizational efficiency in future years.

Where there is an immediate need to set up procedures and processes, it requires the active support of company leadership. Leadership includes such titles as CEO, chief information officer, chief marketing officer, and business unit heads. Involvement would ensure senior management's participation in such data and analytics activities as

- Devising an appropriate organizational structure to support analytics activities
- Providing business groups with access to support for both data and analytics
- Designing effective data architecture and technology infrastructure to support analytics activities
- Securing internal leadership for analytics projects
- Tracking business impact of analytics activities
- Creating flexibility in existing processes to take advantage of new analytics insights
- Attracting or retraining appropriate talent, both functional and technical
- Developing a strategy to prioritize long-term investment in analytics

Competitive Strategy

One of the important applications of data is to shape fresh strategies and tactics so that they are not worn-out repeats of yesterday's actions. As indicated earlier, your strategies should achieve the dual purposes of first, securing a defensible market position against aggressive competitors, and second, shifting to offensive strategies to achieve the growth objectives of the strategic business plan.

Feeding off the results of past market campaigns and introducing predictive data analytics can help you assess which strategies are likely to work and reject those with little chance of success. For instance, you will want to be informed about the following:

- Changes in the character of your markets according to demographic and behavioral characteristics.
- Unmet customer needs that would enable you to respond rapidly in the form of products, services, methods of delivery, credit terms, or technical assistance.
- Competitors' products that are likely to be perceived by customers as substitutes for yours. Included here are usage patterns and any deviations in regional and seasonal buying procedures.
- Innovations in marketing, especially in the use of the Internet. Included are data related to promotional allowances, selling tactics, trade discounts, rebates, and point-of-purchase opportunities.
- Advances in the supply chain, as they relate to electronic ordering, computerized inventory control systems, and use of mobile devices.
- New technologies that would disrupt standard industry practices and thereby create both opportunities and threats.

Competitive Problems

The major issue here is of company leadership remaining unaware of potential dangers, or there is awareness, but leaders rationalize the situation and do little or nothing to respond. The reasonable conclusion is that a slow-to-react, passive corporate culture is in place; leadership is misinformed, lacks judgment, or is fearful about reacting to industry changes, customer behavior, and competitors' actions; and the organization suffers from a cumbersome structural design.

Thus, from an intelligence viewpoint, when and how did the leaders receive the first indication about a competitor's aggressive moves? At what point did they fully grasp the seriousness of what the competitor could possibly do to the company's market position? Who noticed the first signs of a problem: an executive, a junior manager, or a sales rep?

Moreover, if a digital capability was in place, did any signals come from that source? How accurate was the assessment? And how confident were leaders in its reliability? These questions are meant to alert you to where data applies to competitive problems and the need to get other managers on board to internalize the ramifications and pervasiveness of big data in helping respond to threatening situations.

Competitor's Performance

In the event your competitor's strategy failed, it is useful to know at what point in the unfolding campaign that the rival's efforts began falling apart. If you employed data analytics, you should be able to glean meaningful information that could reveal patterns useful to strategizing future campaigns.

For instance, you want to know when the competitor prematurely stopped resisting your efforts. Did the rival simply relinquish a segment of the market to you? Alternatively, did the competing manager back off only for a brief period before mounting an all-new effort?

In addition, you want details about when and in what form the first telltale signs of weakness showed. There can be many reasons for a failed strategy, such as insufficient financial or physical resources, lack of trained and experienced personnel, weak leadership, or faulty implementation. Conversely, if the competitor's campaign was successful, you want the same data about how your strategy failed.

Your Company's Performance

In the event the competitor was successful against you, and to learn from the experience, you want to know at what point your campaign began to unravel. Was it a matter of inadequate data, did the competitor catch you by surprise, or were some managers not paying attention to the clues that began appearing.

Then, there are the specific details about the nature of the competitor's strategy that caused your failed performance. Was it a case of insufficient reserves, unskilled and inadequately trained personnel, a depleted budget, or a scarcity of backup support?

In any event, to augment the data analytics, it is useful to do an after-action report to determine how the campaign failed, in what time frame, and under what conditions. When exactly was the turning point that ensured the rival's success? Was there an instant where events could have changed if you had more precise data?

As important, and where possible, you want information about how your personnel held up during the successive phases of the campaign. What lessons did you learn about your staff, your strategies, and the reliability of your business intelligence system from the unfolding events?

From a leader's point of view, there is another dimension to the above guidelines. It is the magnitude of the total situation and the numerous variables of a volatile marketplace that have a huge impact on you personally. Gnawing misgivings creep into your mind about being seriously mistaken in your analysis. These feelings of uneasiness often take hold, and from uneasiness to indecision are small, scarcely discernible steps.

What are the underlying issues that trigger such negative thinking and subconscious feelings? Are there doubts about the competitor's strength, exaggerated estimates of the rival's size, or concerns about the accuracy of the data? Specifically, what about the people gathering and reporting the intelligence? Individuals by nature are inclined to be timid and tend to overstate danger. Or, as likely, they steer toward self-interests, which can cause inaccurate interpretations of data.

Then, should you be personally involved in a tough competitive encounter, it is altogether possible that you are not fully and honestly informed about the overall strategies and short-term actions of your competitor. On the other hand, you may not be clear about your own strengths and vulnerabilities. Such doubts could include not knowing about the capabilities of your personnel to perform under adverse conditions.

The above scenario is not surprising. Individuals torn with fear and apprehension hinder calm and factual assessments, which often fill reports with miscalculations. In addition, people tend to believe evil rather than good. Consequently, what you get is feedback tainted with bad news and false dangers. Thus, trying to predict the performance of individuals at a particular time and during a tense experience is fraught with uncertainties.

All those issues can weigh heavily on your mind and leave a misleading impression of your rival's intentions and capabilities. And from that mindset arises a new source of indecision.

In spite of those people-related complexities, you cannot take uncertainty as a reason for indecision, nor can you use it as a rationale to forego action. Your best option is to prepare as best you can by elevating digital intelligence and security to the *highest* level in your firm or business group. As already stated throughout this chapter, make data analytics an embedded part of the strategy development and implementation process.

In all, utilizing your judgment, experience, training, and intuition, along with business intelligence, will help you outthink, outmaneuver, and outperform your competitors, as well as provide you with a pathway to growth.

3

Neutralizing a Competitor and Creating a Competitive Advantage

We don't want to be competing on the basis of price and wages. We want to be competing on the basis of generating new products and services that the rest of the world can't make yet.

Tom Kalil
Deputy director, Office of Science and Technology

As an extension of Chapter 2 on how business intelligence and security integrate with competitive strategy, one particular application that is often sidetracked and which deserves an in-depth discussion is the issue associated with *neutralizing* a competitor. That issue should raise strong concerns among managers if they fully internalize the potential dangers from ongoing encounters with determined competitors. These rivals aim to compete for an advantageous position as they look to outperform each other and gain growth in market share, sales, and profits.

If you take a macro look at the marketplace, competitive campaigns consist of actions within two zones of activity: first and foremost, creating and retaining customers by providing a series of physical and psychological satisfactions, and second and essential, preventing competitors from interfering with actions in the first zone of activity by means of maneuvers, strategies, and tactics. From that viewpoint, the primary objective of zone 2 is to neutralize the competitor from effectively activating its own two zones of activity.

In whatever form these campaigns are conducted, they are costly, time-consuming, and potentially risky. They involve committing people, money, and resources to maintain a competitive lead, while at the same time diverting resources from longer-term goals.

And it becomes even costlier as the tools needed to achieve an edge increasingly require sophisticated software, systems, and skilled people to plan the maneuvers. Therefore, if you want to maintain a viable competitive position, a major part of that effort revolves around doing whatever is necessary to neutralize your competitor, who is trying to do the same to you through countercampaigns.

Unfortunately, some managers naively take a somewhat casual approach about neutralizing. This is evidenced by the lack of serious writings on the topic when compared with the amount of space devoted to a single line of inquiry where customers are the only force that requires maximum attention, that is, the first zone of activity.

This complacency is reinforced by some executives thinking they are protected by a distinguished market history and a strong public image. As a result, many once-proud enterprises ended up in shambles against a competitive onslaught. Or they are forced to exit their primary markets through bankruptcy and move in entirely new directions, as in the case of the Eastman Kodak Co., which entered bankruptcy. It has since been reorganized, downsized, and redirected.

Kodak saw the digital photography market coming. The company is even credited with inventing the digital camera in 1975. In the end, however, Kodak management remained focused on protecting its old technology and stoically watched its market presence decline. The result: An industry that is identified with Kodak was relinquished to aggressive and forward-looking rivals, such as FujiFilm, that picked up on digital photography and moved ahead at turbo speed.

Other organizations sought government intervention through tax relief. Or they attempted to win through rulings in trade disputes, as in the case of Whirlpool's bottom-mount refrigerators against those made in South Korea and Mexico.* Still others, through neglect or self-assured attitudes, fell too far behind in technology, marketing, manufacturing, or supply chain logistics and disappeared from the market altogether. It is such a careless approach to the potential damage of competitive conflicts that can shatter an organization.

What, then, are the key concepts behind neutralizing a competitor? First, it means reducing, eliminating, or voiding the competitor's capabilities that cause threats. In its extreme, it could lead to tying up scarce materials used by the rival in the production of its products. China's aggressive investments

---

* Whirlpool lost the case at the U.S. International Trade Commission.

in such areas as Africa and Latin America aim to secure the supply of precious metals and other natural resources, thereby denying them to competitors and effectively neutralizing their capabilities over the long term.

Second, neutralizing can take a course that is less extreme by diminishing a rival's strength relative to your own. For instance, it could result in advancing the timing of a product introduction, offering above-average incentives to intermediaries in the supply chain, or launching advanced technology applications. Each move conceivably places the rival at a distinct disadvantage and achieves a neutralizing effect. Then, there is the use of speed to maintain a digital advantage by using data analytics to concentrate on a market's decisive points, maneuver to create surprise, and boldness to engage a larger competitor. These approaches are discussed in depth in the following chapters.

Third, a singularly dominant approach to neutralizing a competitor is implicit in the opening quote: "We want to be competing on the basis of generating new products and services that the rest of the world can't make yet." That statement clearly infers innovation, inventiveness, and creativity.

Innovation runs the gamut of new-to-the-world breakthroughs, which are well beyond the capabilities of most organizations, although they are embedded in the souls of such organizations as General Electric, IBM, Google, Apple, Tesla, Uber, and Amazon. They recognize creativity and invention as the leader's central job of leading in the digital age.

Yet for the majority of organizations that do not have the time and resources to make giant leaps in innovations that carry the mantra of disruptors, modified forms of innovations can still fulfill the job of neutralizing a competitor. However, the downside is that they could suffer the problem of their modest innovation having a shorter life span before it is quickly duplicated by savvy rivals. The issue, then, is how damaging is the neutralizing action you take and how long will it take for the competitor to revive and confront you with an entirely new strategy?

As an example, consider the following approaches to product innovation that may not include disruptive breakthroughs, yet they can cause some level of neutralization.

- Modify a product by altering its features or adding new applications. Yet the product line consists of the same number of products. It works as a way to combine the new with the familiar.
- Use line extensions by adding more variety to the product line. It consists of the same number of product lines, but a higher number

of products. The result is to segment the market by offering more choices for the customer.

- Diversify by entering new businesses with the product line—or its technology. It creates a new product line with a higher number of products, thereby spreading risk and capitalizing on opportunities.
- Remerchandise to market change and create a new market impression. Doing so maintains the same products in the same markets with the aim of generating excitement and stimulating sales.
- Use market extensions to enter a new market with the same products, which broadens the product's base.

Innovation takes various forms, as shown by Cognizant, an information technology (IT) services company that outmaneuvered its competitors. Known originally as an outsource company that inexpensively handled ordinary data processing jobs for its customers, the company had to change due to many of its clients shifting their work to cloud services that require less hands-on management. "Traditional outsourcing has ground to a halt," according to one industry analyst.

Cognizant's maneuvering to remake itself focused on adding high-level consultants to its staff. The strategy aimed to provide customers with strategic advice on IT and mergers, as well as with help to generate ideas to improve their processes. With that move, Cognizant took on a whole new set of competitors, such as the likes of Accenture, Deloitte, and IBM's services division.

Although the strategy has not neutralized those industry giants according to the above definition, the meaning can be legitimately stretched to include Cognizant's success in achieving a spot as one of the top five global consulting firms in that industry. And according to a recognized research organization, the company is "gaining traction as an increasingly strong technology-based transformation power."

Thus, there are numerous major and minor approaches you can employ to devise innovative strategies and tactics along every dimension of the business. Again, the intent is to place the competitor at such a disadvantage that it cannot continue the campaign without excessive risk, and under extreme instances retreat from the market altogether.

As stated earlier, the neutralizing process means committing people, money, and other resources. Thus, should you lose resources in the competitive campaign equal to those of the rival, then the so-called victory has to be viewed from a variety of perspectives. For instance, what effect did the action have on the morale of your own staff? How many resources were diverted from the longer-term strategic objectives? How many key members of your staff were redirected to support the effort? How many key customers were lost to mainline competitors and new entrants?

Then, there is the issue of which side has the wherewithal to continue a costly campaign. In effect, the draining of resources can be a determinant in whether a company will continue to fight a contentious campaign or use its remaining resources in a more resourceful manner.

In all, when considering physical versus morale losses, it is the latter, or psychological loss, that is the dominant factor in all cases. Put together, there are three elements that make up success in neutralizing the competitor:

1. *Loss of physical resources.* This is where data can be of invaluable assistance. It indicates, for instance, how far you should apply the neutralizing strategy. With the assistance of algorithms, a fairly accurate assessment can be made about how much the rival can afford to lose. You will then be in a better position to know when to cut off your neutralizing strategy. And should you decide to continue with the strategy, it helps in determining the level of effort you should provide and the expenditures to be budgeted.

   There are still other situations that define neutralizing where your sheer presence in a segment could be enough of an intimidating force to accomplish its purpose. Again, one key measure of success is whether the competitor will regain its strength and make a comeback.

2. *Loss of morale.* Throughout this book, much is said about morale as the pivotal point in the outcome of a campaign. The essential points as they relate to leading in the digital age and specifically to neutralizing a rival are these: Morale creates cohesion or a feeling of being united in purpose. Cohesion allows you to tap more readily into the inner strengths of individuals, thus eliciting the resolve and determination to act decisively under competitive pressures.

   As important, it prevents them from faltering when stress increases due to a difficult market situation. Where this powerful force is missing, a competitor can feel the neutralizing effect.

   There is another reality about morale: some managers do not seem to worry too much about morale, or they give it only passing interest. No obstacles seem to bother them. "Here's what I want you to do;

now do it" is a familiar command. Underlying this rather cavalier attitude are signs of disorder in their follow-on moves, which could cause a hobbling effect. They are the great leaders for a day, until the moment that some market reversals overwhelm them—and they are neutralized.

The greater and more reliable reality is that marketplace conflicts rely on positive outcomes through individual fortitude, triggered by the potent force of morale. And that takes ongoing training, excellent leadership, and intimate concern for employees' well-being. To understand morale as a factor that adds vitality to any organization, consider the universality of the issue as expressed by a leader from another time and a different field of endeavor:

Loss of morale ... must not be underestimated merely because it has no absolute value and does not always show up in the final balance. It can attain such massive proportions that it overpowers everything by its irresistible force. For this reason, it may in itself become a main objective of the action.

Carl von Clausewitz*

Thus, where you can determine the rival's levels of morale, through formal research or informal observation, the better your chances of tipping a campaign in your favor.

3. *Loss of interest.* The issue here is the likelihood of the neutralizing effect being permanent or temporary. If your rival has just settled into a market niche and from all outward appearances wants to make it a permanent strategy with no visible interest in expanding, then a live-and-let-live policy may be the prudent path for you.

You can then resume your own expansion plans without concern about diverting additional resources to continue a neutralizing strategy. However, if in your judgment the competitor's strategy is temporary, then you have to move forward while the competitor is in a weakened condition and cannot put up too much resistance against you.

---

* Carl von Clausewitz (1780–1831), a Prussian general and military theorist, stressed the moral, psychological, and political aspects of conflict. He is famous as a military thinker and the author of the widely acclaimed book *On War*. Known for his maxims, his most famous is "War is the continuation of politics by other means." (For further reference, see Norton Paley's book *Clausewitz Talks Business*, Taylor & Francis, Boca Raton, FL, 2015.)

NEUTRALIZING A COMPETITOR

There are five ways to neutralize a competitor: *weaken the rival, prepare successive campaigns, reduce the competitor's effectiveness, make the conflict costlier for the rival,* and *wear down the competitor.*

Weaken the Rival

Weakening a competitor means creating situations that place excessive strain on the rival. If possible, the impact should not be temporary, or the rival would simply make adjustments or wait for events to change. In Cognizant's situation, should the industry leaders wish to derail the company, they could certainly field an army of consultants and overwhelm Cognizant. That move in itself would not necessarily alter the situation, as numbers of individuals can in themselves be neutralized by means of innovative strategies.

Where strategy does play a significant role is in such areas as introducing proprietary technologies, tying up customers into long-term contracts, or placing individuals at the customers' locations to aid in handling logistical problems.

The worst of all conditions in which a competing manager can find himself is in a state of utter defenselessness, where the feeling is that options have run out. These feelings can be real or perceived. Consequently, if you are to force the rival manager to back off by deliberately creating confrontations, you must either make him literally defenseless or at least put him in a position that makes this danger probable.

So long as your rival is a threat, you are not in control. As a consequence, the competitor can dictate to you as much as you can dictate to him. It follows, then, that to overcome the rival, or neutralize him, must always be a fundamental aim of a competitive campaign.

Consequently, you must match your effort against his power of resistance, which can be expressed as the product of two inseparable factors: first, the total means at his disposal, and second, the strength of his will. The total means at his disposal is a matter of the level of data you acquired about his physical resources.

But the strength of the competitor's will is much more difficult to determine and can only be gauged approximately by tracking the patterns of behavior from past campaigns. Assuming you arrive at a reasonably accurate estimate of the rival's power of resistance, you can adjust your own efforts accordingly. You can either increase them until they surpass the rival's, or if this is beyond your means, you can make your efforts as great as possible. But expect the rival will do the same. Thus, confrontation will again result in another round of campaigns.

In practical terms, the strength of the rival's will is an issue with two faces: the will of your own people, which is matched against the strength of will of your competitor. From a leader's viewpoint, that issue refers to the morale of personnel who are directly involved in the conflict.

Returning again to the importance of morale, it is the dominant issue that affects day-to-day employee performance and contributes ultimately to how well a business plan is implemented. More precisely, in the context of neutralizing a competitor, morale is also a prime factor in weakening the rival's resolve and power of resistance.

Morale, then, is shaped by common values, such as loyalty to fellow workers and a belief that the organization will care for them. Where morale is at a high level, it results in a team's absolute determination to win in a competitive confrontation. Successful leaders also know that when the inevitable problems and reversals occur, morale holds a group together and keeps it going in the face of adversity.

Weakening the rival, as a neutralizing strategy, is illustrated in the following case example.

The executives at Mattel Inc. felt quite satisfied with its longtime association working with Disney. They began their relationship in 1955 as the first sponsor of the Mickey Mouse Club. And since 1996, Mattel has been working with Disney as the maker of its famous princess dolls.

That seemingly happy relationship, however, ended in 2016 when Disney awarded Hasbro, Mattel's rival, the license to make its numerous princess dolls. "Disney Princess was probably the biggest coup that Hasbro has had in the last three decades," said an industry executive. Hasbro had not had a hit since the 1980s, when it came up with Transformers and My Little Pony. "We let our brands lie fallow, and were losing lots of money," according to CEO Brian Goldner.

Where does weakening the rival as a neutralizing strategy apply to this case? Around 2013, Hasbro saw an opportunity when it observed that Mattel was spending a great deal of creative time and effort on its own line of princess-themed Barbie dolls. In effect, the shift in attention was at the expense of Disney's princesses. And Disney apparently did not like the direct competition.

Noticing that Mattel's interest was waning, Disney executives set up a meeting with Hasbro. The meeting proved fruitful as Hasbro executives described its FunLab, referring to the room where research teams watch children play with toys through a two-way mirror. Then, in further dialogue, Hasbro touted its ongoing research initiatives of sending teams to travel the country, talking to parents and kids about their toy shopping habits.

The big plus, however, that firmed up the decision to move the business away from Mattel was Hasbro's bold move to coproduce movies with Paramount Pictures. The collaboration proved so successful that Hasbro opened its own film studio in Burbank and made certain its toy designers would "work with the filmmakers to ensure that the characters you see on the screen can be turned into toys." That bold action permitted Hasbro to directly influence the screenplay and characters. In turn, Hasbro centralized control in timing the marketing of the toys, games, and dolls associated with the film and its personalities.

There is still another aspect to the weakening process: *morale*. What effect did the loss of Disney's princess dolls have on Mattel's personnel, given the decades of close relationships? "We took Disney for granted. We weren't focusing on them. Shame on us," according to Mattel's former CEO.

After such a forceful and dramatic public admission, and in the context of neutralizing a competitor, how long would it take to rebuild confidence in the organization and its leadership considering the magnitude of the loss? With Mattel seriously weakened, what type of executive effort will it take to form cohesive teams to once again pull together and look for new avenues of growth?

The length of time for recovery will inevitably fall on the effectiveness of Mattel's leadership. Thus, it is the executives' task to reach the hearts and minds of the staff, regain their confidence, and get them to throw themselves into the upward climb.

Prepare Successive Campaigns

Campaigns rarely consist of a single short encounter. Rather, they are made up of several successive ones, with each campaign providing a point of reference for those that follow. Here again, that is where judgment layered with predictive analytics and other forms of research can provide the calculations, trends, and conclusions needed for neutralizing the competitor.

Underlying the campaign planning is effective leadership. As discussed in the Mattel versus Hasbro case, there were successive steps spanning at least three years that included numerous minor and major events, initiatives, and campaigns that resulted in Hasbro winning Disney's business. For Hasbro senior executives, it meant guiding employees with purpose, direction, and motivation. In turn, it reflected in the attitudes of all levels of management toward the overall marketplace, and specifically with Disney's interests in protecting and perpetuating the princess dolls with its customers.

In another case example, Cisco Systems reflects a similar way of thinking with its all-embracing dedication to the customer, a total belief in employees as intellectual capital, and an energetic willingness to team up with outsiders to develop active partnerships. This passion for molding such an outside-in focus is credited to the leadership of former CEO John T. Chambers, who clearly saw those attributes as a value system to drive subsequent actions.

The essential point: Accepting the idea that neutralizing a competitor entails numerous campaigns, and given that the effort would be supported with adequate resources, leadership is the linchpin to preparing successive and successful campaigns. It demands calmness and patience, which is exhibited in how managers react in various campaigns.

Reduce the Competitor's Effectiveness

Another approach to neutralizing a rival is to create conditions that reduce its effectiveness to carry on the campaign. The key word is *reduce*. In reality, however, the aim of diminishing the rival's effectiveness is not always achieved. Not every campaign needs to be fought until one side exits the market. Mattel found itself in a similar situation when it lost Disney's princess business. There was a point in time when the full realization of the loss took effect and reasons for the failure were fully internalized before recovery began.

Even where the fears of the outcome of a campaign are slight, the faintest prospect of defeat might be enough to cause one side to yield. If from the very start the other side feels that this is a probability, most often it will concentrate on bringing about that possibility rather than completely disable the competitor.

Influencing such a decision to make market peace and not upset the marketplace through negative media stories also means fully internalizing the personnel commitments and the other expenditures of resources to follow. Thus, after considering all the ramifications of the competitive situation, if one side cannot completely weaken the other, the desire for a live-and-let-live approach on either side will rise and fall as future events unfold. Meeting each other half way translates to each side finding a comfortable nonconfrontational niche in which to feel somewhat secure.

On the other hand, should future events dictate otherwise and you wish to expand your presence in the market, then resume the weakening of the competitor's capabilities as the most appropriate action. In that case, the following maneuvers apply to reducing the rival's effectiveness: First, look for ways to apply your strengths against a competitor's weaknesses. The essence of the move is that you position your resources so that your rival cannot, will not, or simply lacks the capability and spirit to challenge your efforts.

Second, focus greater attention toward serving customers' needs and resolving their problems in a manner that visibly outperforms those of your competitors.

Third, search for a psychological advantage by creating an unbalancing effect in the rival manager's mind, whereby he or she hesitates in indecision. The aim is to disorient and unbalance the competing manager into wasting time and making irreversible mistakes.

Fourth, secure a long-term position in a target market by building a brand, company image, or area of specialization that is unique to your company and cannot be easily replicated.

Such is the case with a mobile payments company, Square. The company enables small businesses from local hardware stores to restaurants to accept credit card payments via a small plastic reader that attaches to a smartphone.

In one particular year, the St. Louis, Missouri, firm processed $15 billion in transactions, up from $5 billion during a previous 12-month period. Not unexpectedly, Square was being watched by a strong, deep-pocketed competitor, Intuit. The rival also served a substantial customer base of small businesses with its popular Square-like credit reader called GoPayment.

Square founder Jack Dorsey claimed that his primary approach to reducing the competitor's effectiveness was a line of attack that his rival could not claim, that is, an ability to get his people to come together behind him, to believe in his vision, and to buy into the cool image that Square had managed to attain.

Whereas the Square case illustrates a maneuver against a competitor, the action raises the following questions: Will such an advantage be powerful enough to increase Square's market share? Is the advantage sustainable to spearhead an ongoing offensive and secure a sizable market penetration? To date, progress has been exceptional. The sustainable part, however, will be determined at some later time depending first on when and how Intuit decides to react, and second on the durability of Dorsey's strategy to get people to come together.

Make the Campaign Costlier for the Rival

The next approach to neutralizing is by increasing the competitor's expenditures and thereby overstretching its ability to sustain ongoing campaigns. In other words, make the effort costlier for the opposing company. In all outward appearances, the rival company may be seen as wasting its human, material, and financial resources through a continuing effort to react to competitive moves. In this form of neutralizing, the overall intent is to maneuver the rival into playing a passive role in the marketplace and thereby, from any practical viewpoint, neutralize it.

Then, there is another issue: How far can you push this effort? Obviously not to the point of absolute inactivity; that would not be competing at all. While this process lacks immediate effectiveness as it prolongs the competitive effort, there is a consequence for your firm. How long can you stay on the offensive and outlast the competitor?

Here, a level of judgment is needed. Maintaining even a moderate effort, as in promotional bursts or limited price wars, can be counterproductive if it consumes excessive amounts of your resources and ends up weakening your position. And should you intend to hold out longer than your opponent, you must be content with a more limited objective. The reason is that most major objectives require more innovative approaches and greater expenditures than minor ones.

Wear Down the Competitor

Wearing down the rival applies to numerous situations, some of which are similar to the above factors. These vary from wasting the competitor's resources, to rendering it harmless, to losing a favorable market position. Some of the techniques can result in both a physical and a psychological effect on the competing executive's mind, and thereby influence his will to resist.

Thus, many roads lead to wearing down a competitor, which opens up a wide range of interpretations and applications. For instance, consider the following possibilities:

- If you latch on to new systems and advanced digital technologies as a way to pursue revenue expansion possibilities or cost reduction opportunities, it is possible to create a wearing-down effect. And if the competing manager views such initiatives as direct threats that cannot be easily overcome, the approach would be successful.
- Position your group in the market through rapid maneuvers, so that the competitor cannot anticipate your moves in sufficient time to counter your actions with a meaningful defense. In part, this was the problem facing Mattel. Through their own admission, they did not see Hasbro's maneuvers and anticipate Disney's deep concerns.
- Where you can focus your resources on an emerging or poorly served market segment, you can cause the competitor to spread its resources by attempting to anticipate your moves, thereby weakening its primary efforts.
- Create a differentiated product or value-added service that is not easily cloned. One of Hasbro's winning strategies was to use extensive market research by fielding numerous teams of researchers in all of its primary markets to capture the play needs of kids. That form of data gathering, coupled with its ongoing use of the FunLab to watch children at play through a two-way mirror, provided the grist for product development. It was also the winning combination that permitted Hasbro to obtain the princess doll business. The total effect caught Mattel off guard and created an unbalancing effect.
- By permitting junior managers to take fast action on market opportunities, you allow them to react quickly to a competitor's vulnerabilities. Here, again, Hasbro's bold initiative in opening a movie studio illustrates this approach by allowing midlevel managers to coordinate product development to take advantage of movie releases. This action, initiated with speed and surprise, also had a wearing-down effect on Mattel.
- Forming constructive relationships with customers can lock out competitors for an extended sales cycle. As Hasbro got more involved with movie making and with merchandising its own and Disney's

products simultaneously with the films, it tightened the relationship with Disney and wore down the connection with Mattel.

The essential point: There are numerous opportunities to design your own innovative strategies that would be unique to your company.

In another case, Primark, the British fashion retailer known for its low prices and trendy clothes, illustrates a somewhat different method of wearing down the competitor when it expanded into a highly competitive and crowded market. The company was already well established with more than 200 stores in the United Kingdom and Ireland. And it had successfully spread into Spain, Germany, and France, where it became a household name.

Then Primark management looked to the hotly contested U.S. market. That meant confronting such high-profile competitors as Kohl's, Target, Walmart, Abercrombie & Fitch, and American Apparel, to name several.

Primark's approach to using a neutralizing strategy is illustrated by how it gained a firm foothold in that market. The company played its best hand by leaning heavily on its well-honed skills of reacting faster to changing fashions and trendier clothes than any of its competitors.

With confidence that it could achieve the same level of success in the United States as it had in its home markets, Primark management based its faith on three factors: First, it had to maintain its highly efficient manufacturing and logistics network that permitted pricing merchandise lower than most of its primary rivals could profitably match. However, that meant making certain there would be no serious repercussion if there were mishaps in the supply chain.

Second, Primark relied on predictive analytics about trends and market behavior to signal changes in fashion cycles and buyer behavior. The intelligence allowed for maneuverability without losing momentum, which is an ever-present condition in the volatile field of fashion, where the power of social media can create overnight changes.

Third, it had to depend on a management system that allowed managers at the local level to make on-the-spot decisions, so that designers could react rapidly to fashion and competitive moves.

Enveloping those three factors is a dimension of leadership that is brazenly reflected in the not-afraid-to-take-on-competition comment by Primark's CEO, "The Walmart offer, the Target offer, Kohl's as well—it didn't look like something that would be any more difficult to compete against."

Such a challenging statement encompasses the core ingredients that form the backbone of what defines leadership in the digital age. Even where it is acknowledged that big data is vital to making well-informed decisions, it still takes finely tuned judgment to interpret the nuances that characterize a market.

Then, there are the leader's sensitivities to understand the underlying elements that shape the morale of personnel. Beyond those issues, it takes boldness to address the embedded competitors that are ready to create barriers. As was shown in the previous case examples, such concerns are not always clarified by big data.

As Primark executives forged ahead with its expansion, they paid attention to every detail at the front part of the business that faced the consumer. That included stylizing in-store designs to match local venues by using city maps and local architectural ambiences. At the back end of operations, they were totally responsive to the critical issue of logistics by maintaining strong relationships with its primary manufacturers, chiefly among those in Bangladesh.

They did so by building a reputation for early, aggressive orders of styles their buyers thought would trend, and for sticking with them. Then, they used speed to move merchandise directly from delivery truck to store shelves, thereby eliminating the need for excessive storage areas, which added more footage for selling.

The sum of all the pieces illustrates Primark's strategy of wearing down the competitor.

NEUTRALIZATION PLAN

Having looked at the five ways to neutralize a competitor, now consider how *weakening the rival, preparing successive campaigns, reducing the competitor's effectiveness, making the conflict more costly for the rival,* and *wearing down the competitor* fit into a strategic business plan* (see Exhibit 3.1).

---

* See Chapter 11 for details about the strategic business plan.

EXHIBIT 3.1

Integrating the Neutralization Plan into the Strategic Business Plan

Strategic Section			
Strategic Direction/Vision	**Strategic Objectives**	**Strategies**	**Business Portfolio**
Allows for visualizing the long-term direction of the company, business unit, product line, or service	Indicates major performance expectations affecting the growth of the business over a long time frame	Specifies actions to achieve the long-term objectives	Includes existing products and markets, as well as new products and markets

Note: Neutralizing actions are focused on the strategies and business portfolio sections.

Tactical Section				
Situation Analysis	**Market Opportunities**	**Tactical Objectives**	**Strategies and Tactics**	**Financial Controls and Budgets**
Organized around • Historic performance • Competitor analysis • Market background	Identified by • Targets of opportunity	Prioritized by • Quantitative objectives • Functional objectives	Provides details of offensive and defensive actions	Contains key performance indicators (KPIs)

Note: Neutralizing actions are focused on the market opportunities and strategies and tactics sections.

Neutralizing actions can be incorporated in the strategic and tactical levels of the strategic business plan. As shown in Exhibit 3.1, the basic structure of the strategy section consists of four parts: the strategic direction or vision statement, objectives, strategies, and business portfolio of products and services.

To add neutralizing actions at the strategic level, you would first focus on the strategy part of the plan to specify decisive points in which to concentrate your efforts. These would include market segments where, in your best judgment, supported by data, a neutralizing effect would hit the competitor. Second, your attention would then center on the business portfolio, which permits you to deal with existing markets; new markets, products, and services for existing and new markets; and breakthrough products and technologies.

In the tactical section, the overall structure consists of the situation analysis, which incorporates historic performance and data analytics to reveal areas of vulnerability. Then, market opportunities identify and highlight which of the five types of neutralizing action to undertake.

Next is a statement of objectives consisting of quantitative goals, such as revenues and similar financial metrics, and functional objectives that represent various parts of the business, such as products, services, technologies, logistics, and communications. What follows are strategies and tactics that detail the specific actions you would consider. (See Section II, "Competitive Strategy," for greater detail.) The final part consists of a summary strategy, including financial controls and budgets.

In summary, neutralizing a competitor is an essential component of planning. As part of that process, there are two primary principles worth following for successful implementation. They are covered in greater depth in the following chapters, but are abridged as follows.

The first principle is concentration. This classic principle is in sharp contrast to the overly common planning approach of spreading resources in several directions, covering numerous objectives, segments, and isolated actions. Whereas the thinking may be to play it safe and cover all contingencies, instead it has the potentially damaging effect of dramatically exposing weaknesses and revealing areas of vulnerability. The result: The chances of failure multiply through the excessive thinning out of resources.

What's behind this singular straightforward principle? In practice, it means concentrating your resources at a customer group, geographic segment, or single competitor's area of vulnerability. It means finding the decisive point where neutralization can take effect. The hard-nosed evidence from history and current business practices leads unequivocally to adopting a strategy that aims at concentrating resources where you can gain superiority in as few areas and with the fewest possible actions as possible.

The second principle is speed. "There is no instance of a country having benefited from prolonged warfare," declared the ancient Chinese strategist Sun Tzu. To paraphrase that sage advice for business application, there are few cases of overlong, dragged-out campaigns that have been successful—unless it is one of the neutralizing strategies, such as wearing down the competitor. Exhaustion—the draining of resources—has neutralized more companies than almost any other factor. "Without exception, all of my biggest mistakes occurred because I moved too slowly," declared John Chambers, former CEO of Cisco Systems.

Thus, no halt or detour must be permitted without good cause. Extended deliberation, procrastination, cumbersome committees, and indecisiveness are all detriments to success. Drawn-out efforts often divert interest, cancel the momentum, diminish enthusiasm, and damage morale.

Additionally, employees become bored and their skills lose sharpness. As damaging, the gaps created through lack of action give competitors extra time to develop strategies that can neutralize your efforts. Therefore, it is in your best interest to evaluate, maneuver, and concentrate your forces in the shortest span of time.

The proverbs "opportunities are fleeting" and "the window of opportunity is open" have an intensified truth in today's markets. Speed, then, is essential for gaining the advantage and exploiting an opportunity. Altogether, the sum of these principles, ideas, and techniques form a plan for neutralizing a competitor and creating a competitive advantage.

The Five Forces of Leadership Shaped by the Digital Age

- Digital technology
- Competitive strategy
- Corporate culture
- Organizational structure
- Strategic business planning

Section II

Competitive Strategy

All men can see these tactics whereby I conquer, but what none can see is the strategy out of which victory is evolved.

Sun Tzu

4

Apply Analytics to Concentrate at Decisive Points

There is no higher and simpler law of strategy than that of keeping one's forces concentrated ... to be very strong: first in general, and then at the decisive point.

Carl von Clausewitz

Sun Tzu's* statement on strategy, written more than 2,500 years ago, distinguishes between the broader outcomes of strategy and the more visible dimensions of tactics. Clausewitz's† view on strategy, written more than 200 years ago, relates to its more precise application at a decisive point.

If you transpose those two statements to operating in today's embattled markets where big data and analytics are integrated into long-term and day-by-day decisions, then competitive strategy legitimately qualifies as one of the five forces of leadership—along with digital technology, corporate culture, organizational structure, and strategic business planning.

Specifically, if you acquire competence at seeing the far-reaching market picture that others cannot grasp, and if you can pinpoint where to direct your resources with precision, then you will be able to think with the mind of a strategist and with a skill that is essential to outperforming

---

* Sun Tzu (c. 544 BCE–496 BCE), an ancient Chinese military strategist and philosopher, is best known as the author of *The Art of War*. It ranks as one of the most influential books on military strategy ever written. Increasingly, it has become popular among political leaders and those in business management.

† Carl von Clausewitz (1780–1831), a Prussian general and military theorist, stressed the moral, psychological, and political aspects of conflict. He is famous as a military thinker and the author of the widely acclaimed book *On War*. Known for his maxims, his most famous is "War is the continuation of politics by other means." (For further reference, see Norton Paley's book *Clausewitz Talks Business*, Taylor & Francis, Boca Raton, FL, 2015.)

a competing manager. Doing so, however, means internalizing the principles of strategy and knowing how to apply them to competitive situations. To hone that high level of know-how entails reaching back to the origins of strategy and internalizing the primary concepts that have endured through the ages, and which are applicable in today's digital age.

ORIGINS OF STRATEGY

The origins of strategy date from the ancient Greeks (800–480 BCE), and the term is derived from the word *strategia* or *strategos*, meaning "to lead an army" or "the art and science of generalship." Commanders over the centuries have relied on military strategy to conquer territory and gain power. That meant imposing their will on others and maximizing the impact of their economic and human resources to achieve their goals.

Those generals faced formidable challenges as they crafted plans to outmaneuver competing forces, gain territory and power, and conserve resources, while expanding their influence. To impose their wills on others and achieve their objectives, they had to distract and unbalance their opponents physically and psychologically. Faced with resistance, those leaders were forced to maximize the effectiveness of their resources to achieve their goals.

While the terminology varies, these challenges are not much different from those of other human endeavors—whether business, politics, or athletics. Most confrontations involve a defense protecting the ground or an offense trying to overtake that ground. When transposed to business terminology, it means defending a market position or securing a foothold in a new market. In all instances, confrontations involve influencing the behavior of targeted groups. "We could more accurately compare [battles] to commerce, which is also a conflict of human interests and activities, and it is still closer to politics, which in turn may be considered as a kind of commerce on a larger scale," opined Clausewitz.

Although the destructive aspects of war are not present in business, there is a reasonable parallel when considering the bankruptcy of organizations, including once-mighty global leaders; the vast layoffs of thousands of personnel; and the closing of physical plants, with the devastating economic impact and societal disruption that bring about demoralizing misery to large groups of individuals. In many instances, those powerful shocks result in decimated regions, cities, and local communities, as evidenced by the bankruptcy of Detroit.

Many business scholars, executives, and line managers readily accept the military–business connection and find practical wisdom in studying the chronicles of military conflicts that span 2,500 years of recorded history. By examining the strategic and human elements of clashes, they gain valuable insights that provide an additional dimension to business study.

In particular, the lessons gleaned from military history and strategy can be indispensable in the pragmatic, everyday managing of people and resources, especially when applied to competitive issues. It is through the long lens of time and space that this additional perspective can fortify your judgment in such areas as leadership and employee behavior.

The chapters within this part of the book aim to tap the universal logic and historic lessons of strategy and thereby uncover solutions to today's stubborn competitive problems. Doing so overrides the narrower pathway of focusing only on current business events or job experience, where viewpoints tend to limit the range of opportunities and reduce judgment to a relatively short-term, constricted outlook.

Consequently, the military viewpoint provides foundation principles that can strengthen your understanding of strategy, whether you operate in a multinational firm maneuvering for position in a global arena, or a regional business fighting an everyday battle for survival. It is in this framework, then, that the rules, concepts, and strategies are presented in the following chapters.

The route begins by interweaving the classic works of the masters of strategy: Sun Tzu, Clausewitz, Jomini, Machiavelli, and twentieth-century historian B. H. Liddell Hart, among others. Their collective wisdom provides longevity, general acceptance, and authority to the workings of strategy, which is built on a common foundation of two main factors: First, the underlying patterns of human nature have not changed significantly throughout history. Second, notwithstanding the transforming geographic boundaries, political systems, and technological disruptions, the pragmatic logic supporting strategy retains its value today, as it has since the ancient writings of Sun Tzu.

Some fields, particularly those in science, medicine, technology, and economics, are continually updated in response to breakthrough discoveries. In contrast, many of the historic treatises in the humanities still remain noteworthy and valuable as the day they were written.

It is the study of military strategy, however, that fits a special category. Fighting, rivalry, competition, and power struggles give a human face to conflict. Thus, by focusing on the distinguishing qualities of human behavior that interface with those forces, you can shape your leadership style to fit the digital age.

Specifically, then, what lessons can be taken from understanding the origins of strategy? How does the study of military strategy link to business, so that the time-tested practices, guidelines, rules—and the overall historic body of knowledge—can be transferred and applied?

Let us look at the everyday language of business. It is not uncommon to read in the business press, or hear at seminars and speeches, the war-like vocabulary borrowed from the military, with such phrases as "attacking a competitor," "developing a strong position," "defending a market," "strengthening logistics," "deploying personnel," "launching a campaign," "developing a strategy," "utilizing tactics," "coping with price wars," and "doing battle with ...."

Then, there are the more indirect references that connect military to business, such as holding reserves to exploit a market advantage, developing an intelligence network to track a competitor's actions, avoiding direct confrontation with the market leader, bypassing a market because of high entry barriers, reorganizing the marketing and sales effort to strengthen a market position, or employing a new technology to create a competitive advantage over a weaker rival.

A sampling of such enduring concepts is shown in the list below, which lists statements from the masters of strategy. To gain their full meaning, and to form a historic and experiential foundation for business application, substitute such terms as *war* with *competitive confrontation, enemy* with *competitor*, and *soldiers* with *personnel*.

Classical Thoughts from the Masters of Strategy

"Speed is the essence of war. Take advantage of the enemy's unpreparedness; travel by unexpected routes and strike him where he has taken no precautions."—Sun Tzu

"Money is not the sinews of war although it is generally so considered. It is not gold, but good soldiers that insure success."—Machiavelli

"Now the method of employing men is to ... give responsibility to each in situations that suit him. Do not charge people to do what they .cannot do. Select them and give them responsibilities commensurate with their abilities."—Sun Tzu

"If we always knew the enemy's intentions beforehand, we should always, even with inferior forces, be superior to him."—Frederick the Great

"Supreme excellence consists in breaking the enemy's resistance without fighting. While we have heard of blundering swiftness in war, we have not yet seen a clever operation that was prolonged."—Sun Tzu

"The concept of war does not originate with the attack, because the ultimate object of attack is not fighting; rather, it is possession."—Clausewitz

"To accept superiority of numbers as the one and only rule, and to reduce the whole secret … to the formula of numerical superiority at a certain time in a certain place, was an oversimplification that would not have stood up for a moment against the realities of life."—Clausewitz

"The whole art of war consists in a well-reasoned and extremely circumspect defensive, followed by a rapid and audacious attack. I habitually think of what I must do three or four months ahead; and I always look for the worst."—Napoleon

"They are swift to follow up a success, and slow to recoil from a reverse … they were born into the world to take no rest themselves and to give none to others. You still delay … let your procrastination end."—Thucydides

"For to win one hundred victories in one hundred battles is not the acme of skill. To subdue the enemy without fighting is the acme of skill."—Sun Tzu

Given the origins of *strategy*, now let us single out the term for business applications. While freely applied throughout an enterprise, various definitions of business strategy do exist. The following meanings are used in this book:

> Business strategy is the art of coordinating the means (money, human resources, and materials) to achieve the ends (profit, customer satisfaction, and company growth) as defined by company policies and objectives.

In more pragmatic terms, strategy consists of *actions* to achieve *objectives* at three distinct levels:

1. *Corporate strategy.* At this level, strategy is developed at the top echelons of the company. The aim here is to deploy resources through a series of actions that would fulfill the vision and objectives as

expressed in a long-term strategic business plan—where "none can see … the strategy out of which victory is evolved."

2. *Midlevel strategy.* At this juncture, strategy operates at the department or product line level. Its time frame is more precise than that of corporate strategy. Typically, these strategies cover actions in a three- to five-year period and focus on fulfilling specific objectives—and "to be very strong: first in general, and then at the decisive point."

   Also at this level, strategy embodies two zones of activities: first, actions to create and retain customers, and second, actions geared to prevent competitors from dislodging the defending company from its market position by seizing market share and customers.

3. *Lower-level strategy—or tactics.* This level requires a shorter time frame than those at the two higher levels. Normally, it links with a company's or product line's business plan, marketing plan, and annual budget.

In everyday application, tactics are actions designed to achieve short-term objectives, while in support of longer-term objectives and strategies.

Also, tactics are precise actions that cover such areas as social media, the Internet, sales force deployment, supply chain methods, customer relationship programs, training, product branding, value-added services, and the selection of a market segment to launch a product or dislodge a competitor.

STRATEGY APPLICATIONS

Within the framework of competitive strategy, three primary principles are discussed: *concentration* in this chapter, and *speed* and *indirect maneuver* in the following two chapters.

CONCENTRATION

Finding the decisive point focuses on "keeping one's forces concentrated." It is an essential task that should occupy your thinking as you shape a strategy for your company, business unit, or individual product. Choose correctly and you are likely to win the competitive battle. Choose incorrectly and you could end up spreading your resources thin and slugging it out in the marketplace, which ends up consuming excessive amounts of human, material, and financial resources.

What is a decisive point and how can you find it? It turns out there are numerous possibilities for selecting a decisive point for a concentrated effort. The general guideline is that you target a competitor's specific weakness or a general area of vulnerability.

The search begins by conducting a comparative analysis. This includes reviewing a wide range of factors, from markets, products, pricing, supply chain, and technology to corporate culture and leadership, any of which can affect the timeliness and efficiency of how a company deals with a competitive situation. Encompassing those factors is the psychological or human aspects of people who must perform the work.

The starting point of a comparative analysis is to search for a rival's vulnerabilities, as they compare to those of your company. When completed, you are better able to develop a strategy that singles out a decisive point in which to concentrate your resources. You are thereby in a proactive position to determine a course of action.

Yet, even with the utmost care, there are bound to be gaps in your assessment, especially in less visible areas concerning a competitor that cannot be clearly measured, isolated, or controlled. Then, there are the undercurrents of friction, chance, and luck that emerge at unexpected times to alter your assessment as well.

To further saddle the process are the effects of imperfect competitor intelligence, which increases to the shifting nature of risk. Then add the human element with its unpredictable nature evolving from the personal agendas, creativity, intuition, and experience of those individuals interpreting and acting on the input of data analytics. Supplement those with the policies imposed on you by your firm, its overriding culture toward risk, and its attitude toward expending resources, and taking on excessive debt.

All this volatility can interfere with the objective assessment of your company compared with that of your competitor. Nonetheless, you still have to override those hurdles and identify your comparative advantage, if you are to pinpoint a decisive point of concentration.

That said, much more is at stake if you avoid the irrefutable lessons of history about the strategy development process. Among them, avert a head-on confrontation with a competitor (unless you are in an absolute commanding position), prevent depleting resources and leaving yourself vulnerable, and forestall a prolonged, dragged-out, morale draining campaign. The following guidelines will assist you in developing and monitoring concentration.

Guidelines to Developing and Monitoring Concentration

The first step is to adopt strategies that concentrate resources at a decisive point where you can gain superiority in select areas. These include targeting a competitor's specific weakness or a general area of vulnerability. The effective use of concentration includes the following:

- Recognize that concentration is a strategy with which to challenge larger competitors using a segment-by-segment approach.
- Aim to concentrate your resources to gain a superior position in a selected market segment, even if it creates some exposure elsewhere.
- Use data analytics to pinpoint a segment for initial market entry. Then use that position to expand toward additional growth segments.
- Make certain your staff is adept at reaching beyond traditional demographic and geographic segmentation approaches; employ big data to identify new or underserved segments.
- Maintain flexibility about extracting your organization from underperforming segments and concentrating on faster-growing ones.
- Concentrate your resources against competitors' weaknesses by means of maneuver.
- Understand that every market segment presents opportunities to fill market gaps, allocate resources efficiently, or exploit a rival's limitations.
- Train staff, especially marketing and sales personnel, to seek decisive points for concentration.

Second, watch for possible areas where concentration is not being implemented effectively. These include

- Failure to select market segments that offer long-term growth
- Dissipating resources across too many segments
- Launching a product with disappointing results due to the absence of adequate data about consumer buying behavior and a well-thought-out strategy

- Employing a strategy of concentration where the staff did not completely internalize the advantages of concentration and thereby was not fully involved

Third, use the following guidelines to correct the ineffective application of concentration:

- Actively utilize data analytics and other forms of competitor intelligence to identify a competitor's weaknesses.
- Concentrate on emerging markets, or those that are poorly served, to get a foothold into additional segments.
- Secure your position with dedicated services and customized products to create barriers to a competitor's entry.
- Within customer segments, tailor products and services built around product differentiation, value-added services, and business solutions that exceed those of competitors.
- Conduct internal strategy training sessions, especially for those individuals who do not understand the value of finding a decisive point and resist adopting a strategy of concentration.

The following case example embodies many of the points presented above.

Alibaba, the Chinese e-commerce giant, initiated a "strategy out of which victory is evolved." The process began with trend analytics that indicated Chinese consumers were rapidly adapting to new retail formats and online shopping—a fact supported by 40% of Chinese consumers buying groceries online, compared with only 10% of Americans. That data led to a bold strategic move of forming a partnership with the vast network and systems offered by Amazon, which fit Alibaba's long-term quest for supremacy in its markets.

At the midlevel strategy and tactical levels, however, Alibaba faced an entirely different and more intimidating situation. Its growth was slowing, dragged down by the dual forces of a faltering Chinese economy and aggressive competition from a rising group of start-up rivals. Alibaba responded by "keeping one's forces concentrated ... to be very strong: first in general, and then at the decisive point."

For instance, noting that Chinese consumers held an enormous appeal for U.S. brands, Alibaba concentrated on forming strong relationships with such iconic companies as Procter & Gamble, Estee Lauder, Macy's, and Costco to create a tactical advantage. The target: A huge generation of Chinese consumers who were attaining middle-class prosperity, which is quantified as 109 million Chinese people with a net worth between $50,000 and $500,000 and projected to surpass 500 million by 2022.

To seal the relationship, Alibaba formed a powerful set of major benefits that would be vitally important to those U.S. companies, as well as to support its own strategy of continuing its penetration of the brand-conscious consumer online market.

For instance, Alibaba was quite aware that U.S. companies were experiencing outlandish regulatory and logistical barriers to reach the vast Chinese population. For those U.S. companies that signed on, Alibaba rewarded them with approaches to circumvent tough hurdles by helping with marketing, data analytics, and shipping.

It even went so far as to assist suppliers in avoiding many of the taxes and other regulatory impediments that consume excessive amounts of time, money, and people. To further strengthen the bond, Alibaba arranged to handle transaction processing with the brands' home country banks and even takes care of maintaining inventory through its network of logistics partners. In all, the benefits alleviated most of the frustrations U.S. managers faced in lost years and lost opportunities. "This is an incredibly important strategy for the future of Alibaba," announced chairman and founder, Jack Ma.

The lure for U.S. companies is that Alibaba gives those firms the ability to learn the Chinese market and its culture and understand the Chinese consumers' buying patterns without a massive investment of time and money. (The irony behind Alibaba's efforts is that many of the U.S. products sold through its networks are produced in China, which indirectly helps the Chinese economy.)

What Lessons Emerge from the Alibaba Case?

First, strategically, Alibaba formed mutually beneficial alliances with U.S. companies to concentrate at decisive points, defined as online target audiences pinpointed by measureable demographic and behavioral profiles.

Second, tactically, the package of benefits that formed the partnerships was welded together in a manner that could not be easily replicated by rivals.

Within the context of concentrating at a decisive point, another viewpoint exists: if only the wealthy firms, as those cited above, can afford the types of relationships built on technology, brand leadership, and other high-level support to enjoy an overwhelming competitive edge, what happens to the less endowed organizations?

Are the smaller, cash-strapped companies with fewer resources always at a disadvantage? Do they have to defend their markets and retain customers against the continuing threat of resource-rich organizations that can mount offensives and win over markets on their own terms? The following section provides some answers.

STRATEGY APPLICATIONS FOR THE SMALL AND MIDSIZE ORGANIZATIONS

Returning again to the long history of conflicts, the chronicles of military encounters from ancient times to the present day provide substantial evidence about groups clashing in strong versus weak battles where the weaker side emerges as victor in the proverbial David versus Goliath encounters.

Thus, the resulting lessons that span 2,500 years of conflict-filled history have merged into firmly established concepts, guidelines, and rules. They provide insight into how leaders in those uneven struggles operated with comprehensive strategy plans and implemented them through effective leadership.

The subsequent body of knowledge survived meticulous analysis by scholars and practitioners and has been translated into numerous languages. This knowledge, in turn, has been incorporated into the business curricula at universities and military academies worldwide. And these same time-tested ideas, concepts, and rules continue to flourish today in business books, magazines, and workshops.

Within the context of this chapter on concentration at decisive points, let us begin with the opening statement of this book:

> To harness the enormous power of technology is one of the key measures of your effectiveness as a leader, especially in the active environment of disruptive technologies and intense competition. Your leadership determines how successful you will be in mobilizing your staff and preparing your organization, or business unit, to operate competitively in the digital age.

Amplifying that statement and applying it as guidelines for the small and midsize firms is summarized in the following four-step process, with more complete details in other chapters.

Step 1: Establish a Vision

This initial step means giving perspective to your thinking and planning about such areas as what your business would look like, on what markets your company or business unit would concentrate, what technologies you would likely utilize, and how your firm would be positioned against competitors during a period of at least three to five years.

Doing so means reflecting on your organization's distinctive areas of expertise, the business model you have or need to change, the profiles of the segments you will serve, the additional functions you must add to satisfy consumer needs, and how you will acquire the technologies to maintain a viable market position. Then, there are two additional and fundamental categories to contemplate: first, likely changes in consumer behavior, and second, known and potential competitors you are likely to encounter.

Notwithstanding that unforeseen events can cloud your vision and interrupt parts of your plan, envisioning where your business will be positioned at least 36 months out in time is fundamental to your leadership responsibilities—even in the swiftness associated with the digital age. As important to your leadership, the plan operates as the great communicator, along with other forms of internal and mobile communications, to support your efforts and motivate your staff to seek active involvement.

The plan also allows for innovative thinking by you and others who would explore new products, new product applications, and modifications for entering additional market segments. That includes delving into all-new-to-the-world possibilities. At its simplest level, product innovation can take the form of remerchandising to give the impression of a new product introduction; at its highest level, there is a truly innovative product utilizing cutting-edge technology that is new to the market.

Implicit in this first step is the pragmatic need for your staff to buy into the vision and make it their own. Otherwise, the effort forms into a cliché academic exercise, which is theoretically valid, but operationally questionable.

The implication for you as a leader is that directives cannot be forced on your staff in this critical stage. Rather, the plan's vision, objectives, and strategies have to be nurtured through participation and collaboration with key performance metrics put in place to measure, award, and otherwise recognize achievement. (Details of the process are given in Chapter 11.)

Step 2: Select, Monitor, and Concentrate

At this stage, you have to grapple with singling out on which of the product or service innovations to concentrate your resources. If yours is a small or midsize organization where resources are somewhat limited, the selection is certainly critical and worthy of your strong attention. The obvious reason is that innovations are inherently risky, even where you give the issue your best thinking with the support of reliable data analytics. In a pragmatic sense, your selection can run the gamut from a gut feel (or call it intuition) to sophisticated computer models.

You may also use an initial screen suggested by the questions in Table 4.1. This approach is best considered with a cross-functional team that reflects a collaborative approach and utilizes a scoring system. Initially, each member of the team scores every question privately. The team reconvenes and individuals present and justify their scores. A general discussion follows, and the team members go for a second round, and even a third round, of private scoring until there is consensus. Further, for greater accuracy, questions can be weighted for degree of importance. These weights are then multiplied by the appropriate score to form an evaluation index.

In practice, it is appropriate to screen several projects during one time period; notwithstanding, some innovations or courses of action may appear unrealistic for the moment or beyond your financial capabilities. Doing so can alert you to opportunities that cannot be immediately foreseen, such as joint ventures and outside funding. It is always easy to drop projects from the list or place them in reserve for some future time.

Also, keep in mind that your final assessment should correlate with the vision you described in the first part of your strategic business plan. If it does not, look again at the vision statement. Perhaps it is too narrow a focus and needs to be recast to allow for a more expansive outlook. The essential point, too, is that you want this exploring, screening, monitoring, projecting, and thinking process to take on a strategic, yet highly pragmatic application.

Step 3: Sustain Innovation

Innovation comes in diverse forms, from the geniuses who created momentous inventions that solved major problems, to organizations

TABLE 4.1

Screening, Monitoring, and Concentrating

	Low				High
Product/Service/Innovation Criteria	**1**	**2**	**3**	**4**	**5**
1. What is the long- and short-term market potential for the product or service?[a] Is there sufficient validation from data analytics to support the effort?					
2. What competitive advantage might be gained by adding value, modifying the product, or creating other differentiating features and benefits?					
3. What would be gained by repositioning or rebranding the product to customers and against competing products?					
4. What resources (materials, equipment, people, and financial) would have to be acquired or redeployed from other parts of the organization? Are personnel sufficiently skilled to handle the tasks?					
5. What is the level of risk? Will other parts of the business suffer by diverting resources?					
6. Based on financial calculation of return on investment (ROI), profits, and any other key financial criteria, how much is the product contributing beyond its direct costs?					
7. What value, if any, does the innovation have in supporting the sale of our other company products?					
8. Is the new product or innovation useful in defending a point of entry by competitors?					
9. Is the product innovation sufficiently strong to be used in concentrating on a decisive market segment? Or will it have a marginal impact?					
10. Are the innovation and related strategies compatible with the prevailing culture of the organization, as well as with the long-term vision of the strategic business plan?					

[a] Indicates metrics used to assign a score based on dollar value, unit volume, scalability, or other criteria required by your firm.

that created or transformed industries, to the executives who changed the way organizations operate—all of which impacted the lives of vast groups of individuals. The distinguished ones include Alexander Graham Bell's telephone, Thomas Edison's incandescent lightbulb, Henry Ford's moving assembly line, Clarence Birdseye's food freezing system, Bell

Lab's transistor, Intel's microprocessor, and IBM's personal computer. Numerous others of the same caliber have made a giant impact on the world. Then, there are today's innovators, such as Google and Amazon, working with autonomous vehicles and space explorations, and Microsoft, sinking a data center on the ocean floor where seawater acts as a coolant and waves serve as a source of power.

At a less dramatic level, there are leaders who develop different forms of innovations, such as with specialized joint ventures, as noted earlier with Alibaba's strategy. Notwithstanding that, Alibaba is not a small organization; its strategy can apply to all-size firms.

Common to all those forms of innovation is a practical reality: how to position them in the marketplace to provide a tangible return for the time, creativity, and resources required to commercialize the innovation. Thus, *positioning* a product, service, or technology is central to concentrating at decisive points.

Al Reis and Jack Trout popularized *positioning* during the 1980s as "not what you do to a product. Positioning is what you do to the mind of the prospect. That is, you position the product to the mind of the prospect." Professor Philip Kotler said, "Positioning is the act of designing the company offer and image so that it occupies a distinct and valued place in the target customers' minds."

What follows, then, is for you to monitor how customers perceive your product by examining the image it projects, its applications, the level of satisfaction it delivers, and its comparative position against competitors. Here is where data analytics can make a significant contribution to the process. You should then be able to incorporate the accumulated data from all sources and locate an open position in the market and in the customer's mind.

To consider the broader aspects of positioning, use the following guidelines:

Keep focused. Stake out a position for your products in those niches where there is an above-average chance to achieve a viable ranking among market leaders. Where possible, it is best to avoid the commodity segments, which are often dominated by the low-cost leader. Ideally, find a technology, product design, distribution system, or service that differentiates you and leads to a favorable position compared with that of competitors. That is where Alibaba excelled through its alliances with U.S. brands.

Establish cross-functional teams. The teams that represent the key functions of the organization serve as the collaborative linkage that forges a connection between the organization, product development, and customer. To succeed, however, teams must have a clear definition of how the company wants to be positioned and then be able to implement strategies that align with the vision and objectives outlined in your strategic business plan (see Table 4.2).

Solve customers' problems. The more you are able to solve customers' problems and help them prosper, the greater chance you have for survival and long-term growth. Therefore, look for new product applications, value-added services, and new market segments that may have been overlooked in the initial stages of product development, or which were uncovered from incoming data.

Look globally. Push your products and technologies wherever they apply in the world. Trade barriers continue to crumble in many areas, or

TABLE 4.2

Functions and Responsibilities of a Cross-Functional Team[a]

Functions	Responsibilities
• Identify innovations and market opportunities derived from big data that relate to the environmental, industry, customer, and competitor situations.	• Create and recommend new or additional products and services to fortify a concentration strategy.
• Align the business or product line with the vision, as described in the strategic business plan, as well as with the corporate culture.	• Approve all product alterations or modifications of a major nature.
• Develop long- and short-term objectives and strategies.	• Act as a formal communications channel for the interdivisional exchange of data about new market or product opportunities.
• Prepare product, market, and supply chain tactical plans. Include experimental tests that represent ideas and concepts derived from data analytics.	• Utilize big data to plan and implement strategies at each stage of the product's life cycle.
	• Develop tactics to improve market position and profitability.
	• Identify product and service opportunities in light of changing consumer buying patterns.
	• Coordinate efforts with various corporate functions to achieve short- and long-term objectives.

[a] While a team represents the collaborative thinking of individuals representing the functional areas of the business, the resulting recommendations still require the approval of the senior-level executives at the business unit level.

they can be overcome through alliances, as in the case of U.S. companies joining in Alibaba's supplier networks. However, make sure you are positioned to offer a specialty or customized product that will satisfy local needs, and not use foreign markets as a means to unload a standardized product.

The primary goal of positioning, then, consists of a two-pronged strategy: create a long-term desirable position for your product in the customer's mind, and secure a strong advantageous position against your competition. If the picture of your market reveals an undesirable position for your brand, use the following procedure to assist in improving your situation:

- Identify your product's actual position by inputting data from all the consumer touch points and the analytics derived from those sources.
- Evaluate your product's current position based on the criteria in Table 4.1. If it remains viable, then strengthen your position by creating strong offensive measures by focusing on products and services that continue to meet consumers' needs; then develop defensive strategies to prevent competitors from penetrating your position. Otherwise, select a position that nobody else wants, providing, again, it matches the objectives of your plan.
- Utilize two principal options to achieve an ideal product position: (1) move your existing product to a new position with or without a change in the product itself, or (2) introduce another product with the necessary characteristics for a new position, while leaving the current product untouched, or consider withdrawing it from the market altogether.

  Once you discover that your product's position is far from ideal, marketing has its job cut out for it. Together with the other elements of your promotional mix, such as advertising, personal selling, publicity, sales promotion, and social media, you can create a new position for your product.
- Recognize that achieving a lasting and favorable position is an expensive, time-consuming proposition. It is up to you to get your company's management to firmly commit to a positioning strategy. The dynamics of consumer behavior, the nature of global competitors, and the disruptive ramifications of new technologies are too volatile not to realign your company and product with a more viable position.

- Continue to track your competition and monitor the impact of your positioning on the customers' mind. Follow up with the digital tools of research to examine and compare your product's actual position with its ideal position. After all reasonable efforts have been made and they did not produce the intended results, then a review of your strategy may be necessary.

Step 4: Deliver Growth

Every organization has a range of embedded activities and procedures that are unique and potentially valuable. If uncovered and readied, they can sustain a continuous flow of ideas and innovations. In their extreme, they can take the shape of a leading-edge technology with a projected timeline of decades, as with autonomous automobiles and drones. Or they can be of more limited scope of an updated service or procedure that is unique to your firm and which can enter a new sales cycle.

Or, more likely, they can appear at a lesser level in the form of an innovative strategy or business model, as shown by Alibaba, which delivers growth while fending off competitors that seek to latch onto a winning trend. Any of these innovations could form the underpinnings for a concentration strategy to target segments for niche applications.

Within the context of delivering growth, and given the range of possibilities for innovation, it is valuable to know how far you can scale up, what types of resources you will need to sustain the effort, and what safeguards you need to defend your position over the long pull. After all, a smartphone app, or even a luxury item, has its growth limitations. Over a period of time, they will likely be relegated to defined niches.

Another consideration for delivering growth is a streamlined organization that speeds up communications from the multilayered contact points in the marketplace. As such, it is with increasing frequency that the cross-functional team is becoming a repository for big data and the resulting analytics. Organizationally, it is an outstanding place to centralize and utilize data to assess innovations in their diverse forms.

In its most creative form, delivering growth means marshaling the talents, data, and inputs of millions of people worldwide. For instance, search engine Google can instantly poll millions of people and businesses whose websites link to each other. And companies from Procter & Gamble to LEGO Group use Internet-powered services to tap into the collective beliefs of employees, customers, and outsiders, which are then used to transform their internal operations and product development activities. Procter & Gamble now gets 35% of new products from outside the company, up from 20% a few years ago. That has helped boost sales from R&D by 40%.

LEGO uses the Internet to identify its most enthusiastic customers to help it design and market more effectively. After a new locomotive kit was shown to just 250 train fans, their word of mouth through social media helped the first 100,000 units sell out in 10 days with no other marketing.

Thus, growth means ongoing leadership that fosters innovation through collaborative relationships with customers and other constituents. It is the focal point in which data and ideas can be discussed from a variety of viewpoints through an organizational format of a cross-functional team. It also leads a company or group through continuous learning that can spur creative thinking whereby the accumulated data can be used to intelligently prioritize objectives.

Clausewitz's opening statement that "there is no higher and simpler law of strategy than that of keeping one's forces concentrated ... to be very strong: first in general, and then at the decisive point" is a potent strategy for the allocation of resources. It is now more feasible than ever, with the availability of data analytics, to guide decision making and eliminate some of the risks. It is also a way to even the playing field against larger competitors.

5

Initiate Speed to Maintain
a Digital Advantage

The speed of innovation in terms of both its development and diffusion is faster than ever.

Klaus Schwab
Swiss professor and digital industry analyst

In a digital world where decisiveness, action, and surprise are the ingredients that contribute to the successful outcome of consumer and competitive campaigns, the above comment is a direct and succinct affirmation for utilizing speed in all activities. The pace at which activities and actions are set in motion appears to hit numerous parts of the business. Noteworthy firms that have embraced speed in all its aspects include Facebook, Amazon, and Alphabet. Yet, there are few firms worth mentioning where deferred or delayed actions have been successful, especially when operating in a highly competitive marketplace.

That said, procrastination is outright dangerous and contrary to the intent of what algorithms, big data, and data analytics are supposed to achieve. However, the reality does exist that firms are burdened with embedded organizational issues, such as a sluggish corporate culture that tolerates drawn-out deliberations, cumbersome committees, long chains of command, and a general practice of indecisiveness that stalls action. And even where the much touted movement toward collaboration is utilized, there are built-in delays, as documented in a survey of more than 23,000 employees that reports "60 percent of employees must consult with at least 10 colleagues each day just to get their jobs done."

As a result, the organization is unprepared to benefit from what big data has to offer. Moreover, from a leadership point of view, there is the potential damage that prolonged efforts have on staff morale. Their interest is often diverted, enthusiasm is erased, and the high level of positive expectancy is lost.

Should malaise and complacency creep in, there is the troubling issue of alert competitors taking advantage of the time gap and moving in to exploit the opportunity. Such was the case of Levi Strauss.

Levi Strauss & Co. makes one of the most recognizable clothing items in the world: jeans. Founded in the nineteenth century, it is the creator of that popular category of clothing, which remains the basic apparel for tens of millions of individuals worldwide. However, even with such a proud legacy, it turned into a desperate problem for Levi.

With the ongoing trend of vast numbers of individuals wearing jeans, the inevitable parade of competitors followed, such as Lee and Wrangler, as well as an evolving number of others trying to cash in on the continuing movement. Predictably, intense competition struck heavily at Levi, with the outcome that its $7.1 billion in 1996 sales plummeted to $4.2 billion by 2003. Over the next decade, sales rose only marginally as the San Francisco–based company attempted a turnaround.

What were the underlying problems? First, within the marketplace, Levi faced more aggressive competitors and a deteriorating retail environment where both shopping mall traffic and industry-wide denim sales continued to fall. Second, within the organization, an obstacle existed whereby Levi's design team was late in latching onto key trends, such as colored denims for women and more tailored jeans for men. Third, data revealed that females were the more frequent buyer of jeans, yet the company had the smallest share of that lucrative buying group.

Then other internal problems surfaced, such as a lack of managerial discipline and an inability to correctly identify decisive points on which to concentrate, such as the above-mentioned female segment. For several years, some senior-level executives, by their own admission, acted as if they had a monopoly on the denim market and gave little notice when young fashion-conscious individuals began trading in their Levi's for more trendy styles offered by start-up rivals.

As one Levi executive pointed out, "We have one of the greatest brands in the world, but I think that there may have been periods where we thought the brand itself could carry us through thick and thin. There's no question that we got complacent." After further investigation, it came to light that the embedded company's culture had created a working environment of complacency, which resulted in indecisiveness, followed by delayed actions.

CEO Chris Bergh subsequently formed new teams that addressed numerous issues by initiating programs to control costs, improve internal communications, revitalize morale, and cast off negative employee feelings that led to anxiety and fear. His priorities, then, were to rapidly invigorate the staff with a sense of competitive urgency to streamline operations, market the iconic Levi brand as the inventor of blue jeans, and reverse the sales decline.

Speed, then, is a recognizable advantage in today's competitive environment. Yet it must be supported by leadership that integrates rapid movement into the operating systems. For instance, it must align with the organization's culture through an organizational design that encourages staff collaboration and fosters communication with a spirited staff. The endpoint is to hone a capability that reacts quickly to the outpouring of predictive analytics that signal opportunities in such areas as changes in buying trends, signs of unserved or emerging markets, and indications of competitors' vulnerabilities.

MARKET, COMPETITIVE, AND CORPORATE CONDITIONS RELATED TO SPEED

From a leadership viewpoint, there are a number of diverse conditions that can affect your firm where speed of action would have turned around a negative condition.

First, attempting to recover lost market share, competitive position, and customer loyalty, as in the Levi Strauss example, is often costlier, time-consuming, and riskier than moving swiftly at the initial signs of declining sales. Also, the failure to react in a reasonable time period reaches deep into the organization and affects product development and the ability to react with the appropriate products at the right time. And if market data were available, the implications are that there was a lack of effective communications and a failure in leadership to turn the data into action.

Also affecting Levi was the reluctance by those within the organization to make strategic changes in production or to adopt a new technology, mostly due to objections centered on protecting the investment in its current technology. In all, there was a total miscalculation in missing the fashion shifts in the marketplace, especially in the female segment.

Similar issues existed at Eastman Kodak Co. Thinking its name was protected by a renowned worldwide reputation and a solid public image, its overly confident executives lagged behind in switching to the industry-wide movement of digital photography. When its leadership did respond to the change, whatever action Kodak attempted was too little, too late.

The illustrious company subsequently declared bankruptcy in 2013, at which time it reorganized and downsized into a fraction of its original size, exited its primary markets, and moved in an entirely new direction.

The irony is that Kodak saw the coming of digital photography. It is even credited with inventing the digital camera in 1975. In the end, however, Kodak's management, like that of Levi, remained focused on protecting its old technology and stoically watched as its market presence declined. The result: An industry that is identified with Kodak and a company that pioneered and popularized photography relinquished it to aggressive and forward-looking rivals.

Second, where there is a cultural pattern resembling an apathetic, half-hearted working environment, it is an invitation for a fast-moving competitor to probe and exploit weaknesses and convert them into opportunities. The essential point is that when a company stalls and loses momentum and exposes itself to an alert rival, it takes a monumental effort to regain its footing and move forward. This pattern could also foretell problems in integrating algorithms and big data analytics into the decision-making process—and in implementing the decisions.

Intel is an example of such a situation. The company's leadership had sufficient data to recognize an impending competitive crisis just in time to take rapid action. Initially, it had been caught off guard by the speed of the transition from sagging sales of PCs (in which it had boasted a leading position) to tablets and smartphones, which use lower-powered chips of different designs.

It immediately reorganized the firm and rapidly focused resources on a single dominant objective: move rapidly to latch onto a prevailing industry trend by redirecting its product line to focus on mobile devices to gain a leadership position in that segment of microchips.

Underscoring Intel's reorganization was management's awareness that its situation was more than just an external market condition and more than some random incident. Consequently, what followed was for management to go through an intense problem identification phase that resulted in the company's reorganization and a new management team to identify and root out endemic obstructions that created the predicament.

Third, speed is a factor in preventing a product from becoming a commodity, and even avoiding irreparable harm to a company's reputation. Inevitability, a product moving up the curve of its product life cycle will reach maturity, accelerated in many instances by competitors plowing in with innovations. Some innovations often extend the sales life of a product in entirely new directions, whereas other parts of the product category are commoditized. In many cases, you can delay the dire outcomes through continuous improvement and thereby forestall plateauing for longer periods of time. These market conditions were highlighted in the previous examples of Levi Strauss, Kodak, and Intel.

The central point is that you now have such tools as predictive analytics to drive product research, whether it is with new-to-the-world products, additional features to existing products, new applications of the product, or simply cosmetic changeovers. It is speed of reaction that can contribute to extending the sales cycle of the product or service.

In its most fundamental application of speed to prevent the further downward slide of its services and revenues, the U.S. Postal Service (USPS) has become an extension of Amazon's delivery network. As of 2014, the USPS made an estimated 40% of Amazon's deliveries. With the troubled USPS looking for additional utilizations of its vast services, Postmaster General Megan Brennan calls the move "just leveraging our infrastructure." She is transforming the USPS into a technology-supported delivery service for the e-commerce era, thereby beginning a new services life cycle using its enormous resources of sorting centers, delivery trucks, and hundreds of thousands of personnel.

Such a makeover for the USPS means hauling more packages and fewer letters. And it does so by designing customized service solutions to a variety of organizations. For its corporate customers, timely and efficient distribution is the bedrock requirement. Losing a position within a well-organized supply chain creates a break that is sure to be filled by a rival firm. Thus, recognizing that need, the USPS promises its corporate customers that it will make timely delivery at almost any hour of the day, including Sunday, nationwide.

For the USPS and others, speed adds vitality to a company's operations and serves as a catalyst for growth. It tends to elevate employee morale and energize an entire organization or group. And where an organization's product strategy integrates speed with the infusion of big data analytics, it is in a better position to secure a competitive lead. This point has been implied and clearly stated numerous times up to now. Consequently, before your competitors preempt you, it is in your best interest to integrate digital technology to gain and sustain an advantage.

There is still one more set of conditions related to speed that should have your attention: how effective you are in responding to market opportunities and competitive threats. Specifically, such issues are illustrated by the problems experienced at several high-profile retail chains: J. Crew, Aeropostale, Ann Taylor, and Gap. They all suffered market share losses and profit-draining write-downs, which collectively resulted in hundreds of store closings.

The central issue underlying the damages was the inability for those retailers to respond fast enough to changing consumer needs. On average, they took nine months to get a product to market. That is twice as long as the response time of fast-moving and -growing organizations like Sweden's H&M, Spain's Zara, and Japan's Uniqlo. Finally, recognizing that speed to market is the strategy that correlates with one of the major advantages of big data analytics, Gap and the others adopted newer, quicker, and more flexible manufacturing models—to get up to speed.

IMPLEMENTING SPEED

The guidelines outlined in the following subsections can assist in implementing (or enhancing) speed within your organization.

Align Big Data with the Corporate Culture

This point was emphasized in Chapter 4, as well as in this one, and it is important enough to deserve a dedicated chapter (Chapter 7). The central idea is that your corporate culture is one of the key supporting connections that allows for the successful integration of big data into your everyday operations.

As pointed out in the Intel case, culture guides how your employees think and react when entangled in a variety of competitive situations that require quick reaction. A supportive corporate culture drives forward-looking business decisions, generates customer loyalty, and ignites employee involvement in obtaining meaningful impact from big data.

Require Managers at All Levels to Submit Proposals Based on Data Analytics

It is in your best interest to immerse managers at all levels, including those in everyday contact with managing sales territories and product lines, into submitting proposals for market-expanding and revenue-generating opportunities. The key point: These proposals should be specific recommendations based on the output of data analytics.

If the recommendations are approved, they would be incorporated into the respective manager's business plan. Utilizing this approach would then filter through several layers of the organization and involve numerous managerial levels in implementing speed.

At General Electric, a similar procedure is used for its C-suite executives. Known as "Imagination Breakthrough" proposals, each executive must submit at least three per year for evaluation and possible funding. The criteria for submitting the proposals must include taking GE into new lines of businesses, geographic areas, or customer groups.

Reduce the Chain of Command and Increase the Speed of Communications

Collaboration is the objective. What follows is establishing cross-functional strategy teams that bring about multiple perspectives and heighten the chances of integrating algorithms and data analytics into strategy discussions and business plans. (The duties and responsibilities of a cross-functional team are shown in Chapter 4.)

Communications is central to your leadership effectiveness. From a broad point of view, effective communications provide consistency and positive reinforcement that can influence employee behavior, strengthen a team culture, revitalize morale, and cultivate an entrepreneurial mindset.

From a specific viewpoint, you have the opportunity to inspire teams through personal contact, or reach entire groups using internal communications networks. In either approach, you could recount successful stories where data analytics were used. There is yet another benefit of a strong internal communications network, namely, to report changes in the character of your markets in terms of your customers' demographic and behavioral characteristics.

Maintain Reliable Market Intelligence

Even where data analytics is utilized in your organization, you and others in your group should still get actively involved in doing your own grassroots, hands-on intelligence gathering. Depending on your role in the organization, it is highly useful to make customer visits with salespeople. You thereby get multiple points of view about the changing character of the markets.

You also have the opportunity to observe close-up your competitors' marketing practices and see how they are viewed by your customers. Then you will be in a prime position to compare and, if necessary, adjust your own strategies.

There is one further issue of importance: through your personal involvement, you become more knowledgeable and are apt to ask more insightful questions, for example, when presented with information about how algorithms are developed. This approach is summed up with the sage comment by a former president of the American Management Association, "Don't expect what you don't inspect."

Uphold Your Indispensable Role as a Leader

As an extension of the above, that means understanding the gradations of the marketplace, which consist of two zones of activity: first, knowledge about your customers and an understanding of the depth of your firm's relationships with them, and two, your ability to profile the actions of your primary competitors and know how to develop competitive strategies.

Within the organization, your roles require that you work with the best data available and act boldly, with speed. Even where some facts may be lacking and there is a veil of uncertainty coupled with periods of apprehension, you must rely on intuitive guidance, your years of experience, and your base of knowledge to make decisions.*

As for upholding your role as a leader, it is useful to gain insight about your fundamental personality traits. It is axiomatic to desire strongminded, confident, and decisive character traits, although these may not always be present at the level you wish. Notwithstanding, courage, discipline, and determination are essential qualities for effective leadership.

---

* General and former secretary of state Colin Powell indicates that 60% of the available information should be sufficient when a decision is required and action needed.

And of necessity, these qualities must be consciously employed until the other personality traits are strengthened.

As for intellect, certainly intelligence is important to function effectively in a complex technology-driven world. However, it is not a substitute for courage. There are ample numbers of brilliant managers in organizations who simply do not have the fortitude and boldness to act decisively. It is for you to arouse the inner feeling of courage and then act.

Beyond self-motivation, your indispensable role is to unlock the creativity and vigor of your staff and keep them motivated to fit the accelerated pace offered by data-driven opportunities.* U.S. Steel, for example, was once the world's largest steel manufacturer, as well as the world's largest company. However, that was before global overcapacity in the steel industry led to a significant rise in steel imports to the United States. Then, there were other factors, such as replacing steel with various new-age materials.

Now in the midst of a turnaround, the century-old company is attempting to grow through innovation based on finding solutions to customers' problems within the framework of what the company produces. For instance, part of the innovation process is utilizing digitization to simulate processes, embedding sensors into materials to capture temperatures, pressures, and other information.

It is relying on data to provide correct decisions. "In today's world, you can die just by the amount of data that gets dumped on you. You have to prioritize what's really crucial and important and then apply judgment to how you go about doing it," declared CEO Mario Longhi.

BARRIERS TO SPEED

A slow-moving, plodding organizational structure can be a major deterrent to speed. It results in drawn-out efforts that divert interest, diminish enthusiasm, and depress morale. Similarly, a sluggish corporate culture that is out of tune with the rapid movements dictated by the digital age is equally out of step with fast-changing consumer tastes. This point is reinforced through the following company example.

Haier Group, the Chinese appliance maker, first considered entering the U.S. market in 1999. It did so very cautiously by turning out low-priced

---

* For an all-inclusive review of leadership, see Chapter 1.

niche appliances like mini-fridges for college dorms and small wine cellars for city dwellers. Progress was slow, even though Haier built a manufacturing facility in South Carolina as a means of embedding itself in the marketplace. The company also attempted innovations, such as remote monitoring of its appliances' functions via the Internet. Yet, it was stalled in presenting its product line to Walmart for almost a year.

All told, it has taken almost 17 years for Haier to reach a point where it was able to take a giant leap forward by acquiring General Electric's appliance unit, the second largest U.S. manufacturer of major appliances. Now with an important brand name, a loyal customer base, and a solid distribution network, the expected breakthrough began taking place.

There are numerous reasons that can derail efforts to implement speed, even where there is intense desire in the C-suite to move with greater agility. Staff relationships may be strained, so that there is little or no trust that employees have the skills, discipline, and capabilities to handle a big forward move.

The needed component for implementing speed—a willing and spirited staff—is absent. It also means the best-laid plans, the most ambitious goals, and the most audacious business strategies are not going to work with inexperienced employees who lack the essential business and psychological competencies.

Also, if they do not display at least a moderate level of discipline, or if they cannot demonstrate an aptitude for the job, the organization is in deep trouble. The reason: Discipline, training, morale, and skill form the underpinnings of speed.

That requirement ties to yet another contributing factor to support speed and the push for performance: the amount of time an individual stays in one position. "There is kind of a natural evolutionary process where at some point people have been here a long time and they go off and do something else. That's healthy for an organization," explained a C-suite executive of a large bank.

What's behind that statement? First, speed of reaction is needed at the lower echelons—from field personnel through midlevel managers—so that they can adapt quickly to the unexpected with alertness and drive.

Second, success in the marketplace is an ongoing process consisting of several campaigns. Thus, it is the job of leaders to identify and expand on market opportunities. These may have been initially highlighted through the resourcefulness of junior managers, especially among those with hands-on access to market data. Providing there is enough initiative, they are the ones who can see the point for taking rapid action, even where senior executives are reluctant to make a commitment.

Third, long training and extended time at one job level may make managers experts in execution, but such expertise is bound to be gained at the expense of fertile ideas, originality, and flexibility—the essential elements for swiftly meeting the day-to-day demands of the marketplace. Midlevel managers, therefore, should demonstrate those qualities needed for speedy reaction. This is particularly relevant as the scaled-down organization takes hold and field personnel begin taking responsibility for on-the-spot decisions.

Consequently, from a leadership viewpoint, if you acknowledge that speed is essential to successful performance, it is your responsibility to maintain an environment where knowledge, training, and discipline are ongoing activities.

The categories outlined in the following subsections indicate the most common barriers or deterrence to speed.

No Confidence by Employees in Their Leader's Ability to Make Accurate Decisions

This is especially problematic when confidence reaches such a low point that employees do not trust in their leader's ability to determine a proper course of action. It is incumbent on that individual to get to the core of the problem and find out what is driving such opinions.

The situation becomes an intolerable barrier not only for speed, but also for pursuing any action at any pace. The dire outcome can cause morale to deteriorate and place the business unit or company in an unrecoverable situation.

If the leader is confident that the course of action is correct, it is up to that person to gather meaningful evidence, ideally from reliable data, and open face-to-face dialogue to explain the reasons for the strategy. That same platform could also set in motion a procedure for a collaborative approach to strategy development and a pathway to ongoing communications. Conversely, if the leader is incorrect in his or her opinion, that individual should take immediate action by admitting the error to the staff and making every effort to recover the situation.

It is only speculative at this point to wonder how Haier's employees felt about management's 17-year-long effort before making a significant breakthrough in the U.S. market with its GE appliance acquisition. What was the level of confidence employees had in their management's decision making? Did morale suffer? Or, on the positive side, did Haier's executives maintain an ongoing dialogue with employees to explain the strategy at every step in the long journey and thereby mitigate the problem of deteriorating morale?

Ineffectual Support from Senior Management

There are few encounters with management to equal the unsettling feeling of being cast aside by those in the C-suite—or, at best, given only marginal attention with an occasional meeting spiked with indifferent questions. Admittedly, in some situations a manager may relish the idea of being left alone to run his or her operation without interference.

However, assuming the business unit or product line is relevant to the welfare and advancement of the organization, then inadequate support and gaps in communication can signal deficient command and control. In turn, such a vacuum prevents senior management from providing timely support in such areas as approving additional funds to increase market share, shifting resources to secure a competitive position, or improving a supply chain network.

Then, there is the need for prudent guidance and support from management on technology sharing, integrating data into new product development, and personnel training. In some instances, however, correct direction is not provided. Such is the case with Honda leaders shaking up all levels of management when the company was plagued by an excessive number of recalls and problems in introducing too many car models too quickly, without achieving market success. The ineffectual support from management abused the intent of speed by not providing adequate support across all levels of the organization in the development and launch of new products.

Confrontations among Line Managers about Objectives, Priorities, and Strategies

Turf battles can create dissension and slow down the organization's progress. This is especially so where managers of equal rank cannot resolve difficulties independently. It is therefore important for senior management to intervene at the appropriate time. In a multiproduct, multimarket organization, disagreement is typical and understandable, since most contentious issues deal with power and the availability of resources.

That means resources must be allocated among many business initiatives, all of which are vying for attention. Inevitably, some plans get shortchanged or receive an outright turndown from management. And even the winners suffer the effects of lost time that slows their efforts. Painfully, the lapse in time may give the edge to an alert competitor.

Notwithstanding that there are some leaders who feel internal competition is beneficial, where it interferes with implementing plans that are time-sensitive, there is little justification for allowing such controversy to boil over into adversarial relationships that stall operations.

A Highly Conservative and Plodding Corporate Culture Places a Drag on Speed

Here, again, corporate culture enters the scene. In this framework, it shows as one of the toughest barriers to speed. Yet, it is one that managers must face. If the culture is out of sync with the competitive environment, and if managers are not in a position to change the culture, they must adapt plans to the existing culture with the aim of moving as rapidly as possible.

At Royal Dutch Shell, a sluggish culture existed due to the joint British and Dutch management structure, which trudged along with two chairmen and two executive committees. It finally took the courage of a new CEO to streamline the organization. One immediate priority was to speed up the "overly analytical culture," which made it difficult for the company to land big deals in a timely fashion.

Lack of Urgency in Developing New Products to Deal with Short Product Life Cycles

The life cycle issue has a wide range of applications. For instance, in California's Napa Valley, wine growers have used workers on foot or tractors to apply nutrients and pesticides to the vines that produce grapes. Recognizing the cyclical nature of that business and the importance of timing, Japan's Yamaha Motor has introduced drones equipped with onboard GPSs to precisely and rapidly spray chemicals on acres of vines. The aerial spraying can be done as much as five times faster than with tractors and is able to reach vineyards that are hard to reach with tractors and backpack sprayers. There is also the human benefit in keeping individuals away from the actual location where the chemicals are being discharged.

Then, as noted above, it would appear that Honda management was quite aware of the life cycle issue and the need to introduce new models at a rapid pace. However, it did not provide effective support, which resulted in product recalls and failed product introductions. Yet the marketplace continues to react to the "new" in all products with predictable regularity. Where that basic knowledge is not fully internalized by management or acted upon quickly to clear away organizational barriers, results can be ruinous.

Fear of Hardline Competitors Can Damage Morale and Suspend Plans

Impressions can create perceptions, for instance, of actual physical encounters with competitors, so that the images, attitudes, or ideas the mind can conjure, believe, and then react to shape employees' reality.

Such perceptions feed their emotions, which generate a set of attitudes and opinions. Some are correct, others distorted. That means people will choose to interpret and believe as doctrine through observation or the inevitable rumors—right or wrong.

What follows is that staff morale could flounder based on the slightest signs of what they perceive as a reversal. Such warnings could include failed performance of a new product, reduced profits, changing customer behavior, or competitors grabbing key customers.

Then, there are the sudden changes in management structure, the resignation of a key executive, or the downsizing of operations that can send shivers through the employee ranks.

Who, then, are the new employees in this digital age? Specifically, who are the millennials who are being recruited, trained, and nurtured for today's work and tomorrow's leadership?

MILLENNIALS OF THE DIGITAL AGE

Born after 1980, various studies have generally profiled these individuals, labeled millennials, as those who have grown to adulthood during a global financial crisis. Many in the United States were loaded down with heavy school debts, faced with an unsettled corporate environment where numerous organizations stripped away benefits, and it was commonplace for various functions to move offshore.

On the positive side, millennials are probably the most digitally connected group with a natural affinity to technology. Typically, they are registered with one or more websites, such as LinkedIn, Careerbuilder, and Monster. Overall, they can be characterized as looking for a career that provides meaning and purpose in a troubled world.

Even with a somewhat generalized profile, how do you lead the current generation of young digitally connected individuals? Are the classic behavioral and motivational theories, such as Abraham Maslow's hierarchy of needs, Frederick Herzberg's motivation-hygiene theory, or Douglas McGregor's XY theory still valid?

The following section reviews these theories, followed by current leadership techniques for your comparison.

Maslow's Hierarchy of Needs

Maslow viewed people as basically trustworthy, self-protecting, and self-governing, and when put to the test, they would come together and put forth their utmost efforts. Further, he believed that individuals' innate tendencies are toward growth.

According to Maslow's theory, there are five types of needs that must be satisfied before a person can act unselfishly. Table 5.1 shows these needs, which are arranged in hierarchical order and usually shown as a pyramid. The path is to satisfy one set of needs at a time, beginning with the physiological need, moving upward to self-actualization.

TABLE 5.1

Maslow's Hierarchy of Needs

Physiological needs: These cover the basic functions of comfort and maintenance of the body, such as food, drink, heat, shelter, sleep, and health.

Safety needs: These refer not just to physical safety and protection from harm, but also to such areas as financial security, employment, medical and legal assistance, and all means that maintain stability.

Belonging needs: These indicate the need for human contact: family, friends, relationships, teams, and general contact in society.

Esteem needs: These recognize the need for status, power, prestige, acknowledgment, respect, and responsibility. (Such requirements are provided to individuals in higher positions within the organization.)

Self-actualization needs: After all the previous needs have been satisfied, the top of the pyramid deals with the individual's need to reach for his or her full potential and strive for individual destiny.

TABLE 5.2

Herzberg's Factors Affecting Motivation

Factors Leading to Dissatisfaction	Factors Leading to Satisfaction
1. Organizational policy	1. Sense of achievement
2. Quality of management	2. Level of recognition
3. Relationship with boss	3. Intrinsic value of the job
4. Working conditions	4. Level of responsibility
5. Wages	5. Opportunities for advancement
6. Interpersonal relationships	6. Status provided

Herzberg's Motivation-Hygiene Theory

The most important part of Herzberg's theory is that the primary motivating factors are embedded in the satisfaction gained from the job itself. He reasoned that to motivate an individual, a job must be challenging with sufficient scope for enrichment and interest. Motivators—often called satisfiers—are directly concerned with the satisfactions gained from a job.

In contrast, a lack of motivators leads to overconcentration on what Herzberg called hygiene factors—or dissatisfiers—which form the basis for complaints. Table 5.2 presents the top six factors causing dissatisfaction and satisfaction.

McGregor's XY Theory

McGregor maintained that there are two fundamental approaches to managing people, popularized as Theory X and Theory Y. Theory X tends to use an authoritarian leadership style. In contrast, Theory Y leans toward a participative approach. In today's environment, Theory Y generally is accepted as producing better performance, in that it allows people more latitude to grow and develop in self-motivating surroundings. The two styles are contrasted in Table 5.3.

Now contrast the above theories with the actions that companies are taking to adapt to the incoming generation of workers who will be replacing the baby boomers and generation Xers.

1. Use digital tools and data analytics to routinely monitor and understand day-to-day behavior of employees. Doing so adds greater precision to evaluations and thereby permits a better form for engaging them. Managers are then able to shape the job to the individual and the individual's skills to the job, as well as guide types of training.

TABLE 5.3

Contrasting Views of Theory X and Theory Y

Theory X (Authoritarian Management Style)	Theory Y (Participative Management Style)
• The average person dislikes work and will avoid it, if possible. • People must be forced to work toward organizational objectives. • Individuals prefer to be directed, look to avoid responsibility, generally lack ambition, and want security above all else.	• Effort in work is natural and enjoyable. • People will apply self-control and self-direction in the pursuit of organizational objectives, without external control or the threat of punishment. • Commitment to objectives is a function of rewards associated with their achievement. • People usually accept and often seek responsibility. • People use a high degree of imagination, ingenuity, and creativity to solve business problems.

2. Elevate internal communications to the highest level. The key point is that employees want to hear from those in the C-suite—and they want to do so rapidly with the ability to maintain two-way communication.

3. Develop a proactive and open culture that allows individuals to experiment and flex their intellectual and, increasingly, diverse ethnic backgrounds.

In these brief descriptions of current actions, there are noticeable parallels with the above classic theories. Today's young workers can fit any one of the stages, from physiological to self-actualization, in Maslow's hierarchy of needs. As for Herzberg, there are also suitable matches among his listing of satisfactions. And there is an excellent match with McGregor's Theory Y, participative management.

In addition to these comparisons, there is still one major area that flows through all the theories and guidelines: *communications.** With the growing trend of workforces combining staff, freelancers, and contract workers, plus telecommuters across various divisions and geographic areas, keeping in real-time touch through an active communications channel has never been more urgent.

---

* See the Appendix.

Consequently, inspiring employees, quasi-employees, and nonemployees has become more challenging than before. Motivating and directing them to continuously improve, perform, and grow becomes a major issue, especially for the digital worker. Thus, helping employees to understand the volatile changes that exist in a global and competitive market takes a good deal of leadership skill and sensitivity to alter their attitudes and behaviors. This is particularly so when the natural inclination is to shrink from the realities of an uncertain and inconsistent environment.

Therefore, your aim is to inspire individuals to make courageous save-my-company, save-my-job efforts and turn potential defeat into victory. Accordingly, maintain a continuing humanistic awareness of the psychological effects on your business strategies—and on your ability to manage your subordinates.

For instance, if individuals are placed in a no-escape predicament and if faced with the bleak outcome of dismissal, there can be a fight-or-flight reaction. Instead, your role as leader is to utilize the utmost creativity to energize them to struggle out of the tight spot—if not for the sake of the organization, then for their own self-interest. Thus, a real or perceived threat can evolve into remarkable behavior among individuals, that is, if inspired by an energetic manager with a disciplined strategy for survival, followed by a plan for a burst of growth.

There is also a pragmatic truth that if employees are unaccustomed to the rigors of travel and long hours of work, they will worry and hesitate at the moment when levelheaded decisions are needed to handle tough competitive conditions. It is here that ongoing interactions can justify the investment of time and money to support an internal communications network.

What is needed is clear, uncluttered communications that convey information about the strategic objectives of the organization, goals related to strengthening customer relationships, the long-term outlook for a technology's impact on the market, and data about customers and competitors. Then there are the tactical details that influence advertising, selling, and customer service objectives.

Communications, then, should be seen from the viewpoint of employees as intellectual assets that must be nurtured and developed. Thus, indispensable to acting with speed and decisiveness is an organizational culture that helps all personnel acquire a way of thinking and an orientation that is totally customer driven.

Speed: A Core Rule of Strategy

Looking at the big picture, speed is one of the core rules of competitive strategy in the digital age. As for the global marketplace, the impact of speed is evidenced by how companies prioritize their long-term objectives and how they see their competitive standing.

In summary, if you move with persistent speed, you can significantly improve your chances to secure a competitive lead. Apply speed in the following ways so that your timing preempts competitors' moves to frustrate your efforts:

- Explore opportunities to cut costs for you and your customers.
- Investigate strengthening quality assurance and introducing new warranties related to product performance and reliability.
- Speed up internal communications and decision making, particularly where it involves approval of products and services that are time-sensitive.
- Track product life cycles for possibilities to replace products or systems and introduce new product applications.

Thus, where speed is coupled with decisiveness, action, and surprise, sufficient force exists to sustain momentum to take on opportunities.

6

Activate Indirect Maneuver to Create Surprise

Pure intuition without any data gets you in trouble.

Marvin Ellison
CEO, JCPenney
(from Wahba, 2016)

The previous two chapters within this competitive strategy section dealt with concentration and speed as essential steps toward maintaining a digital advantage. This chapter focuses on the use of maneuver to activate a business plan's strategies. Maneuver is understood to combine *direct* and *indirect* approaches. To provide some perspective for you to internalize the full meaning of these two approaches, reference is again made to their historical foundations, which stem from their military roots. Consider the following enhancing references:

> There are not more than two methods of attack: the direct and the indirect. Yet these two in combination give rise to an endless series of maneuvers. The direct method may be used for joining battle, but indirect methods will be needed in order to secure victory.

Sun Tzu
Ancient Chinese military general, strategist,
and philosopher (c. 544–496 BCE)

> History shows that rather than resign himself to a direct approach a Great Captain will take even the most hazardous indirect approach. He prefers to face any unfavorable condition rather than accept the risk of frustration inherent in a direct approach.

Sir B. H. Liddell Hart
Distinguished military historian (1895–1970)

103

The direct and the indirect lead on to each other in turn. It is like moving in a circle; you never come to an end. He who knows the art of the direct and the indirect approach will be victorious. Such is the art of maneuvering.

Sun Tzu

How, then, are the indirect versus direct approaches applicable to activating strategy and implementing a business plan?

One of the primary principles underlying the indirect approach is that, where possible, you avoid a costly direct confrontation with a competitor. Rather, your strategy would circumvent your rival's strong points of resistance by means of maneuvers. At the same time, your aim is to serve the current and evolving needs of your markets.

Applying an indirect approach as a strategy operates in three dimensions: First, the strategy is anchored to a line of action whereby you apply your strength against a competitor's weakness. The essence of the move is to maneuver so that your rival lacks the capability to challenge your efforts.

Second, concurrent with activating indirect moves against a competitor, you focus your attention on serving customers' needs or resolving their problems in a manner that measurably outperforms those of your competitors.

Third, your aim is to achieve a psychological advantage by creating an unbalancing effect in the mind of the rival manager. That is, by means of distractions and false moves, you make it appear that you are launching your effort directly at the competitor's strengths, whereas your true purpose is to target his vulnerabilities.

More precisely, the psychological effects of the indirect strategy seek to disorient the competing manager, causing him or her to waste time, effort, and resources in the wrong direction or, expressed differently, make costly and irreversible mistakes.

All three applications serve the strategic purpose of reducing any resistance leveled against your efforts. Yet it is the psychological effect that has the greatest effect on the outcome if a competitive confrontation. Look at it as an encounter of manager against opposing manager, mind against mind. It is your experience and skills pitted against those of your opponent.

The following references further solidify some of the psychological properties that impact maneuver. U.S. Air Force colonel John Boyd, in the 1960s and 1970s, shaped his ideas into a formula that has influenced the development of modern-day strategy.

He summed up his views as the "OODA loop," which stands for observation, orientation, decision, and action. The parallels begin to take form for conducting business in the digital age when you consider that the OODA sequence starts with observation. Thus, looking at the marketplace means observing through the wide lenses afforded through big data. That leads to the next stage, orientation, which allows for data analytics to assist in making decisions, and then taking action. Boyd indicated that the OODA loop applied to any situation in which it is necessary to keep or gain the initiative.

Another integral part of Boyd's concept is that the aim of maneuver is always to disorient the opponent. That condition reflects in an individual's inability to clearly and quickly grasp an evolving situation. For instance, as an evolving competitive situation develops more quickly than anticipated and in unexpected ways, it can cause a kind of mind paralysis, which leads to stalled indecision. Boyd's ideas had wide appeal in that they resonated with individuals using varied approaches to strategy development, such as supporters of statistical analysis and those who take a broader, more visionary strategic view of a situation.

In practice, Boyd acknowledged that there is physical contact with an opponent, but he focused strongly on the psychological element to generate surprise by introducing ambiguity, mobility, and deception into the encounter. To do this, he stated, "We must make decisions and act more quickly than the opponent to ... keep him off balance." This unbalancing idea formed into what Boyd called a "primary objective" of breaking "the spirit and the will of those opposing by creating unexpected and unfavorable operational or strategic situations."

The lasting importance of Boyd's concepts focuses on disrupting the opponent's decision-making capabilities, thereby encouraging uncertainty and confusion. Under his influence, systems were amended to take account of how data was collected, interpreted, and then communicated. By the time of his death in 1997, the revolution in information and communication technologies was well underway.

This psychological dimension* as applied to maneuver states that the most important points are in the opponent's mind. In turn, that exposes the human elements of positive emotions that help employees obtain favorable outcomes leading to achievement and success. Then, there are

---

* The psychological dimension was discussed in Chapter 1 within the framework of the organization. Here, it is used as a major factor in maneuver.

the negative emotions that produce fear, anger, stress, hostility, and anxiety. Activated by maneuver and surprise, these undesirable ones form disorder to produce a mental dislocation and, if left unattended, lead to a kind of mental shutdown.

Such positive and negative emotions are ever present in the development and implementation of a business plan, and they contribute more than most managers suspect to the ultimate outcome of a competitive campaign. Consequently, the state of employees' emotions should be factored in as a powerful source of competitive advantage.

Supporting the psychological dimension are the following affirmations from other times and places in history*:

> The psychological is to the physical as 3-to-1.
>
> **Napoleon**

> The final deciding factor of all engagements … is the morale of the opposing forces. Better weapons, better food, and superiority in numbers will influence morale, but it is a sheer determination to win, by whomever or whatever inspired, that counts in the end. Study men and their morale always.
>
> **Field Marshal Archibald Wavell**

> Pay heed to nourishing the troops; do not unnecessarily fatigue them. Unite them in spirit; conserve their strength. Make unfathomable plans.
>
> **Sun Tzu**

> Heart is that by which the general masters. Now order and confusion, bravery and cowardice, are qualities dominated by the heart. Therefore, the expert at controlling his enemy frustrates him and then moves against him. He aggravates him to confuse him and harasses him to make him fearful. Thus, he robs his enemy of his heart and of his ability to plan.
>
> **Sun Tzu**

What, then, are the key emotions that pertain to leadership and the psychological dimension of maneuver that would impact your role as a leader?

---

* As in previous chapters, to gain the most from these statements, substitute such words as *troops* with *employees*, *weapons* with the *traditional parts of the marketing mix*, *general* with *executive*, and *enemy* with *competitor*.

EMOTIONS

Maneuver unleashes streams of emotions that strike individuals in a variety of ways through complex patterns of physical arousals, inner feelings, and thoughts in response to significant situations. Typically, these result in surprise by introducing ambiguity, mobility, and deception into the encounter.

Also, emotions are greatly affected by the way leaders communicate, not only within the organization but also to the marketplace, especially during the opening stages of a campaign against a competitor contesting for the same market space. Such events have great emotional impact on behavior and attitudes on both sides of the encounter and are instrumental in deciding the eventual outcome.

Consequently, your ability to detect, assess, and control the emotions of your staff (as well as your own) is one of the predictors of success. Being able to read emotional cues in employees is a learned skill that can allow you to motivate them in ways that cause positive performance. It can release positive emotions of optimism, mood, and emotional resilience to persist under uncertain conditions.

However, one of the primary conditions that you must keep in mind is that in the event of a failed competitive campaign, blame should not be placed directly on any of your subordinates. The ultimate responsibility is centered on you as the leader. Instead, your thoughts should focus on uncovering the underlying causes or circumstances surrounding the outcome. Once determined, changes are possible by redirecting your staff's efforts on changing the strategy (see the list below).

Determining the Causes of a Failed Campaign
- Was the approaching competitive threat wholly unexpected, or could it have been avoided if there were a streamlined organization that permitted the flow of intelligence from the field to the right decision-making managers, who could have responded rapidly to the danger?
- Could a properly developed strategic business plan have averted the crisis and turned around the situation, assuming it contained a long-term strategic direction based on substantive data that included contingency scenarios that were not subject to the emotional reactions of the moment?

- To what extent did the staff internalize the seriousness of the conflict, which depended on astute maneuvers to neutralize the rival's actions?
- Were key members of the staff—including sales staff—trained in incorporating data analytics into developing competent strategies to turn around a negative situation by going on the offensive, and then defending what would have been won?
- Did cross-functional teams exist at various levels with responsibilities to develop business plans? And did team members understand that their collective actions must complement the corporate culture for plans to succeed?
- Did management recognize and take into account how unexpected forms of market resistance, friction, and the vagaries of chance could bring a plan to a standstill, and did it grasp the need for agility as an essential component of management practice?
- Did the senior executives and line managers display the leadership qualities that would inspire individuals, did they maintain the strength of mind at times of stress, and did they display the determination and boldness to move forward and implement a plan with a winning attitude?
- Did managers understand that a competitive crisis is not solved in a single campaign; rather, it is made up of a series of linked events, each leading to the next, so that one campaign should not be viewed with any sense of finality?
- To what extent did the organization and its personnel maintain unity even in crisis, so that it could support a turnaround with a competitive spirit and high morale?
- Did the managers fully comprehend an essential aim of strategy: to uncover those decisive junctures or focal points that would then become the primary objectives of a turnaround plan?
- Did the leaders understand the importance of identifying the ending point of the effort, that is, the point at which further expenditures of resources would be counterproductive?
- Was there a poststrategy in place to secure success by setting in motion contingency plans to actively defend a market position against a competitive attack?

As a leader, therefore, displaying positive emotions consistently is more likely to motivate those around you. And being able to bring out positive emotions in your staff is indispensable to success.* There is yet another favorable outcome in that such an environment tends to enhance creativity and innovation, especially where there is an effective internal communications network (see the Appendix).

Conversely, in instances where negative emotions are prevalent, these can be traced to ineffectual leadership, an inability to develop effective plans, and insufficient resources. They show most often where employees display a lack of confidence in a leader's ability to make timely and correct decisions. Worse yet, the negative attitude and behavior in one individual has an insidious way of infiltrating the minds and subsequent behaviors of coworkers. As such, they should be viewed as an urgent problem and handled immediately.

A failure to recognize and control emotional cues among staff can be detrimental within a team and progressively ruinous to the organization. It can cause interpersonal conflicts, result in missed opportunities, and lead to botched campaigns—all of which could have long-term negative ramifications.

The emotions discussed in the following subsections represent those that would affect your ability to introduce maneuver into your plan.

Anxiety

Anxiety is a type of emotion that individuals display when experiencing an inner disturbance and is usually accompanied by visibly nervous behavior. Anxieties contain sensations of uneasiness, alarm, and worry. These often result from an overreaction to a future-oriented situation that is perceived by individuals as threatening. It is usually accompanied by muscular tension, restlessness, fatigue, and problems in concentration.

There is still a deeper form of anxiety tied to agony, dread, terror, apprehension, feeling tense or jumpy, anticipating the worst, and irritability. Any of these are hardly states of mind you want your employees to experience when getting ready to launch a competitive campaign.

Frustration

Frustration is a common emotional response to opposition. It comes about from some form of resistance to fulfilling an individual's will or desire. So

---

* At this point, it would be useful to review Chapter 1.

the greater the perceived obstacle, the greater the frustration. Causes of frustration may arise from internal conditions, such as interference with some individual's personal long-term career goals, or with more immediate concerns about obtaining a promotion and making more money.

Then, there are external competitive situations of running into unexpected roadblocks due to start-up competitors interfering with key parts of a business plan. Some problems may be within a manager's ability to resolve, and if handled swiftly, the frustration is short-lived. Others may reach beyond the company's capabilities, especially if the problem deals with government regulations and the like.

And as the problems lengthen and build, so too do the levels of frustration deepen. Again, early detection of the causes of frustration is vitally important. At that point, it is essential to communicate openly and explain the full situation to the staff. Then, seek their active involvement to resolve the issues—or find creative maneuvers to circumvent the problem and neutralize the obstacles.

Stress

Stress is a reaction to an event that causes an individual to feel endangered or vulnerable. The severity of the stress depends on the nature of the event and the individual's reaction to it. Whether real or imagined, the body responds with a reaction that affects the mind, body, and behavior in many ways.

From a psychological viewpoint, the symptoms can appear as poor memory, inability to concentrate, poor judgment, excessive worrying, moodiness, agitation, or the feeling of being overwhelmed. These symptoms in varying degrees create an unbalancing effect on a manager and consequently on his or her decision-making capability. In turn, there is a progressively negative effect on total performance.

These visible shifts in behavior also tend to trickle down from the affected leader to members of the staff who can easily see the changes in mannerisms. As an outcome, the leadership qualities of objectivity, calmness, optimism, strength, and clear thinking are marginalized.

Fear

Fear is closely related to, but should be distinguished from, anxiety. The emotion of fear is caused by a perceived present and immediate danger that occurs within an individual. Or it can be in anticipation or expectation of a future threat perceived as high risk. It is characterized by such changes in behavior as the fight-or-flight response, hiding, or getting into a frozen state of nonresponse. Thus, fear would appear as rational or appropriate and irrational or inappropriate. An irrational fear becomes a phobia.

During one time period in 2016, CEOs of major organizations cited their common fears, most of which were centered on economic issues such as crashing oil prices, manufacturing in a recession, tumbling profits, and falling stock prices. "Over my several decades in business, I've never seen this combination of sustained headwinds across most economies, combined with high volatility across global financial markets," declared Indra Nooyi, CEO, PepsiCo.

Fear of the unknown, fear of uncertainty, and unpredictability accelerate the symptoms of negative emotions. Fear, then, is a deeply rooted part of human nature and can be triggered in various forms and through numerous circumstances.

JCPenney provides a pragmatic example of these physical and psychological dimensions during the company's tumultuous attempts at remaking itself between 2012 and 2016. The main event began when former Apple retail executive Ron Johnson was brought in as Penney's CEO to turn around the ongoing decline in sales, as well as reverse the company's weakening market position.

He spent a year attempting to remake Penney's into a high-style retailer of upscale merchandise. Johnson incurred huge debt by totally redesigning stores, replacing internal systems, and revamping marketing approaches. The result was a failure. Once-loyal customers fled in droves, sales nosedived, and Penney's was crippled financially.

Then, in 2013 a former Penney's CEO, Mike Ullman, was called back to salvage what was left of the company. His task was to return the store to its middle America roots and reverse the continuing sales slide, which he achieved with some success. In 2015, still another CEO took over, Marvin Ellison, with an urgent mandate to plug the stores' countless leaks in operations, strategy, and technology, problems left over from the chain's nearly fatal attempt to reinvent itself.

He immediately set in motion internal changes, such as relying on real-time data to handle inventory and logistics and refining pricing decisions. That meant building databases to better synchronize markdowns and promotions with changes in consumer demand. As a data enthusiast, his decisions were grounded to reliable information, which linked to his overall strategic goal of full recovery to its celebrated past. These changes, in part, made up the physical dimension.

What of the psychological dimension? Where do employees' emotions fit into the scenario? What were Penney's employees feeling and thinking during the chaotic attempts at turnaround? What anxieties, fears, and frustrations were they experiencing? To what extent were their emotions taken into account during the times of executive turnover and the day-to-day disruptive changes?

It now appears that Ellison displayed a greater awareness than the recent CEOs about employees' psychological issues. It was during his first few months at the helm that he conducted more than 60 employee town halls and visited hundreds of stores, talking to managers and floor clerks. It was an all-out effort to establish face-to-face interactions with employees and recognize them as valued human capital, and vital to Penney's recovery.

The essential point: Anxiety, worry, fear, anger, insecurity, doubt, indecision, stress, and threats relate to activating indirect maneuver. In the hands of an effective manager, emotions serve as an active competitive weapon. As such, they should be an integral part of every competitive strategy.

ACTIVATING AN INDIRECT MANEUVER

Activating an indirect maneuver is anchored to three fundamental points: (1) thinking strategically, (2) destabilizing the competitor, and (3) seeking areas of differentiation. In practice, maneuver consists of interlocking physical and psychological forces to circumvent a direct confrontation with a competitor, since marketplace fighting is not the aim of strategy. Rather, its purpose is to achieve a series of strategic and tactical objectives, such as nurturing the continuing growth of the market and occupying a profitable and sustainable position in a market segment, in addition to achieving an organization's specific goals.

Thinking Strategically

Ellison's initial order of business after coming on board as CEO was straightening out Penney's day-to-day operational and merchandising issues. For him, thinking strategically meant developing maneuvers that would have a long-term effect on restoring the retailer's position in the marketplace. Ellison initially followed three pathways: First, regain customer loyalty. He started by installing data-driven processes to manage inventory better, so that in-demand products would always be in stock with the aim of satisfying customers' immediate needs. Ellison also introduced a variety of new services and product lines to entice them to remain in the stores for longer periods of time and spend more.

Second, build on private labels. In addition to its in-house brands like St. John's Bay and Liz Claiborne, Ellison began building on its clothing lines by adding big-and-tall and plus sizes. As important, he hastened to install data-driven systems to shorten production cycles and bring popular styles to stores faster, thereby engaging more fully at the leading edge of fashion cycles.

Third, use smarter shopping technology. Ellison moved rapidly to catch up and, if possible, exceed other retailers by enabling same-day in-store pickup of online orders, improving its website, and overhauling its shipping app to make it easier for in-store customers to find discounts and deals.

However, from a macroviewpoint, strategic thinking forms the underpinnings of strategic planning in that it aims to generate more expansive ideas, concepts, and innovations that shape longer-term objectives and strategies. And where strategic planning is a formal process that takes place periodically, within the context of this chapter, strategic thinking is an ongoing mental activity that seeks creative indirect approaches to maneuver.

Thinking strategically also spans time and space. That is, it transcends global borders and regional markets and steers the mind to think of broader strategies and precise tactics. Within that space, there are also the pragmatic considerations of how to outthink, outmaneuver, and outperform existing and emerging competitors.

BMW, the luxury car maker, illustrates the far-reaching considerations related to strategic thinking. The company had to figure out how to maneuver through the biggest disruptive challenges facing transportation since the early days of the horseless carriage: autonomous driving, electrification, and car sharing.

Beyond those were the entirely new changes in competition. BMW faced off against some of the tech world's most powerful companies: Google, Apple, Tesla, and numerous start-ups that were investing billions to build electric, self-driving cars made of lightweight materials that could reduce greenhouse gas emissions and air pollution. Also competing were the traditional auto manufactures that were beginning to react at their own speed to the changing industry.

And the competition did not end with those companies. BMW opposed still another kind of rival, Uber, which was aligning with the market's changing demographics and shifting market behaviors. The car-hailing company partnered with robotics experts at a major university to design a self-driving vehicle. The maneuver aimed at a somewhat different goal from other organizations in the autonomous field. Uber envisioned a time when there was an end to private car ownership. The vision extended to a period when Uber would have a fleet of autonomous vehicles ready to pick up passengers whenever and wherever they liked.

What, then, are the predictive changes and trends compelling you to think strategically and envision maneuvers that would point you to the future? Consider the following issues and then add your own industry, company, and competitive concerns to the list:

- Intensifying competition from developing countries continues to worry many executives and prompts them to devise fresh strategies to respond to competitive prices that often range from 30% to 40% below prevailing market pricing. Then, shifts in energy sources, human rights concerns, and higher wages in those countries that originally offered low-cost manufacturing have forced fresh strategic thinking about the future.
- New flexible manufacturing techniques, digital breakthroughs, and advances in three-dimensional printing, for instance, convinced even the most cautious executives about vast new opportunities and competitive advantages for developing and distributing specialized products and services targeted to dissimilar customer groups.
- Shifting behavioral lifestyles influenced marketers to focus on how different groups live, spend, and act—all of which are continuously being highlighted by social media and influenced by diverse political, economic, and cultural movements.
- Shortening product life cycles due to the proliferation of new products and the continuing flow of dazzling new and affordable technologies convinced executives to probe emerging or previously unserved market segments. In turn, those circumstances triggered even greater efforts to push for faster, cheaper, and energy-efficient products.
- Continuing pressures to improve profitability and productivity activated the pervasive movement toward downsizing, reengineering, and outsourcing. The result: A rush by many forward-looking

executives to create market-sensitive organizations committed to total customer satisfaction. And with that movement, there came a demand for attracting the right type of people to managerial positions with the skills and experience to take on essential responsibilities.

- Disruptive technologies, skyrocketing progress in Internet commerce, cybersecurity, widespread industry regulations and deregulations, new sources of energy, alternative financial sources, and the expansion of cross-ocean relationships in Asia and Africa created additional challenges for executives to think about, anticipate, and act on.

Strategic thinking, then, encompasses numerous issues. Yet to avoid being totally overwhelmed by their complexity, consider the following six-part process to activate your mind to think strategically about maneuver: First, focus on the leading-edge trends that would affect your core markets. Include peripheral regions that represent growth opportunities, as well as expose vulnerable positions through which competitors can attack you. As part of the process, rely on networks of information anchored to data analytics that can expand your vision and get you to think beyond your current boundaries.

Second, think critically about the information you receive through such outlets as seminars, industry sources, and the media. Even question the data and underlying assumptions of the algorithms as you seek to open your mind to new pathways of thought.

Third, as an extension of the above, integrate information from a variety of sources before prioritizing your objectives and committing resources. Look for convincing patterns among those multiple sources of data. Then verify your conclusions by matching them against the strategic direction of your plan.

Fourth, recognize that at some point, thinking strategically must convert to action. The late management scholar Peter Drucker framed the idea succinctly as "all plans must deteriorate into action." Thus, a proper balance is needed by thinking in terms of two zones of activity: first, responding to the changing needs of the marketplace, and second, staying alert to traditional and upstart competitors that want to upend your efforts.

Fifth, understand that any strategic thinking that reaches out in space and time must align with the operating culture of the organization. For instance, embracing disruptive technologies that aim to serve new customer groups is not likely to succeed within a self-satisfying, complacent culture. Either the culture changes or the expansive thinking shrinks. (The impact of culture on organizational performance has been cited in various chapters.)

Sixth, communicate to all levels within your authority. Much has been said about internal communications in Chapter 5, and an implementation plan is included in the appendix. Continuing to strive for excellence by effectively communicating, motivating, and inspiring are qualities of excellent leadership.

Destabilizing the Competitor

The next underlying principle for activating an indirect maneuver is combining the physical with the psychological elements to create a destabilizing effect on the rival manager. The physical forces consist of such primary areas of operation as the product mix, logistics, pricing, marketing, and various internal systems.

As noted above, however, it is the variety of psychological forces (recall Napoleon's 3:1 ratio) in the form of diversions, distractions, maneuvers, devices, feints, and even misinformation, that would cause an unbalancing effect on the competing manager. Achieving such a destabilizing outcome heightens emotions within the opposing executive's mind and influences him or her to look in other directions and arrive at faulty decisions about the actual situations.

In its most practical application, the question is, what effect would actual competitive campaigns have on the minds of competing managers? While personalities vary, a psychological effect of some sort does takes place in the form of stress, frustration, fear, or other negative emotions that contribute to an unnerving effect, especially where there is an unexpected maneuver mounted with speed, boldness, and surprise.

Competitive campaigns that can potentially create a destabilizing effect take many forms, as noted by the following types of marketplace encounters:

Campaigns to reclaim a lost position in a market segment. Reclaiming a lost market position begins with determining what initially created the loss. Forging ahead blindly where there may have been lax leadership, flawed strategies, or undisciplined and unmotivated personnel will probably lead to a replay of the original event. The psychological effects from failure would likely deepen. For example, Ellison's challenge was to remain on red alert for changes in employees' emotions as he maneuvered to reclaim Penney's lost position.

Defensive campaigns to retain a key market. Defensive campaigns enjoy a psychological advantage, as long as they are handled in an active manner and not as a passive defense. For instance, there are distinct benefits in understanding the nuances of market behavior, assuming the defender has sufficient systems in place to monitor behavior and predictive data to interpret and anticipate evolving trends. The major issue here is avoiding the complacent no-one-can-beat-us attitude that results in self-satisfaction.

Therefore, defending a market position is never to be handled in a reactive manner. Rather, any pause should be considered time to assess strategy options and continue on the offensive to destabilize the attacker. Thus, for the defending leader, the issue is to recognize the transition point when mindsets need to change among staff members from defense to a spirited offense. Stated another way, every defense must have an offensive element connected to it.

Preemptive campaigns to block a competitor's entry. Moving aggressively to block a competitor's entry entails a well-trained, highly motivated staff that is deft at interpreting incoming data. It also calls for an organizational design that is fluid enough to sustain a free flow of information exchanges, and which allows for maneuver with speed, agility, and surprise. Within such an organizational framework, the central points pivot on accurate data about a competitor's intentions, effective leadership to unravel data and make correct decisions, and skilled employees to implement the preemptive campaigns to block, or at least downgrade, the competitor's entry.

Campaigns related to joint venture obligations. Joint ventures, acquisitions, and various types of marketing relationships often require participation outside a company's normal operating space. In such instances, it is the leader's obligation to be alert to where those employees are frustrated about being pulled away from their work. That means maintaining transparency and open dialogue to show the staff that a confident and collaborative approach is needed to fulfill obligations.

That also means providing details of the partner's overall strategy and why their willing cooperation is obligatory. In turn, it is useful to remind them that they may need help at some future time. If appropriate, it is also worth prompting them to be alert to marketing, service, or technological applications that would be transferable to their own operation.

Campaigns of opportunity. In today's business environment, opportunities can occur in many ways and at any time. They appear through predictive analytics or from media citing new trends. Such was the case of BMW described earlier that reset its strategic objectives and allocated substantial resources to match, and even exceed, the commitments made by Google, Apple, and Tesla, as those companies moved at breakaway speed to develop autonomous vehicles.

Such opportunistic campaigns tend to instill a sense of excitement among employees as they attach themselves emotionally to the opportunity. Alternatively, a destabilizing effect can occur when advances shift from one organization to another due to any minor or major breakthrough. Thus, emotions change from negative to positive and are continuously in motion. As such, the instability of feelings is an ongoing challenge of leadership.

Campaigns that expand into additional markets where there are embedded market leaders. This type of campaign warrants skillful maneuver. What should be avoided is any semblance of a direct approach against an entrenched competitor. Instead, attempt to circumvent the competitor through skillful entry maneuvers. See the following list of classic company examples (see page 119). Such maneuvers require accurate market data, an emotionally stable staff, and competent leadership that employs creativity, boldness, concentration, and surprise.

Campaigns to solidify an existing market positon and make it more defensible. This type of campaign was partially addressed above under "defensive campaigns to retain a key market." The key point, here, is that some managers take on a false sense of security that their company's strong market presence provides a sufficient defense against incoming rivals. What often results from such a passive attitude is that vulnerable areas are exposed through which competitors can enter. That was the case when Eastman Kodak did not pay sufficient attention to solidify its company's position. That is, Kodak management did not move fast enough to deal with the changeover from film to digital technology.

The irony is that the company saw the coming of digital photography. It is even credited with inventing the digital camera in 1975. To the end, Kodak remained focused on protecting its old technology and stoically watched as its market presence deteriorated. The outcome? Forward-looking rivals took over a mass market that was once dominated by Kodak.

Campaigns into new markets, or new businesses, to support long-term strategic objectives. Moving into new markets requires a high level of maneuver to initially establish a foothold from which to expand. Systematic analysis is needed to seek out an embedded leader's weak points in its product mix, pricing, marketing, or supply chain. It also means locating unattended market niches.

Then, there is the instance of entering a new and emerging market opening with the recurring question: What are the advantages of being first in, second in, or last in? Numerous opinions exist. For those advocating first in, the dominant reasons center on locking in key customers and forming solid relationships within the supply chain. Doing so also affords the opportunity for establishing a strong brand presence.

For the second-in firm, the main points focus on letting the first-in company make the heavy expenditures in developing the market, while observing and learning from the inevitable errors of the pioneering firm. For the last-in organizations, the reasons frequently focus on dealing with limited resources, cautious leadership, or a passive culture, which often means employing a niche strategy.

The following types of campaigns are variations of the above and tend to employ similar strategies:

- Campaigns by an aggressive competitor attempting to weaken a defender's resistance
- Campaigns that are short-term tactical moves
- Campaigns that attempt to reverse declining sales and loss in market share
- Campaigns that intentionally make it costlier for the competitor to maintain a market presence
- Campaigns initiated by internal pressure to take some action.

What follows are classic company cases collected from past decades to illustrate parts of the above campaigns. The main point is that they used indirect maneuver to intentionally avoid costly direct confrontations with competitors. In so doing, they succeeded in bypassing the competitors' strong points by means of clever movements.

- German and Japanese automakers indirectly maneuvered into the North American automobile market with small cars during the energy crisis, a market essentially neglected by domestic manufacturers during the 1970s, and poorly served during the 1980s and into the 1990s. Once embedded, they expanded into full lines of cars covering all price segments of the market with resounding success.
- In a somewhat similar approach during the above time period, Japanese companies entered North America with small copiers that targeted small and midsized companies. Xerox, the acknowledged brand leader, instead focused on large companies with its large copier machines. Once entrenched, those new entrants developed a full line of copiers for all segments of the market. The maneuver unhinged Xerox, from which it has taken decades to recover.
- Dell Computer initially bypassed the traditional distributor channel through retailers and other intermediaries. Instead, it sold directly to the end user with a build-to-order strategy, which complemented its low-price approach.
- Apple Computer became a dominant factor in schools early on, specifically serving that segment with computer hardware and software, which was left vacant by IBM.
- Walmart originally avoided a head-on confrontation with market leaders by opening its stores in towns with populations under 15,000, which were totally ignored at that time by the leading retailers.

Should those organizations have taken a direct approach by challenging stronger competitors head on without sustainable advantages, they would have awakened their respective competitors to aggressively defend their markets. Under those circumstances, losses would have been enormous in terms of human, financial, and material resources. Instead, they developed plans and maneuvers that probed for unserved market niches with minimal resistance from larger competitors, and where opportunities existed to eventually establish a foothold and expand into mainstream markets.

Overall, then, where there is little or no differentiation in product features, quality, performance, and service, or where there is no identifiable advantage in price, promotion, distribution, technology, leadership, or caliber of personnel, the result would likely result in failure. Thus, a company that moves directly into markets controlled by a competitor can exhaust itself before reaching its sales, market share, and profitability goals. And should the company achieve some minor objective through a direct effort, such as scoring minimal sales or nominal market share increases, meager resources would remain to move forward and secure enough market share to reach profitable levels.

In summary, indirect maneuver consists of interlocking physical and psychological forces that require strategic thinking, the ability to destabilize the competitor, and the creativity to identify areas of differentiation. The object is to circumvent direct confrontation, since competitive fighting is not the object of maneuver. Its purpose is to achieve a business objective, such as occupying a profitable and sustainable long-term position in a market.

Nor is it the mark of a successful executive to withstand excessive losses of capital and other resources that end up exhausting a company. Rather, it is the two-pronged effort of creating relationships and consummating a sale among customers as it fends off threats from competitors.

Referring again to other fields of endeavor where rivals are contesting ground or fighting to achieve success, there are clear-cut references to indirection that hold a large measure of wisdom:

> For to win one hundred victories in one hundred battles is not the acme of skill. To subdue the enemy [rival] without fighting is the acme of skill. Supreme excellence consists in breaking the enemy's resistance without fighting.
>
> **Sun Tzu**

> If we always knew the enemy's intentions beforehand, we should always, even with inferior forces, be superior to him.
>
> **Frederick the Great**

Thus, an indirect maneuver applies strength against a competitor's weakness, and resolves customer problems with offerings that outperform those of your competitors. As for your competitor, your aims are twofold: First, achieve a psychological advantage by creating an unbalancing effect in the mind of your rival manager by distracting him or her into making false moves and costly mistakes. Second, create approaches as described in this chapter that would neutralize the rival's capabilities to prevent you from achieving your objectives.

Next, integrate maneuver into your plans by engaging your staff, ideally through the focused energy of a cross-functional team, to open their minds to fresh ideas about innovative ways of developing such maneuvers. You thereby reduce the risks as you increase the chances of success, especially when going after market leaders, even where limited resources are available.

The Five Forces of Leadership Shaped by the Digital Age

▓ Digital technology

▓ Competitive strategy

▓ Corporate culture

▓ Organizational structure

▓ Strategic business planning

Section III

Corporate Culture

The culture of a company to me defines how excellent it will be, how help-ful it will be, how ambitious it will be, how innovative it will be. Everyone at Apple knows how deeply the culture of the company is ingrained. And in my mind the company wouldn't nearly be where it is today without that strong culture.

Tim Cook
CEO, Apple Computer
(from Lashinsky, 2015)

7

Align Big Data with the Corporate Culture

Apple's Tim Cook treasured the culture created and nurtured by the late Steve Jobs. When he took over as CEO, he also knew that he would have to delicately massage the existing culture to subtly redefine Apple in his own image. In part, that meant keeping the core values that made the company great.

One highly visible change was Cook's managing style of behaving more like a coach to his people and letting them get on with their work. Perhaps due to his primary work experience in operations, he wisely recognized that he was not equipped with the special expertise needed in such critical areas as product development, design, and marketing. This approach is opposite of Jobs' pattern of impulsive micromanaging at virtually every point, from the conception of a product to its delivery into a consumer's hands. Thus far, Cook's style has resulted in a level of greater stability within the senior management ranks than had previously existed.

Cook's leadership during his tenure has resulted in the Apple Watch, the large-screen iPhone 6 and its even bigger iPhone 6 Plus, and a new payment system, Apple Pay. Although Cook's more reasoned and deliberate approach in leading Apple is substantially different from that of the company's founder, his focus on developing innovative products and maintaining a long-term strategic orientation is the same.

He also expanded on Jobs' view of Apple's culture when it came to training and innovation. To that end, Cook keeps in mind the critical importance of a cultural fit with those he hires. He revamped its existing in-house education unit, Apple University, to focus on helping employees think critically and remain open to new ideas that are the underlying concepts that support his strong view of culture.

Cook's view of culture extended to how Apple stores interfaced more directly with consumers by hiring the former CEO of Burberry, Angela Ahrendts, to head the operation. Within that framework, it is fair to assume that Cook had access to the sophisticated logarithms, big data, and analytics to assure him that his decisions were on the right path. That is, he felt secure with the knowledge that technology was on his side.

What predictive power, therefore, does culture have over an organization that can support Cook's dramatic statement that "the culture of a company to me defines how excellent it will be?" In turn, what can a strong culture mean to your group or firm?

Specifically, how should your organization's culture interface with your role as a leader, given the rapid advancements in digital technology and artificial intelligence? What, then, is this amazing force called corporate culture that should form the underpinnings of an organization's success or failure?

DEFINING CORPORATE CULTURE

Corporate culture defines the unique spirit of the organization. Lodged within its DNA are the behavioral patterns, ideas, history, traditions, and mannerisms that can drive it forward. Or it can leave the organization languishing in a dormant state, ineffectual against competitive threats. Culture goes deep and shapes how your employees think and react during competitive threats, or when faced with the many disruptive technological and marketplace forces.

Thus, culture forms the backbone of your business strategy. It is a generally accepted truism that the best business strategy will carry a horrendous burden with the strong risk of it not being implemented where there is a troubled, doubt-filled, and flawed culture. Whereas a similar strategy supported by the foundations of a healthy and inspired culture enjoys the greatest chance of winning.

Corporate culture seeps into every part of organizational life. It defines and delimits the types of strategies you can realistically undertake without exposing your firm to excessive risk. Yet it affords you some measure of assurance that you will realize your objectives. "Very often you have to be willing to make a big move even before most of your advisers are on board. You have to be bold. And you need a culture that lets you figure out how to win even without a blueprint," declared John Chambers, Cisco's former CEO.

Culture infiltrates the extreme boundaries of corporate performance, as shown by growth or retreat, viability or stagnation, or in its extreme, survival or bankruptcy. To grasp the underlying nature of your organization's culture and to internalize what makes your organization tick is to foretell whether your plans have a reasonable chance of succeeding.

Accordingly, if you take the time to sort through the core values, deep-seated beliefs, and historical traditions that shape your organization's culture, you can control how successful you will be in running your operation. Such awareness is the primary step in formulating a digital strategy.

Doing so also strengthens your ability to engage the minds and hearts of the personnel who must take responsibility for its implementation. As a tangible outcome of that effort, you will be able to develop more exacting business strategies and tactics that can win in hotly contested markets.

The following visionary comments from heads of leading organizations illustrate these points:

A business can become stronger by making itself a community of people who share the same ideals and goals, the same corporate culture.

Hitoshi Mizorogi
CEO, Disco Corp.

Sharp has a heritage of creating one-of-a-kind products. It is part of our corporate DNA.

Tai Jeng Wu
President, Sharp Corp.

My personal credo of three Cs: Challenge, Create, Commit. I tell all my staff to approach life with a pioneer spirit—several steps ahead of the competition.

Masahiro Okafuji
President, Itochu Corp.

We have many challenges ahead of us, but perhaps our biggest challenge is the one we have created for ourselves. I mean growing Toyota into a company that truly matters to our customers, our employees, and to the societies where we live.

Akio Toyada
CEO, Toyota Motor Corp.

ATTRIBUTES OF A HEALTHY CORPORATE CULTURE

Each organization's culture has its own defined characteristics that give it a unique set of qualities that set it apart from other firms. Yet, when viewed from a leader's perspective, these attributes combine to become a competitive form of differentiation that permit an organization or business group to

1. Respond more rapidly to changing market conditions than a rival, particularly during a digital transformation
2. Exploit fresh opportunities with a bold and unified approach from the various functional parts of the organization
3. Strengthen customer relationships as an ongoing corporate imperative, especially where the potential power of data analytics is utilized
4. Create innovative products and services based on a blend of creativity and emerging digital technologies
5. Implement clever competitive strategies that employ the intensity of concentration, speed, and indirect approach
6. Gain the initiative through high employee morale and effective leadership
7. Sustain a disciplined staff that seeks personnel growth through ongoing training and support

Referring again to Cook's opening comments that culture "defines how excellent [you] will be, how helpful [you] will be, how ambitious [you] will be, how innovative [you] will be," these expectations pivot on the following areas: *beliefs and values* and *employee treatment and expectations*. In turn, they influence organizational structure, applications of competitive strategy, and leadership.

Beliefs and Values

Fundamental to an organization's beliefs and values is the total commitment to customer satisfaction. There is certainly nothing startling about such a belief. It has been touted in every conceivable manner and shouted through every form of modern communications over several decades. The issue, however, is the level of commitment to such an ideal, and how deeply it is ingrained in the policies, actions, and mannerisms emanating from the C-suite to the factory floor. And it goes beyond, to a commitment that has a physical and psychological interface with a satisfied customer who ideally returns another day to transact business.

Consequently, this belief stands out and fits the cultural pattern of high-performing organizations. It is one that should permeate the entire organization. One of the ways to systematize such a commitment is to form cross-functional, multidisciplinary teams at various levels of the organization. Team members can then readily share data and collaborate in problem solving that brings together their best thinking.

Doing so also tends to trigger meaningful dialogue that results in a collection of new ideas that emerge from the analytics. Thus, the tangible results can spring from the diversity of individuals bringing their unique cultural backgrounds, experiences, and skill sets to the meeting's agenda. "When we speak about diversity, we're not only talking about race, nationality, and orientation, but we are also talking about diversity in the broadest sense, meaning of educational backgrounds and life experiences too," declared Lloyd Blankfein, chairman and CEO, Goldman Sachs.

As team members generate fresh product concepts and innovations that become drivers of growth, the end result often exceeds expectations through individual achievement and overall improved corporate performance. As important, the process permits the energized mindsets and attitudes of individuals to delve into the possibilities of new technologies that may elude even the best hopes of those executives in the C-suite (see Table 7.1).

In practice, beliefs and values also incorporate a human dimension, thereby making certain the intuitive inventiveness of individuals flourishes. This idea is expressed by one Google employee as "the company culture truly makes workers feel they're valued and respected as a human being, not as a cog in a machine." This is especially critical when it comes to developing and implementing competitive strategies, which require creativity to neutralize a rival's efforts and prevent it from interfering with a team's plans.

Employee Treatment and Expectations

Within the framework of culture and as an extension of the above beliefs and values, this category encompasses such areas as valuing discipline, maintaining an entrepreneurial outlook, encouraging personal growth through continuous learning, and motivating employees to take pride

TABLE 7.1

Duties and Responsibilities of a Cross-Functional Team

General Functions

- Align the organization's or business unit's broad vision with the new possibilities resulting from digitization.
- Utilize big data when assessing the environmental, technological, industry, customer, and competitor situations.
- Develop long- and short-term objectives and strategies based on predictive analytics.
- Prepare product, market, supply chain, and quality plans to implement competitive strategies.
- Maintain a viable competitive market position by means of offensive and defensive strategies.

Responsibilities

- Recommend new or modified products and services.
- Plan strategies throughout the product life cycle that utilize big data and analytics to determine courses of actions that can be implemented with speed at decisive points.
- Develop tactical plans to secure markets against competitive threats.
- Identify product and service opportunities in light of changing consumer buying patterns resulting from the outputs of data analytics.
- Collaborate with various corporate functions to achieve short- and long-term objectives.
- Organize interdivisional exchanges of new market or product opportunities through the internal company communications network.
- Cooperate in developing a strategic business plan for a business unit or product line so that it aligns with the corporate culture.

in their organization. "We encourage our people to reframe and elevate the meaning and purpose of their work and give them the opportunity to share how their work makes an impact," stated a senior executive of a global consulting firm. As a leader, therefore, encourage your staff to find ways to create possibilities for differentiating your organization's product and service offerings.

To that end, your initial approach is to bring your employees to a point of living in tune with their surroundings. Specifically, get them to reach an expanded state of *awareness*. Awareness, in this context, takes into account such diverse issues as how competitors' actions could disrupt company plans, how to interpret big data and determine its impact on your strategies, and how to integrate data analytics into the product development process.

Therefore, your purpose is to get your staff to look outside their four walls and understand the wider competitive world. Through online communications, informal meetings, and weekly or monthly briefings, update your staff about markets, industries, and competitive conditions.

From a leadership viewpoint, these get-togethers will be worth your time and effort as they serve several purposes:

- You recognize the value of providing your staff with substantive market data and competitor information.
- You motivate them by providing a communications channel through which they can participate with fresh insights.
- You tap their diversity, thought patterns, experiences, and collective knowledge, thereby integrating individuals and their functions.
- You obtain viewpoints that can provide useful perspectives and constructive comparisons.
- You bring unity to your group.

Such sessions typically benefit from another major outcome. They awaken your staff to internalize that you and they walk together on a very narrow path, which includes numerous visible and unforeseen obstacles. Doing so helps them deal with apprehension, rather than give into fear. Stated another way, you want to develop in them a balance of a positive mindset linked with an objective interpretation of market events, so that success is weighted in your favor.

Increasingly, a wide variety of communications vehicles permit you to take the high road and initiate programs and exchanges of information. In addition to the formats described above, there is the burgeoning use of social networks, blogs, e-mail, instant messaging, videoconferencing, corporate wikis, and the like. That includes individual face time, thought to be outmoded by electronic communications, but still prevalent and noticeably on the increase.

And with increased diversity in the workforce, the need is to unite individuals to a common goal. The reason: Individuals tend to be wherever their thoughts are. You want to make certain their thoughts, as well as your own, from a business viewpoint, are where you would like them to be.

As one bank executive points out, "We spend a lot of time listening to team members through town-hall meetings, roundtables, and surveys. And we are very good at following up on the feedback we receive. There is nothing worse for employee engagement than asking for feedback and then ignoring it."

Therefore, stay close to your employees, so that you can sensitize yourself to their thoughts, moods, temperaments, and increasingly the nuances of their respective cultures. All the while, your aim is to integrate them into the mainstream of your company's goals.

Doing so also allows you to focus individuals' attention on constructive projects, such as taking even a sketchy idea that may have been hatched through big data and converting it into a new product or service. Consequently, the exciting possibility exists for an embryonic innovation to sprout into a new revenue stream. Otherwise, without some guidance, their creative thoughts would radiate like sunbeams. At first, they seem solid, until you try to grasp them. You thereby lose the potential value of huge business-building resources.

Thus, reach out to the special needs of your employees and focus on sustaining their psychological well-being. As a result, you should see tangible improvements in performance, innovation, and employee harmony.

As part of that effort, commercially available people analytics software helps to better evaluate the key employee touch points listed above. More specifically, the data assists in understanding the external and internal relationships. Such organizations as Boeing, Facebook, Qualcomm, and Genentech have embraced people analytics. "We know that associates who are fully engaged in their jobs take significantly greater accountability for business result. We listen to our associates and do our best to continuously make their jobs better," stated a CEO of a toy manufacturing company.

Some of the key listening areas of people engagement is determining if

1. The company is seen as an outstanding workplace to forge trust across the enterprise
2. There is confidence that leaders are making correct decisions
3. The company effectively directs resources toward company goals
4. There is open and honest two-way communications
5. Leaders actively demonstrate that people are important to the company's success

Consequently, the human behavioral factors affect the outcomes of a company's performance, especially in ways by which leaders treat their human resources. Specifically, such treatment relates to the employees' states of mind, attitudes, and overall ways of thinking.

In turn, these states of mind can be likened to deep pools of possibilities that are set in motion by thoughts that come to the surface as intuitive insights. They can be positive or negative, depending on the input of the controlling beliefs. And the controlling beliefs can be influenced by a leader's display of such qualities as wisdom, sincerity, humanity, courage, and strictness. These attributes positively affect morale, achievement, and performance.

In turn, the psychological outcomes shape an individual's core behavior. On the positive side, insights can lead to innovative thinking that translates to competitive advantage and bold new opportunities. On the negative side, insights that are chained to fear produce pessimistic attitudes that can strangle creativity, shut down ideas, and blind the individual to problem-solving possibilities. These emotional states are detailed in Chapter 6.

DEVELOPING A CULTURAL PROFILE

To assist you in profiling your firm's culture with the intent of influencing employees' mindsets and attitudes, consider the guidelines that follow. The aim is to reach out to those who are generally positive and compliant, the not so compliant, individuals with negative feelings, and even persons with insubordinate behavior. From a managerial viewpoint, the purpose is to bind your employees' hearts and minds to achieve success when they face the inevitable competitive battles that lie ahead.

Culture is displayed in unusual, unplanned, and unforeseen ways. Such was the case of Amazon, which at the time of this writing was the dominant name in cloud computing through its Amazon Web Services (AWS). Although it did not create the cloud renting system,* CEO Jeff Bezos did see its vast potential as a new revenue-generating division of his company. Recognizing that he had fashioned a fast-to-react and opportunistic culture, he was able to react before any of the other high-tech companies could respond.

From a virtual standstill, Amazon almost single-handedly developed the system into what is now a mainstream part of the technology business. AWS, however, is still projected to generate more revenue than its retail operations. Such high-profile organizations as IBM, Dell,

---

* The cloud renting system was initially introduced by Sun Microsystems and subsequently became part of Oracle, but that program never took off.

Hewlett-Packard, Microsoft, and Google are still attempting to play catch-up with their competing systems. Now the battle lines are more defined through product innovations, pricing battles, and improved services as competitive weapons to win a commanding position in the marketplace.

Table 7.2 provides a four-level structure to evaluate the efficacy of your firm's culture. The outcome would serve as a usable cultural profile of your firm. The following sample profiles describe cultures of four different firms:

- *Hardworking and conservative firm.* This firm prides itself on working steadily and slowly toward its goals. Its history and pattern of behavior indicate that management does not tolerate a great deal of risk, dislikes operating in a state of uncertainty, and tends to act in a deliberate and cautious manner.

  The firm sticks to the markets it knows best and is reluctant to venture out of its comfort zone. As a result, opportunities are often missed. This type of culture generally relies on a diligent work ethic and depends on solid customer relationships as its primary defense against competitors.

  The organization has a top-down structure with clearly defined levels of authority. Although there is an effort to keep up with current technology, the firm would be considered a late adopter. As for leadership, executives attempt to absorb the incoming data about its industry and consumer needs, but movement still consists of a slow methodical approach. And the operating culture looks to maintaining long-term and stable growth as a follower rather than as an innovator.

- *Aggressively led firm.* This company is personified by a dominant, hands-on leader. She requires rapid market feedback and is willing to tolerate high risk. She is action oriented with a focus on winning in the present and letting the future take care of itself.

  This viewpoint is rationalized by the notion that maintaining an aggressive style rather than a cautious management approach will ensure ongoing success. This leader seeks collaboration, but in reality relies on his or her own forceful personality and micromanagement style to keep the organization in constant movement.

  Company history, myths, and stories of the past are not important, since the leader is bent on making his or her own history. Such an attitude is justified by a marketplace that is viewed as in constant

TABLE 7.2

Four-Level Structure to Profile Your Corporate Culture

Levels	Criteria[a]
Level 1: Values and beliefs	*Relates to your*
	Organization's history and core values
	Ethical behavior
	Product lines carried and types of services provided
	Markets served and positions held, e.g., innovator or follower
	Technologies developed internally or acquired
	Capabilities for developing offensive and defensive competitive strategies
	Leadership style (see criteria in Chapter 1)
	Employee development and training
	Fundamental beliefs and attitudes toward employees
	Organization's place in the surrounding world
	Assumptions about the future of your industry and organization
Level 2: Organizational behavior	*Attitudes related to*
	Planning with long-term vs. short-term focus
	Consumer-driven vs. company-driven orientation
	Developing an agile organizational structure
	Bold vs. cautious responses when pursuing opportunities or reacting to competitive threats
	Toleration for risk
	Employee collaboration through cross-functional teams
	Types and diversity of employees
	Decision-making authority at various levels of the organization
	Internal communications and feedback
Level 3: Symbols and rituals	*Elements include*
	Facilities
	Perks
	Offices
	Furnishings
	Visible awards and recognition
	Company slogans and logos
	Stories
	Myths
	Special privileges
Level 4: Hidden influences	*Areas include*
	Unseen stimuli
	Hidden power among individuals or groups within the organization
	Conflicting subcultures
	Upward pressure from middle managers urging senior executives to take action
	Add criteria for your firm's hidden influences

[a] You can add criteria to the listings that are unique to your organization. Also, the criteria can be ranked on a numerical scale according to their value to your firm, or each item may be weighted to reflect its level of importance.

flux from digitization and big data that are rapidly creating new management paradigms. Thus, the cultural patterns are shaped by boldness, speed, and opportunity. In turn, employees are selected with a matching entrepreneurial spirit.

- *Inward-focused firm.* This type of firm is characterized by a plodding and lethargic culture. It leans toward a low market profile and is inward driven by comfort and security. Wherever there is employee stress, it comes about through internal politics and minutia that tend to hamper the firm from moving forward. Consumed by internal problems, it neglects the needs of the marketplace. As a consequence, there seem to be power struggles, some open and others hidden, which also results in conflicting subcultures.

- *High-risk culture.* This firm has some of the characteristics of the aggressively led firm. There is also a tendency toward speed, boldness, and a willingness to experiment and take more chances. Most often associated with start-ups, there is somewhat of a throw-caution-to-the-wind attitude.

  Since there is no particular history to latch onto or stories to tell of past successes, the view is forward looking, with innovation and cutting-edge technology as its weapons. Ostentatious trappings or outlandish facilities do not seem to have a place during the opening stages of operations. Thus, a bold, consumer-driven, goal-oriented, opportunistic, and collaborative team environment that welcomes employee diversity exemplifies the firm.

ALIGNING BIG DATA WITH THE CORPORATE CULTURE

Giving your business unit or organization a realistic chance of success in today's digital environment requires that you give corporate culture the same degree of attention as you would in preparing a business plan. It is the inherent energy generated through corporate culture that gives your organization its unique identity, and which forms the special personality that is a fairly accurate indicator of your probable success.

Therefore, if you want to maximize your ability to reach your objectives, then become totally familiar with the prevailing culture that supports your objectives and strategies. This is one of the infallible rules for leading a successful group or organization.

Avoiding that issue, especially in today's hotly contested markets, can prove fatal. The essential point: Even if you devise a brilliant strategy, implementing it with any measure of success relies on its alignment with your organization's culture.

For that reason, it is in your best interest to sort through the core values, beliefs, and traditions that shape your organization. You thereby retain better control of your operation.

Let us now form a still higher platform for understanding the interrelationships of competitive strategy and corporate culture. In particular, look at the following workable techniques to reenergize your company's culture for the digital age:*

- Stay on the offensive. A good measure of boldness is desirable, depending, of course, on the availability of resources and the level of confidence you show in employees—and they in your leadership. If the risk succeeds, offer ample rewards; if failure results, avoid damaging repercussions.
- Encourage creativity and innovation. Seek maximum input from all levels of employees. Try new ideas that could lead to new products, evolving markets, or new businesses. Maintain a cultural sensibility that retains an open mind and avoids the idea-killing verbiage, "We've tried that."

  Also allow sufficient time for ideas to incubate and hatch into new technologies, products, and services. Develop concrete formats for employees to submit ideas. These can be in the form of what General Electric refers to as "Imagination Breakthrough," whereby executives are required to submit three major reports a year that could lead to new businesses, new products, and new revenue streams.
- Learn to live in a dynamic competitive environment. Dynamic also infers volatility. As a leader, that means maintaining an outward display of calmness and confidence. For some employees, however, extreme change creates an unsettling situation where any perceived upheaval in conditions in or out of the organization is difficult to

---

* If you are operating as an independent business unit, there tends to be a subculture that has distinct characteristics, usually patterned after the leader of the group. Here, too, it is important to track the nuances of behavior.

endure. Still, flexibility is a singular characteristic that must be maintained, if you are to perform successfully in the digitized world.

This is a cultural attribute that is often difficult to embed within an organization—and equally difficult to instill in employees. It also needs senior management's full support, especially during this period of such severe market volatility.

- Build a solid market position. Create a unique market position from which competitors cannot easily dislodge you. To the extent you are able, try to create brand equity and brand recognition. Your managerial efforts should be directed toward mounting a long-term positive image for your firm.

  Some research indicates that high market share equates with high return on investment. Some executives go so far as to advise building market share at any cost. (This latter viewpoint, however, remains controversial.)

  Beyond a certain level, others believe that chasing market share no longer guarantees profitability. Instead, preference would be given to investing resources elsewhere. One point that is not controversial is that customer satisfaction and long-term customer relationships remain the enduring principles.

- Stay close to evolving technology. Tune in to what is happening in those technologies that can help transform your business to the new economy models, which is generally accepted as a digital one. Several choices exist: build an internal system, partner with a compatible company, or outsource the entire system.

- Act as an aggressive competitor.* Here, you are able to discover where your firm has an advantage, or is at risk. It indicates strengths and weaknesses in your products, services, logistics, and overall organizational structure. It examines relationships with suppliers, intermediaries, and customers along the entire supply chain.

  The process exposes strong points and vulnerable areas in technology, manufacturing, human resources, and capital resources. It also uncovers other areas that might endanger your firm to competitive attacks—or exposes any that prevent you from taking advantage of ripe opportunities. It also unmasks sensitive information on employee behavior and suggests clues on how to undertake change.

---

* This approach often works well as part of a training session where the group is divided into teams, with one team acting as though it is a competitor.

Such exposure also sheds light on those senior executives who cannot (or choose not to) make determined efforts to take on an aggressive posture. In practical terms, few executives are effective for all seasons. And not all individuals are capable of performing optimally through successive stages of a corporate cycle—start-up, growth, maturity, and decline—or even within different cultural environments.

You can employ all or some of these steps to drive cultural change and energize your company. How drastic those changes are depends on the severity of your company's problems. Therefore, you can react to problems as they arise or be proactive and anticipate changes. It is all part of exercising leadership and managerial competence, which encompasses your internal and external environments, including competitors, suppliers, and most of all, your customers. In addition to the above techniques, Table 7.3 further defines the components and benefits that align big data with corporate culture.

One firm that is a champion at the energizing and aligning process is Publix. The supermarket chain prides itself with a culture that has an annual turnover rate of a mere 5% versus the retail industry average of 65%. Throughout its 1,100 stores, the average store manager has been with

TABLE 7.3

Energizing a Healthy Corporate Culture

Components	Benefits
Diversity	A company's strength comes from its diversity, where respect prevails for different backgrounds and personal convictions, as long as they do not conflict with the core values of the organization.
Fair treatment of employees	Employees support company efforts as long as equality exists—and where rewards and disapprovals are applied consistently.
Generation of pride and enthusiasm	Employee zeal spills over to business partners and customers.
Equal opportunity for employees	A heightened spirit of innovation helps employees achieve their full potential, leads to team cohesiveness, and elevates morale.
Open communications	Having open communications provides a channel to pass on beliefs and values and unite personnel toward a vision for the future of the organization.
Respect for employee contributions	Such respect enhances involvement and enthusiasm to work toward common goals and strategies.

the company for 25 years, with some remaining at the company for 30 years and as much as 45 years.

With a history dating to its founding in 1930, its cultural values never wavered from providing the highest level of customer satisfaction, as well as regarding employees with the uppermost level of care. Such values are continuously reinforced at every opportunity through personal contact, meetings, and company-wide communications. "The reason Publix is such a great place to work is that nothing has changed in 86 years," says one store manager.

What make those values come alive is demonstrated by the following actions:

Employee ownership. Publix is the world's largest employee-owned company. After one year of service, employees who work 1,000 or more hours are awarded stock, with an option to buy additional shares.

Regular reviews and frequent raises. The company provides workers with frequent feedback. If performance reviews pass muster, they are eligible for salary increases every six months.

Promote from within. Publix uses a "succession planning" process. Any employee who wishes to take a next step in career advancement submits a "registration of interest" to explain his or her goals. The form is submitted to the company's human resources department and the person's name is kept on a list for six months to be considered for open positions matching the request. As part of the advancement process, Publix will foot much of the cost of college tuition for any employee with six months of service. In 2015, the company paid out a total of $5 million in education reimbursements.

Underneath these visible benefits is a prevailing tone of satisfaction that can only be attributed to a corporate culture where employees call Publix a "happy place to work," where no employee has ever been laid off in its entire history.

In summary, culture is the nerve center of the organization. Therefore, as a leader you want to be alert to what makes your organization tick. That means actively tuning into the company's traditions, values, beliefs, and history.

Further, the purpose of corporate culture is to develop an internal work environment that encourages individuals to perform efficiently. Yet a corporate culture will be relevant only if it is aligned with the organization's vision, objectives, strategies—and the dynamic forces that make up the competitive marketplace. Publix embodies such a culture as the organization converges with a near-religious attachment to customers and a total belief in employees as intellectual capital.

By turning to corporate culture and using it as an additional managerial tool, you derive a significant competitive advantage. From a people viewpoint, you can achieve high employee motivation and increased team cohesiveness. You thereby create an ironclad connection with big data, business planning, and corporate culture.

8

Apply Offensive and Defensive Strategies

If you operate in almost any kind of competitive environment, you will have to face the inevitable decision between going on the defensive or moving to the offensive. What are the issues?

Beginning with defense, the immediate aim is to protect your position from being overrun by a rival. That means you face a challenge considering the volatility of markets, disruptive technologies, and changing nature of buyer behavior. As for the long term, your purpose would be to perpetuate your company's presence in a market where it has a long history, and in all likelihood has made a substantial investment.

In both instances, a central issue is buyer behavior, which affects many organizations. Coca-Cola is an example of a company that experienced a long-term trend of declining consumption of its core soda product. In defensive moves, the company attempted numerous product modifications, packaging changes, and inventive marketing programs to stem the losses. Notwithstanding a considerable effort, the downward trend continues.

Then, shifting to the offensive, Coke acknowledged that the decline in the cola segment would continue and growth would have to come from other directions. The company moved into noncola drinks by venturing with Zico coconut water, Honest Tea, and Fuze juice drink. It then identified an entirely new category, new, that is, to Coke: milk.

There, too, consumption over the years has declined, but data tracked a growth segment in specialty milk, or designer milk, which is defined as filtered, high protein, low sugar, and lactose-free. Coke's strategy included taking a minority stake in a dairy cooperative to create Fairlife, which produces the product. As a Coke executive points out, "They know dairy better than anybody. We know consumers." Backing up those encouraging words is Coke's vast distribution network with its access to hundreds of thousands of supermarket shelves across the country.

The central ideas behind defense are twofold: First, it is generally easier to defend a market position than it is to take it from a firmly entrenched rival, so that the defense is somewhat easier than the attack, assuming both sides have somewhat equal means.

Second, *time* is on the side of the defending company. Waiting does not mean being passive. It does require discipline to wait, the ability to block a forceful action by an attacking competitor, and then shift to the offensive.

In practice, it is this two-pronged feature that is the only test by which defense can be distinguished from offense. If an organization were acting in pure defense, meaning there is no response from the defender, then there would be no competitive confrontation, since only one side wants to fight.

A competitive campaign, then, is defensive if the defending company awaits the offensive moves of the rival with the intent of protecting its market share. It is also defensive if the company waits for its market position to be penetrated. In each of these situations, the characteristics of waiting and blocking are germane to the overall aim of protection and continuation. Consequently, where there is an active campaign in motion, the defender would at one point develop counteractions, since they would be taking place within a defender's own market area.

The following classic case of Xerox (previously mentioned) illustrates this concept.

Decades ago, when Xerox created the market for xerography, the company initially focused on large companies with its large copiers. If we introduce the concept of defense into this example, Xerox used passive resistance to defend its position. That is, it left exposed a vast market of small- and midsize companies for small, tabletop copiers without an adequate defense plan.

Astute Japanese makers of copiers, such as Canon, Sharp, and Ricoh, saw the opening and attacked that vacant market with virtually no opposition. Once secured with a solid foothold in North America, they made the next expansive move of going upscale, where they moved against Xerox's stronghold in big company copiers.

Those events occurred in the 1970s at the introductory stage of the industry and product life cycles. Arguably, Xerox could be excused since various user applications were not fully explored at the time, nor had all user segments surfaced.

Xerox eventually woke to the threat and actively defended its position over the following decades, where it successfully counterattacked to recover a good deal of its market share. Even today, "make a Xerox copy" remains a generally accepted term for the copying function, regardless of the brand of copier. The essential point: Defense is not a simple shield, but a way to upend a competitor's strategies by means of well-directed offensive maneuvers.

ADVANTAGES AND DISADVANTAGES OF DEFENSE

In the event a competitor's attack does not materialize—whether from bad judgment, fear, or lethargy—the defending company accrues the advantage. Time, as was pointed out, is an intrinsic benefit rooted in the nature of defense. It provides the valuable breathing space for the defending company to support its market position in various ways, such as seeking marketing alliances, employing new technology applications, strengthening a presence in the supply chain, or fortifying relationships with customers through aggressive programs and incentives.

To illustrate these points, General Electric found itself in a defensive mode with an urgent need to protect its position within core markets of electric power generators, jet engines, locomotives, and oil refining gear. After suffering through several years of flat performance triggered by the financial upheavals of the early 2000s, the time came for GE to begin moving from defense to offensive.

Defense for GE meant overcoming several demanding problems: First, it needed to block the ongoing threats from low-cost, low-priced competitors that were making continuous attacks on GE's industrial markets. Second, it had to solve the problems associated with the lengthy product development cycles that, for instance, took five years to redesign one of its turbines. Third, GE had to deal with the challenge of persuading customers to accelerate the replacement of equipment, where repurchase buying patterns typically stretched to a decade or more.

Thus, to defend and protect GE's presence in those industrial sectors, CEO Jeffrey Immelt moved to the offensive. He began with a monumental shift in the company's direction by remaking it into a software company, which included exiting such markets as capital financing and consumer appliances.

The initial effort resulted in a proprietary operating system, Predix, which had the capability to absorb and analyze the vast amounts of data generated from its sensor-equipped machines. The synthesized data was then used for such major applications as making it possible for planes to fly more efficiently, extending the life of power generators, and allowing trains to run faster.

Beyond that, Immelt continued with plans that included selling the software to other manufacturers that were involved in the Internet of things. These maneuvers became the offensive component of defending its market positions. As part of the total company makeover and to provide the proper internal environment for carrying out the defense, Immelt recast the operating culture within GE from a slower-moving, more rigid organization to a fast-moving, aggressive culture that could take on a new set of competitors, such as Amazon, IBM, Microsoft, and Oracle.

Thus, for any company experiencing below-average performance, a necessity to protect core markets, a shaky economy, aggressive competitors, or any other compelling need to turn around a company, every market encounter is defensive if one company leaves the initiative to the rival and awaits a competitor's aggressive actions. Yet, once the attack occurs, the defending company must employ all offensive means without losing the advantages of the defensive.

The defending organization thereby enjoys the benefits of waiting, as well as the advantages of taking assertive action to hold its position. The central issue, then, is possession of a market position, and not necessarily through competitive fighting, but by maneuver.

As already indicated, the defense is generally easier than the offensive. Yet there are other viewpoints to fully internalize the concept: whereas defense has a purpose of protection and continuation, the offensive has the aims of market penetration and possession. Therefore, a company on the offensive that continues its aggressive actions is expending resources as long as it is on the offensive, whereas the defending company is conserving its strength. That makes the defender intrinsically more formidable than the firm on the offensive.

Consequently, if defense is fundamentally the stronger form of activity, it should be used *only* as long as the situation compels the company to do so. The reason: When the defender has successfully completed its defense and feels strong enough, it follows the natural course and goes to the offensive. Thus, the natural course begins with the defense, goes on the offensive, and returns to the defense to protect what it has gained. And a new cycle begins. The mere notion of defense as its final purpose is contrary to the entire concept of defense and a misunderstanding of its competitive value.*

RELATIONSHIP BETWEEN OFFENSE AND DEFENSE

Where there is a competitive campaign with a dominant rival, three primary elements influence the outcome:

1. Surprise
2. Market position
3. Indirect maneuvers

Surprise is effective should you be the defender and a rival suddenly comes up against you with far more resources than anticipated at a decisive point in your position. If penetrated, the market you are trying to protect might place you in an untenable situation. As bad, your defense plans could be in a total state of disarray and staff morale would certainly be demoralized.

The remedy, then, is to foresee possible pathways the attacking company might use and make them part of your blocking plans. That is where data analytics can sort through entry patterns that could reveal types of strategies the attacking competitor may have used in past campaigns to expand into other markets. At times, organizations are predictable, as they often repeat similar approaches, unaware they are being tracked.

Also, focus on any obvious areas within your immediate market that might be viewed by an attacking competitor as vulnerable to an unexpected surprise. One susceptible area is the customer, and specifically the level of customer relationships. Your attention here would rely on data about changing buying and product usage behaviors within your markets.

---

* The sports world and other institutions commonly use the phrase "The best defense is a good offense." However, that does not go far enough to explain the deep meaning of the concept as explained throughout this chapter.

Consider, too, the use of any technologies or special services that could improve interactions with customers and thereby shore up defenses.

For example, Caterpillar (also referred to in the introduction), the giant construction and mining equipment maker, collects, stores, and analyzes huge volumes of digital information. To that end, the company installed sensors, radios, GPS receivers, and specialized software into its trucks, backhoes, bulldozers, and other machinery.

The move was part of Caterpillar's global technology platform that connects to an intelligent network that monitors its equipment. The system provides beneficial reports on equipment repairs, operator usage patterns, and other valuable bits of data. By disseminating those reports to equipment owners and dealers, Caterpillar solidifies relationships along the supply chain.

Consequently, the ongoing flow of intelligence delivers meaningful data for scheduling service calls. In that manner, Caterpillar engineers are able to set up additional defenses by preempting and solving potential equipment problems. In turn, the real-time information provides substantial amounts of data to product developers for new product designs and applications, all of which offer fresh marketing and selling opportunities.

As the above case points out, even where the defending company is tied to its position and presumably presents the attacker with numerous objectives, it is the defending company that can respond throughout the campaign by the strength and direction of its countermoves. The big advantage, however, is that the defending organization benefits from its enhanced knowledge and experience in the marketplace. As pointed out, Caterpillar was able to use surprise through technology maneuvers in a way that could not be easily duplicated by an attacking rival until the campaign was well underway.

As for the attacking company, surprise does permit the flexibility to move against the defender at any time or location, and with any amount of resources it chooses. Further, it is easier for the attacking competitor to go in numerous directions and surprise the defender in the collective areas identified by the traditional marketing mix.

If for some reason the company on the offensive should allocate only limited resources to the campaign, the defender would also reap the benefit by concentrating its own full strength against the attacker. The essence of such a move depends on the skill of the leader to maintain positive and ongoing observation through data analytics, sound lines of communications from those in everyday contact with customers, and on-the-scene observations of the competitor's actions.

If, however, the company on the offensive were to invent some major new maneuvers, the defender would also have to change its methods. But it will always be certain of having the benefit of market position, and this will generally ensure its initial superiority.

Once the blocking has taken effect, the defending company must prepare to go on the offensive or suffer negative consequences of being easily routed. A sudden powerful transition to the offensive is the defining moment for the defender. If you do not have a presence of mind and an acute awareness of timing from the start, and as important, you have not primed your staff to the importance of rapidly switching their mindsets from defense to offense, you have missed the strategic essence of defense.

Accordingly, consider incorporating this thinking into orientation sessions for those managers who formulate competitive strategies for their respective territories and product lines.* Similarly, it is appropriate to bolster the training by adding these offense and defense concepts at the tactical level. That includes individuals with titles of marketing manager, brand manager, product manager, and sales manager.

Further, a case can be made for including similar training for sales personnel who are assigned to dedicated territories. The idea is based on thinking of each sales representative as a general manager of his or her territory. That means each rep would take a long-term strategic outlook for both the growth and development of his assigned territory, which would require making defensive and offensive strategy decisions. (Some forward-looking organizations have already implemented this approach.)

APPLYING OFFENSIVE AND DEFENSIVE STRATEGIES

Beginning with the defense, a concrete framework based on the previous discussion consists of three distinct phases:

1. Waiting
2. Blocking
3. Moving to the offensive

---

* See Section II, Chapters 4 through 6, for content.

Waiting

As has already been pointed out, the essence of defense entails waiting, which is also one of the main distinguishable features of defense, as well as its chief advantage. Throughout this phase, it is best to maintain ongoing dialogue with your staff, so that they become aware of the direction of your thinking. That is, they need to internalize that the advantage of waiting is to gain strength, at the same time observing if there is a weakening of the competitor's efforts as it continues expending resources.

During this waiting period, there is a major psychological issue that surfaces, which you should be ready to face. That is, you are likely to find a heightened level of negative emotions among members of your staff.* This is where you, and they, must use disciplined patience to wait for better timing. The essential point: Between acceptance and anxiety, choose acceptance, with the proviso that patience is only a pause that allows you to prepare for the offensive.

You can help your people during this waiting period by avoiding negative surroundings. That means creating compatible relationships with others. If this implies assuming the role of an active mediator, do so to maintain a stable environment and make ready for transitioning to the blocking and offensive phases.

Yet instances of anger, frustration, and continuing dispute could go beyond reasonable limits. You may then have to take an active role in setting a pathway for conflict resolution with the aim of creating harmony and unity of effort.

Here, too, you have to expect that the traditional strained relationships among various functional areas of an organization will continue, such as marketing versus finance, product development versus distribution, and manufacturing versus sales.

For the most part, however, as you keep the strategic picture in mind, the central idea is that hostile feelings are counterproductive, especially when flaring anger, resentment, or jealousy dominates the scene. Clashing groups seldom arrive at an acceptable solution. Within such a fractured situation, your aim is to promote workable outcomes based on internal

---

* Chapter 6 outlines types of negative emotions that affect performance, such as anxiety, frustration, stress, and fear.

operating conditions, the dynamics of the marketplace, and the activities of competitors—and above all, the objectives of your strategic business plan.

Then, you are more likely to come to a peaceful and healing condition among all parties, even where groups work as opposites, but not opponents. It takes a measure of sensitive awareness on your part to raise them up and make them feel good.

Consequently, when orienting your staff, the more vivid and persuasive you make your presentation, the greater the chance of strengthening their commitment to the concept of defense. To that end, the talking points outlined in the list below summarize areas for emphasis.

Applying Defensive Strategies

- The defense is valued as the stronger form of confrontation and one that is more likely to initially blunt the rival's efforts.
- The more time lost to the attacking company, the greater the drain of resources that is bound to weaken it, thereby making the defender's actions potentially more effective.
- The defense is not a passive activity; it depends on the active use of data analytics to determine the force, direction, and timing of the rival's offensive action.
- Waiting is a fundamental feature for the organization defending its market positon; such a campaign is hardly conceivable without it.
- Defending a market position is usually centered on a short-term tactical campaign.
- The end of the waiting and blocking period triggers the starting point of offensive action.

The endpoint of waiting will be reached when the defending company's leader has successfully blocked the aggressor and when it is apparent the advantages of waiting have achieved their purposes. There is no infallible means for determining when that time has come, other than with the use of data, personal observation, market feedback, and judgment that the attacker is slowing down.

Thus, many conditions and circumstances would contribute to the decision. For General Electric, flat performance over a lengthy period and the threat of offshore competitors attempting to commoditize several of its product lines forced Immelt to set in motion blocking moves to defend its key markets, followed by definitive actions to redefine itself as a software company. For Coke, it was a long-term downward trend of cola consumption that forced it into new drinks.

Blocking

The key activity during the blocking phase is to utilize predictive analytics that provide clues about possible courses of action the competitor will use in its offensive moves. Being armed with such highly prized information helps in setting up specific defense barriers.

The blocking action begins as soon as the attacking company actively enters your market. Or you may wait for the rival to actually challenge your positon; then you can respond with enough of your resources to block the rival, while still holding in reserve the rest for the offensive that follows.

As part of the blocking action, you can use the following seven areas to examine possible approaches for strengthening your defense, as well as for developing offensive strategies:

1. *Market segments.* You want to identify which market segments the attacking rival is likely to go after. This assessment will help determine weaknesses through which you can be attacked. These might relate to your firm's reputation, level of services, technology, or overall commitment to the market's growth.

2. *Product or service.* If you consider the classic definition that a product consists of a bundle of benefits, and a product is new when it is perceived as new by the prospective audience, then look to the following areas to strengthen your defense: quality, features, reliability, packaging, after-sales service, level of technology, warranties, brand name awareness, or any other area that provides customer satisfaction.

3. *Pricing.* Your attention should be given to how your product compares with competitor's prices, types of discounts, allowances, credit, and financing terms.

4. *Communications.* This comparative analysis deals with advertising commitments, size and experience of the sales force (if any), level of sales promotion, and use of social media.

5. *Supply chain.* Look to strengthen your position on the supply chain by examining such areas as storage facilities and proximity to customers, gaps in market coverage, efficiency of inventory control systems, availability of physical transportation, on-time delivery, usefulness of support systems, and perceived value of incentive programs.

6. *Competitor's intelligence.* This is a vital area to scrutinize. Examine the data you have collected from the marketplace. What is known about the rival's level of morale? How much technical or industry experience does the staff have? Can they sustain a long-term offensive?

7. Rival organization. This area is an extension of the above. What is known about the competitor's culture? Can it be characterized as passive, reactive, active, or aggressive? Is it a start-up or an old-line company with a strong reputation? What is its financial condition? Is it up-to-date in technology? How competent is its leadership?

Moving to the Offensive

This third phase combines physical and psychological factors. The physical aspect deals with the seven components listed above under blocking.

It is the psychological factor, however, that is the dominant key to success. As a leader, you must do all that you can to change the mindsets of your staff from defense to offense.

This point is illustrated by the Japanese company Sharp. In the early 2000s, Sharp made a major commitment with flat-screen televisions to replace boxy analog sets. Initially, the investment paid off, with the company reaping big sales and profits from its Japanese factories. Then calamity struck and it was not able to defend itself.

Sharp executives failed to anticipate major shifts in the global electronics industry. China had emerged not only as the home of cheap manufacturing, but also increasingly as innovators at making electronic devices that could rival Japan's in sophistication and quality. The industry's center for innovation had shifted from Japan to places like China, South Korea, and the U.S. Silicon Valley.

Any defense that Sharp came up with, in the size of TV displays, touch screens for smartphones, and tablet computers, was too little, too late, as each was quickly matched by rivals. And they came to market at a pace that Sharp executives did not anticipate. "First computer monitors became commoditized. Then it was TVs, and finally smartphone screens," according to an industry analyst.

Numerous reasons can be cited for the debacle, such as an inbred Sharp culture that lacked flexibility to move to the offensive within a rapidly changing industry characterized by short life cycles, where manufacturing was increasingly dominated by the likes of the Taiwanese company Foxconn.

Then, there was an internal condition where a myopic management took too many missteps. That was the case even where data was readily available to document ongoing trends within the industry, as well as in technology breakthroughs and changes in buying behavior. Collectively, those forces put Sharp on a pathway of maintaining a constant defense. But it could not effectively block rivals, and it could not mount a meaningful offensive.

The essential point: The defense works, but as it has been repeatedly mentioned, it must connect with solid offensive strategies to win. And that requires astute leadership, a flexible corporate culture, a spirited work-force, business intelligence that incorporates big data analytics, and a plan to neutralize or prevent a competitor from creating a competitive advantage (see Chapter 1).

Many of the above considerations in organizing an offensive at the defender's end also apply to the attacker. Yet a number of salient points remain to fully internalize the process:

1. The immediate objective of moving to the offensive is to attain a viable position in a market that is actively defended by an embedded competitor. That means you have to be prepared to expend greater resources to make up for the intrinsic advantages held by the defender, such as superior knowledge about the market, a lock on key parts of the supply chain, and overall experience.

   However, these built-in advantages have to be confirmed. If not, they become weaknesses that can be exploited, which is what happened in the Sharp case. Then, there is the advantage of speed and the shock of surprise that can upend a defender. To a great extent, those two elements also overwhelmed a lethargic Sharp management.

2. Even if an attacker lacks material superiority, it must have morale superiority to make up for the deficiency. And should morale superiority be lacking, there is a high level of doubt that an attack can expect to succeed.

   Conversely, if the defender's morale is weak, which could be associated with a laid-back corporate culture, the more daring the attacker's actions, the greater the chances of winning. Morale and culture have been discussed at great length. These qualities are often the tipping point where encounters often operate in the dark, or at best in twilight. Thus, there is still the element of human judgment that is needed, notwithstanding the input of sophisticated algorithms and data analytics.

3. If the defender feels utterly defeated and chooses to exit the market, which is altogether possible, or if it cannot match the attacker due to superior technology, a low-cost structure, or any other major weakness that is perceived as an overwhelming competitive advantage, that means the defender holds an indefensible position. Again, several of these issues appear in the Sharp example.

4. When developing strategies, the manager of the attacking company should be consciously aware of two factors: First is how the marketplace views the strategies used in the offensive as they relate to product, branding, positioning, service, distribution, pricing, communications, and customer relationships.

   These entry strategies establish the image. Yet should the attacker be more concerned with using ploys or shady tactics or misrepresentations to outwit the defending company, these methods set up potentially vulnerable areas through which it can be attacked at a later time.

   Second, the attacking leader must consider how to exploit his or her initial success. Gaining an initial position is only the first step, and it could be a vulnerable one. Follow-on strategies are needed to solidify the position by expanding in depth, which can be calculated by sales volume, geographic coverage, or market share.

5. Concentrating at a decisive point is a key strategy principle. Thus, an attacker should not be lured into diluting his marketing effort by moving into another market segment, unless it is absolutely warranted to protect its initial moves. For any leader, to divide time, personnel, and other resources may be chalked up to confusion, overconfidence, or lack of strategy knowledge.

   If, however, the attacker finds that the defender has divided its resources to protect more than one market segment, then options are possible for the attacking company to concentrate on one segment or divide its forces, as long as there is still superiority in one of the segments and there is flexibility to maneuver. In that instance, dividing resources would be justified.

6. The concept of attack indicates that once that phase ends, defense begins. Therefore, the attacker should plan to defend his hard-won success. At this point, the leader will then set in motion the three-part defense outlined in this chapter.

HOW OFFENSIVE CAMPAIGNS CAN FAIL

Since the defense is favored over the offensive, let us deal with the possibilities of failing attacks. For instance, the attacking company enters a defender's market, but then begins to have doubts about risking going head-to-head in a decisive price war or by any other contentious challenge. The attacker would hope to face the defender as if its physical presence or brand name were enough to make a successful market entry.

In short, the attacking leader behaves as if it were the defender's responsibility to seek a confrontation. All of these are mere pretexts, which a leader of the attacking company uses to delude his organization and even himself.

The more reasonable explanation is that the leader discovered the defender's position has been found too strong and a victory would be of no use to him, especially since he does not have enough resources to face a prolonged campaign. In other words, the attacker may have exhausted his resources and whatever is available must be directed at the consumer.

Then, there is another condition where the campaign gets bogged down and the outcome is uncertain. At that point, the attacker would wait for a favorable turn of events to exploit the situation. Yet, in reality, there is no plausible reason to expect that the situation will turn in the attacker's favor—unless there is the possibility of an alliance with another firm. Until confirmed, the leader in this instance is nurturing a delusion.

By way of excusing this turn of events and subsequent inaction, the leader is likely to make excuses of inadequate funds or lack of management commitment and support. He may talk of insurmountable obstacles, and look for motives in the most intricately complicated circumstances. As an outcome, he will fritter away his strength in doing nothing and place the entire campaign at risk. In the meantime, the defender gains time, which is what he needs most.

There is one underlying concern in some of these issues, particularly in the delusions. Where there was outright failure, it may have been due to fear of the defender. Often, such expressions are the result of negative emotions triggered by a range of psychological forces. Individuals in leadership position do harbor deep-rooted fear of failure, which has the insidious effect of closing down the mind and creating a type of paralysis or inability to take action.

Such responses are particularly troublesome when courage is the essential ingredient when preparing for an offensive action. "The requisite for a man's success as a leader is that he be perfectly brave," declared the eminent strategist Baron Antoine-Henri de Jomini.

Courage is defined as the act of determination in a specific situation. It becomes a character trait only if it becomes a mental habit. There are ample numbers of brilliant individuals who simply do not have what it takes to recognize that bold actions are essential elements for timely and appropriate actions—in this instance, defense and offense.

Often, it is up to the individual to arouse the inner sense of courage and push aside the awful feelings that can creep into the mind and take control of his or her actions. That is where training, discipline, and experience need to kick in to overcome negative emotions.

It is also useful to think of a competitive campaign as a contest of one mind against another mind, the mind of one manager pitted against the mind of a competing manager who may be challenged by similar emotions. In practice, however, few leaders, if any, would admit that the decision to stop a campaign, or to give up entirely, was motivated by the fear that his strength would run out, or that he might encounter new competitors, or that other rivals might become too powerful. Those are the suppressed issues or rationalizations that are rarely, if ever, revealed.

In summary, numerous factors contribute to how offensive and defensive campaigns are handled. The commonalities consist of the objectives of the strategic business plan, availability of resources, quality of leadership, and corporate culture driving the organization.

Then, there are the all-important psychological dynamics that encompass the organization's discipline, resilience, morale, and courage, as well as the full range of positive and negative emotions. These forces exist within the market gyrations of individuals shifting mindsets from a defensive mode to an offensive posture, and back again, as campaigns progress.

Finally, if total success could be linked to the offensive elements that are present in every defensive campaign, no basic strategic difference between an offensive and a defensive campaign would exist. Yet all evidence supports the conclusion that the form of confrontation known as defense offers greater probability of success than attack.

The Five Forces of Leadership Shaped by the Digital Age

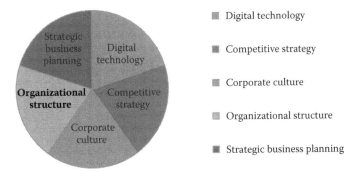

- Digital technology
- Competitive strategy
- Corporate culture
- Organizational structure
- Strategic business planning

Section IV

Organizational Structure

As leaders, if you don't reinvent yourself, change your organization structure; if you don't talk about speed of innovation, you're going to get disrupted. And it'll be a brutal disruption, where the majority of companies will not exist in a meaningful way 10 to 15 years from now.

John Chambers
Former CEO, Cisco Systems

9

Evolution of the Modern Organization

Various approaches to organizational designs for the digital age abound from numerous academics, consultants, and executives. The solutions are somewhat different depending on their respective points of view. Yet commonalities do exist in many areas, including several of the concepts expressed in the previous chapters.

For instance, these include speed, surprise, collaboration, responsiveness, and agility, as well as the use of cross-functional teams to maintain a strong interface with customers. Then add a market-to-organization communications network that permits switching from defense to offensive, and back again to defend on short notice due to sudden actions by competitors.

In today's digital environment, an organizational structure that incorporates those characteristics requires a design of openness, fluidity, and flexibility. Overlying such a structure is a prevailing force that is felt but not seen. It permeates the work environment with feelings of changeability, volatility, urgency, and uncertainty. It is within these disquieting emotional states that individuals rise to accomplish outstanding feats through innovation and inventiveness.

Such was the case at Microsoft when CEO Satya Nadella first took office. He saw a research project that held his attention. It was a demonstration that used speech recognition and artificial intelligence to translate a live conversation into another language. Immediately noticing the commercial possibilities, Nadella wanted the tool combined with Skype as a working prototype, and he needed it in three months to announce at his first public event.

Ordinarily, the task of turning a research project into a demo, or ready-to-use product, would happen more slowly and methodically. But an urgent order is an order. The responsible business unit working at crisis-level speed immediately assembled a team and went to work to meet the deadline. The resulting product: the Skype Translator, which eventually would become available in seven languages.

The type of responsive organization that could produce such a result is quite opposite of what prevailed in the early twentieth century. At that time, the typical organization operated in a hierarchy where every decision was subject to constant challenge and reexamination. Organizations were slow and ponderous, and attempts at mobilizing corporate functions to react in a short time frame would be unreasonable to expect.

Individuals during that period typically worked in their functional areas within large impersonal organizations that one critic described as "dreariness, not so much of physical deprivation but of a psychological void." Productivity was a major concern, and studies were continuously in progress to find approaches to increase efficiency and output.

The most famous of these research studies was conducted at the Hawthorne Works (a Western Electric factory) in Cicero, Illinois, from 1924 to 1932. Observers meticulously tracked results in worker productivity as changes were made in lighting, relocation of workstations, working hours, break times, and other areas. Lighting, however, formed the basis of the study. In all instances, where changes were made, productivity initially improved. When the observers completed their observations and left, productivity dropped to its previous levels.

Over the years, numerous organizational behavioral experts and industrial psychologists put forth unique and scholarly interpretations. The widely accepted view—known as the *Hawthorne effect*—is that the workers reacted positively in response to their awareness of being observed, rather than by any physical changes in their work space.

During that period, other researchers observed organizations, workers, and society through the written word. One of the more noteworthy books was William Whyte's *Organization Man*, which suggested a degree of uniformity in the American middle class, reflected in standardized career paths, consumer tastes, sensibilities, and workplace obedience. Much of the writing about this group included David Riesman's *Lonely Crowd* and C. Wright Mills's *White Collar Workers*. Each suggests that the rise of this working class was joyless.

EVOLUTION OF THE MODERN ORGANIZATION

How did the organization evolve from that early period to where it is today? What were the drivers that prompted the business scholars and pragmatic businesspeople to devise and design the organization that is suitable for the digital environment?

To begin, the mere notion that management was a profession originated with the founding of business schools. The first was the Wharton School at the University of Pennsylvania, established in 1881. The central course of study at that time dealt with labor issues, preventing strikes, and maintaining discipline. The curriculum also dealt with handling great amounts of capital and other business processes.

It was not until 1908 that the Harvard Business School opened. At first, it promoted and taught science and engineering. Eventually, the university opted for business, where the courses of study were influenced by the ideas of Frederick Taylor.

Frederick Taylor

Taylor claimed he found a form of management that was "a true science, resting upon clearly defined laws." He based his method on the belief that for each task of an organization, there should be "one best way" found through careful analysis and measurement. Those who analyzed and measured, and acted upon the findings, would become part of a new profession.

Taylor distinguished between *planning* and *doing*. He thought planning required very clever people, whereas with doing, it did not matter if people understood "the principles of this science." The more a worker could be treated as an unthinking machine, the better, because without the complication of independent thought, it would be possible to calculate how best to extract optimal performance.

Part of what Taylor called science was the reliance on quantification and mathematics to establish the most efficient way to work. In turn, that approach called for "time-and-motion" studies with stopwatches to measure achievement, so that a rate could be set for its completion.

He also wrote in his best-selling book *The Principles of Scientific Management* that workers were natural "loafers" who failed to work as hard as they could. Without greater efficiency, he argued, management would have to reward workers with means other than pay, although he thought that pay was the best motivation of all.*

Considered the father of scientific management, which was inscribed on his gravestone after he died in 1915, Taylor's followers included Henry Gantt and Frank and Lillian Gilbreth, who continued to develop and spread his ideas. They promoted a form of science, "aggressive rationality," which swept away custom and superstition for the benefit of management and labor.

Even though labor unions rejected Taylor's concepts, overall his philosophy was in tune with the tempo of the times. He urged efficiency as a great national goal, rather than just an idea for companies. He hoped the principles would apply to all social activities, from the management of homes to that of churches, universities, and government departments.

Efficiency, as he viewed it, fits well with the progressive connection that science, rather than intuition, could provide. He also felt his ideas worked as an objective basis for evaluating policies and reorganizing society to serve the needs of the majority rather than the self-interest of the few. A group of theorists followed Frederick Taylor to form what became the human relations school.

Human Relations School

As management theory evolved, the adherents to this school went beyond Taylor and stressed the importance of social networks in making organizations work. A key figure here was Elton Mayo, who gained fame as an interpreter of the Hawthorne experiments described above. His research spoke directly to the core of executive concerns: how to calm the worker's irrational, agitation-prone mind, and how to develop and train managers and executives to do so. Mayo's underlying philosophy was deeply conservative, seeing conflict as a "social disease" to be remedied by a healthy cooperation across groups.

Others in the movement also had the idea of organizations as social systems, analogous to human bodies seeking some sort of equilibrium. To achieve equilibrium, the organization needed to achieve both efficiency

---

* Some of Taylor's theories are not unlike the ones contained in Douglas McGregor's well-known Theory X and Theory Y, which consist of two fundamental approaches to managing people. Theory X tends to use an authoritarian leadership style. In contrast, Theory Y leans toward a participative approach. Theory X is characterized by individuals' dislike for work. Though forced to work toward organizational objectives, they prefer to be directed. Above all else, they want job security, whereas with Theory Y, work is natural and enjoyable, it is self-directed to achieve organizational objectives, and individuals often seek greater responsibility.

and effectiveness. Efficiency means the ability to satisfy the individuals who make up the organization; effectiveness involves the ability to meet goals.

Therefore, management must formulate the organizational goals and decide how to meet them. But it must do so in a manner that keeps all members involved through every available form of direct and accessible communications. This notion, which now gets closer to today's organization, emphasized the importance of respect and cooperation, suggesting that collaboration was more important than material incentives and threats.

Along the same lines, and in addition to technical and social skills, managers needed to work actively to infuse the organization with appropriate values—which is now the cornerstone for developing a sound corporate culture. Otherwise, according to the theory, the organization would fail. It was therefore important "to educate and to propagandize" people to "inculcate" appropriate motives and perceptions. Therefore, executives must not only conform to a moral code but also create moral codes for others, which would be reflected in high morale.

As the century progressed, the possibilities for maintaining a docile, regimented workforce receded with the growing strength of labor unions and the increasingly demanding nature of work requiring specialists. Moreover, while the original inspiration for the human relations school might have been to draw workers away from socialism and unions, it encouraged managers to recognize that their organizations were complex social structures rather than simple hierarchies, and that their workers would respond positively if treated as rounded human beings.

The approach risked replacing autocracy with paternalism as it struggled to work out how these developing views of organizational life would affect structures of power. The more these structures had to be addressed, and the more they had to be related to the wider social and economic changes underway, the more managers would need a strategy. What followed were the influences of the giants of industry on the evolution of the organization.

GIANTS OF INDUSTRY

Of all the business leaders spanning several decades, from the late 1800s through the 1930s, a few stand out who influenced the development of organizations and management. The primary ones include John D. Rockefeller, Henry Ford, and Alfred P. Sloan.

John D. Rockefeller

Ironically, Rockefeller's claim to fame cannot be used as a model for others to follow. He is best known for building an industry and developing Standard Oil into a virtual monopoly. As a leader, however, he had an exceptional ability to size up a market situation by seeing the full picture of its potential. Yet he could deal effectively with its individual components, such as sources of supply, distribution networks, government regulations, and competition, although at times his methods used a variety of questionable techniques. By 1900, Standard Oil had reached the peak of its influence. The size of the international market, which already included significant competitors, meant that its relative position was bound to decline.

Rockefeller used skill, boldness, and power to overcome competition. Alliances and combinations, which were ingeniously developed as trusts, were used as a way of guaranteeing efficiency, stability, and most importantly, control. However, he was already in a state of transition when forced to break up the trusts with the enactment of the Sherman Antitrust Act and the active intervention of President Theodore Roosevelt.

Even where it looked as if Rockefeller was defeated, the opposite was the case. As the market expanded, it turned out that it was increasingly beyond the capacity of any single company to control a developing market of such size and complexity. The ability of smaller units to respond flexibly to new conditions eventually made for a stronger and more profitable industry, which was perpetuated by the likes of Henry Ford and Alfred P. Sloan.

Henry Ford

Ford framed an organization that linked to his strategic vision. He wished to "construct and market an automobile specially designed for everyday wear and tear," a machine to be admired for its "compactness, its simplicity, its safety, its all-around convenience, and its exceedingly reasonable price." To accomplish this monumental task, he needed to get the price down to ensure the needed volume for a mass market—which did not exist at the time. That effort required new forms of manufacturing and assembly.

Thus, Ford's strategic thinking of a "universal car" that was built with high-quality materials and simple to operate resulted in the famous Model T. He then concentrated on manufacturing the one model in large numbers for, as it turned out, a longer period than warranted. When asked by his salesmen for more models, Ford famously remarked, "Any customer can have a car painted any color that he wants so long as it is black." That said, the Model T was not to be a luxury item for a few, but one for "the great multitude."

To accomplish this feat, he installed the first assembly line in 1913. Tools and men were placed in sequence as each component moved along until the car was finished. This reduced the "necessity for thought on the part of the worker and his movements to a minimum." Ford claimed that his approach was a breakthrough not only in car manufacturing, but also in the development of the industrial society.

In effect, he gave a decisive impetus to two critical and related developments: the techniques of *mass production*, which in turn fed the desires of *mass consumption*. In his leadership approach, Ford sought personal control and oversight over what had become a massive company, with hundreds of thousands of employees and sales in the millions, yet he ran it "as if it were a mom-and-pop shop."

The company reached its peak in 1923, when it produced 2 million cars, including many tractors and trucks. By then, however, competition was developing from General Motors and Chrysler. While Ford stuck with the Model T, the others set the pace with a greater range of new cars. By 1926, Ford's production barely reached 1.5 million vehicles and prices dropped from $825 to $290. The rivals also began offering new forms of payment, such as accepting credit and installments. Ford was unwilling to offer similar inducements.

By the 1930s, almost submerged by competition, defeated by the unions, and suffering from a shameful reputation of anti-Semitism, Ford had little to offer the next generation of customers. The company's resurgence would have to wait until the beginning of World War II with the production of military vehicles, which would benefit from its vaunted assembly-line heritage. The industrial world was now ready for another type of leader.

Alfred P. Sloan

Sloan, president and later chairman of General Motors from 1923 through 1956, was responsible for shaping the modern corporation, as well as the automobile industry. His initial idea upon becoming president depended on two propositions: First, the company should be split up into divisions, each with its own chief executive with commensurate responsibility for all its operations. Second, specific organizational functions, absolutely necessary to the overall corporation's development, needed to be controlled at one level, notwithstanding that they might cause some contentious issues with division executives.

Sloan also had to face the reality that Ford, in the early 1920s, accounted for some 60% of all cars sold in the United States. To advance against such a formidable competitor, General Motors deployed its several divisions with 10 models, from a basic car to a luxury vehicle.

The brilliance of this product-line strategy at that time is that these models did not reflect any existing market concept. That is, before market segmentation as a calculated marketing strategy became popular, Sloan's way of thinking represented a new way to view the market. It was about how different classes of customers might respond to variations in price and quality.

Consequently, the company could be organized to suit an evolving market. At that time, Sloan was not just relating to the market, he was actually reshaping it. The boldness of the strategy was not unlike Ford's initial approach to making a mass market. Sloan's approach to an organizational structure fit precisely with his strategy of marketing a full range of models under the slogan of a car "for every purse and purpose."

For instance, at the low end of the market, Sloan went up against the Model T with the company's Chevrolet model, but at a somewhat higher price than Ford's car. He astutely recognized that going head-to-head against Ford would be a wasteful strategy. Instead, he targeted the low end of the market by aiming for higher quality in order to justify a higher price.

Sloan's intention was to get sales from customers prepared to pay a bit more, but also to pick up sales from those at the next higher class who might prefer to pay a bit less. That maneuver would leave Ford locked in at the very low end of that segment. And if it wanted to go upscale, it would confront Chevrolet, which was quickly solidifying its position. Within six years, General Motors led the market, selling 1.8 million vehicles in 1927.

ORGANIZATIONAL THINKINGS AND STRATEGISTS

A diverse range of thinkers contributed to organizational development. One of those renowned organizational thinkers was an academic, Peter

Drucker, who explored what it meant to manage a modern corporation. His book *The Concept of the Corporation* was the first to consider business as an organization, and that management is a specific organ doing specific kinds of work with specific responsibilities. He is credited with having established management as a discipline and the organization as a distinct entity; as such, they qualified as a discipline and a recognized field of study.

Drucker acknowledged Taylor's contributions, but was skeptical of scientific management. He thought good results could be achieved by intuition and hunch. Further, Drucker blamed Taylor for separating planning from doing. Rather, he believed the job of management was "to make what is desirable first possible and then actual."

The essence of his philosophy was to alter circumstances by consciously directed actions. To manage a business was to "manage by objectives." To this end, he understood that whatever the long-term vision, it had to be translated into immediate and credible goals when it came to implementation.

Drucker very clearly took into account the complexities of both organizational structures and business environments. His numerous books set him up as the first contemporary management theorist. During his career, he became a consultant to leading companies such as Ford, General Motors, and General Electric.

The Business–Military Connection

Other leaders and writers came on the scene. One specific group saw a meaningful and pragmatic connection between military concepts and business applications, specifically as they related to organizational development and business and competitive strategy.

Bruce Henderson of the Boston Consulting Group was one of those individuals who in the 1960s dealt with issues of strategy by relating them to their military roots. He referenced the work of Sir B. H. Liddell Hart, the eminent British military historian who was famous for his concept of the *indirect approach*, which is still viewed as a valid strategy not only in its original usage in the military, but also in business, sports, and other endeavors.

For instance, Liddell Hart's two fundamental principles turned out to be recognizable and applicable for corporate executives and midlevel managers in competitive business situations: First, direct approaches against an adversary (think competitor) firmly in position almost never work and should never be attempted. Second, to defeat an adversary, one must first upset its equilibrium, which is not accomplished by the main effort, but must be done before the main effort can succeed.

Henderson especially valued Liddell Hart's emphasis on maneuvering through the indirect approach and concentrating strength against a rival's weaknesses.* He also sensed the drama of competition and discussed the trickery that might be employed to divert competitors. Strategy, he thought, could be applied to differences in leadership style, as well as to matters of overhead rate, distribution channels, or corporate image.

Other noteworthy references to the military–business connection came from a 1981 article, "Marketing Warfare in the 1980s," by Philip Kotler and Ravi Singh, where the authors indicated that the need of businesses "to develop competitor-centered strategies to win market share [would] lead managers to turn increasingly to the subject of military science."

Then Al Ries and Jack Trout in 1986 wrote the highly popular *Marketing Warfare*, which used the Prussian general and military theorist Carl von Clausewitz for inspiration.† The authors focused on the psychological aspect by asserting that at stake was occupying the mind of the consumer rather than territory. And just like the strongest armies, the strongest companies should be able to use their power to stay on top.

They also maintained that for small companies to have a chance, like small weaker armies, they must employ cunning and not brute force against a large organization in a well-entrenched defensive positon.‡ Altogether, Ries and Trout became well known for how they applied four strategies—defensive, offensive, flanking, and guerrilla—with market share determining which was appropriate.

Possibly the most influential military reference, which had its origins more than 2,500 years ago, is Sun Tzu's *Art of War*. This remarkable work is often quoted in modern business books, in articles, and at management seminars for its enduring wisdom and capacity for meaningful applications to business situations. As such, Sun Tzu was the common source on which many business leaders and other commentators based their ideas (see Table 9.1).

---

* References come from *Strategy* by B. H. Liddell Hart, Frederick A. Praeger Publishers, New York, 1965. Also see applications of these strategies in Chapters 4 and 6 of this book.
† Also see my book *Clausewitz Talks Business*, Taylor & Francis, Boca Raton, FL, 2015.
‡ See Chapter 8 for a comprehensive discussion on the advantages of defensive positions.

TABLE 9.1

Quotations from Sun Tzu's *Art of War*

For to win one hundred victories in one hundred battles is not the acme of skill. To subdue the enemy[a] without fighting is the acme of skill.

Supreme excellence consists in breaking the enemy's resistance without fighting.

With many calculations, one can win; with few one cannot. How much less chance of victory has one who makes none at all! By this means I examine the situation and the outcome will be clearly apparent.

One mark of a great strategist is that he fights on his own terms or fights not at all.

Although everyone can see the outward aspects, none understands the way in which I have created victory. Therefore, when I have won a victory I do not repeat my tactics, but respond to circumstances in an infinite variety of ways.

Speed is the essence of war. Take advantage of the enemy's unpreparedness; travel by unexpected routes and strike him when he has taken no precautions.

Now to win … and take your objectives, but to fail to exploit these achievements is ominous and may be described as wasteful delay.

Any unnecessary expenditure of time, every unnecessary detour, is a waste of strength and thus abhorrent to strategic thought.

Victory is the main object in war. If this is long delayed, weapons are blunted and morale depressed. When troops attack … their strength will be exhausted.

While we have heard of blundering swiftness in war, we have not yet seen a clever operation that was prolonged.

Engage … only when odds are overwhelmingly in your favor. Always identify and exploit your comparative advantage.

Know the enemy and know yourself; in a hundred battles you will never be in peril. When you are ignorant of the enemy, but know yourself, your chances of winning or losing are equal. If ignorant both of your enemy and of yourself, you are certain in every battle to be in peril.[b]

[a] Substitute *enemy* with *competitor*, *fighting* with *market confrontation*, *war* with *competitive campaign*, and *troops* with *personnel*, as well as other appropriate substitutions, to get the most value from Sun Tzu.

[b] This particular quote, and several others in the listing, is of special value when thinking of the themes of this book and the high value of big data and analytics to determine where you are positioned, as well as to know about your rival.

ORGANIZATIONS: A PANORAMIC OVERVIEW

What follows is a historical review by decades that highlights key events that formed the foundations for today's digitally based organizations.

The 1950s

As Europe and Asia began rebuilding after the devastation of World War II, the 1950s became a period of overwhelming economic influence by the

United States throughout most of the world. During that time, corporate planning dominated most of the larger U.S. companies.

Consisting primarily of production plans, this type of planning focused on satisfying an insatiable demand for consumer goods within the United States, as well as supplying industrial products to help those European and Asian countries ravaged by war to rebuild their economies and redevelop consumer markets.

At the highest organizational levels, senior-level executives developed corporate plans, which maintained a dominant financial focus. Rarely did lower-echelon managers participate in strategy planning sessions.

In contrast, lower-level managers geared their planning to maximize productivity for the short-term satisfaction of market demand. Marketing as a distinct unifying function enveloping product development, marketing research, advertising, sales promotion, and field selling did not exist at that time.

The 1960s

Strong consumer demand for products characterized the 1960s. The business environment was marked by intensified economic growth in most of the industrialized countries. Yet serious competition still remained limited. And there was no urgency to change procedures, other than to keep the production lines moving efficiently. In general, what was produced was consumed.

In addition to developing markets in European industrialized countries, third world countries slowly emerged as customers for products to sustain the basic needs of life. Such products included simple machines, some types of agricultural equipment, and basic transportation in the form of buses and bicycles.

Organizations began to look to business planning as a way to involve those executives who represented the core activities of manufacturing, research and development, sales, and distribution. As part of the longer-term strategy, there was a conscious effort to integrate diverse business functions through a coordinated plan of operations. In spite of this planning breakthrough, however, long-term plans were still kept separate from those short-term plans prepared by middle managers.

The 1970s

This decade triggered a transitional phase in planning and strategy. With the postwar rebuilding process almost complete, its full effect was about to impact the world. European companies burst onto global markets. It was the Japanese companies, however, that generated the most aggressive and penetrating competition.

The full thrust of their competitive assault hit virtually every major industry, from machine tools and consumer electronics to automobiles and steel. The new competitive situation ignited the surging movement to embrace marketing planning and competitive strategy.

In turn, marketing strategy during the 1970s signaled a period of market identification and expansion. In North America, customers demanded more varied products and services, and they were willing to pay for them. Responding to the continuing population shift out of the cities, businesses followed increasingly affluent customers into the expanding suburban shopping malls. In Western Europe and Asia, new markets continued to unfold, thereby increasing consumption of consumer and industrial products.

Executives reshaped their organizations and merged the individual plans of the once-scattered activities of merchandising, advertising, sales promotion, publicity, and field selling into a unified strategy to identify and satisfy changing market demands. Typically, the marketing plans developed by middle managers covered only a one-year period.

Within those plans, managers emphasized emerging geographic markets, new technology applications, and international markets. They made extensive use of demographic profiles to define markets with greater precision. Beyond demographics, a new approach to market definition emerged that utilized psychographics, a profiling system that described prospects by lifestyle and behavior.

Marketing as an independent business discipline expanded rapidly into undergraduate and graduate degree programs at universities worldwide. In keeping with the evolving and changing market conditions, a broad definition of marketing developed:

> Marketing is a total system of interacting business activities designed to plan, price, promote, and distribute want-satisfying products or services to organizational and household users in a competitive environment at a profit.

That definition emphasized understanding customer needs and developing comprehensive programs to satisfy the wants of different market segments. Further, a "total system of interacting business activities" called for integrating various business activities, such as manufacturing, research and development, promotion, and distribution. In turn, the definition also called for the use of strategy teams consisting of individuals from each of those diverse functions. It reaffirmed the integration already begun through business planning.

Managers viewed the planning document as a "housing" to contain all of the above functions and the resulting strategies in a logical and organized format. Then, to encourage clear and precise communications throughout the organization, the plan became the medium to reach all levels of the organization.

By the late 1970s, still another form of planning took hold: *strategic planning*. Strategic planning aimed to build onto the long-term, financially oriented corporate plans of the 1960s by adding a strategic focus to the process. More precisely,

> strategic planning is the managerial process of developing and maintaining a strategic fit between the organization and its changing market opportunities. It relies on developing
>
> * A mission, vision, or strategic direction
> * Objectives and goals
> * Growth strategies
> * A business portfolio consisting of markets and products

Corporations still used the generalized terms *strategic planning, corporate planning*, and *business planning*. And managers considered them part of a common business vocabulary. Regardless of the term used, the intent showed that volatile environmental, economic, industry, customer, and competitive factors require a more expansive and disciplined strategic thought process for effective planning and strategy development.

No longer could top-down 1950s-style corporate planning driven by a production orientation suffice. The evolving competitive international marketplace of the 1970s required a more precise orientation satisfied by strategic planning and marketing planning.

The 1980s

The 1980s spurred the next stage of planning—strategic marketing (or market) planning—which merged two planning formats: the long-term strategic plan and the short-term marketing plan.

There are several reasons why the strategic marketing plan evolved to this stage of the planning cycle:

1. While strategic planning permitted managers to create a long-term vision of how the organization could grow, for the most part, it lacked implementation. A survey conducted by Deloitte & Touche Consulting during this period indicated that while 97% of the Fortune 500 companies wrote strategic plans, only 15% of that elite group of companies ever implemented anything that came out of the plan.

2. Marketing planning, in turn, incorporated only those activities associated with the marketing function into an action-oriented plan. The planning period, however, was usually confined to one year. No formal process linked the longer-term strategic plan that required an implementation phase to the shorter-term marketing plan that warranted a strategic vision.

3. Typically, each plan developed independently within the organization. No procedure unified planning efforts consistent with the marketing definition of "a total system of interacting activities designed to plan, price, promote, and distribute want-satisfying products to organizational and household users in a competitive environment."

Under those exceptional conditions, the strategic marketing plan evolved to create a linkage of the strategic plan with the marketing plan. It connected the internal functions of the organization with the external and volatile changes of an increasingly competitive global environment. In turn, the plan became the storehouse for marketing strategies.

The 1990s

As corporations of the 1980s and 1990s reengineered and downsized to create cost-effective, efficient, and lean organizations, a further innovation evolved. The middle-level manager was asked to develop a formal strategy plan for his or her product, service, or business unit.

Using the strategic marketing plan as a hands-on format, the manager could now conceptualize a product with a long-term strategic direction that focused on future customer and market needs. He or she could project what changes would take place in a framework of industry, consumer, competitive, and environmental areas and identify ways in which technologies would change business practices. In addition, new groundbreaking software could identify buyer patterns and interpret their implications, so that business strategies could be adjusted to maximize profitability.

The 2000s

With intensive worldwide competition from developed and developing countries on virtually every continent, and especially from China, extensive use of strategic alliances continued with major corporate mergers, as well as through minor joint marketing efforts by a wide range of companies. Thus, the effective application of competitive strategies continued to saturate managers' time and energy as they immersed themselves in initiating efficient operations, outsourcing numerous functions, and adopting new technology innovations.

In particular, executives faced various types of competitive campaigns. Each had a distinctive purpose and required a customized action plan with objectives aligned to the business plan and the organization's culture. These appeared in various forms, as displayed in the business press during the recent decade:

Walmart stores attack one of the largest consumer electronics chains, Best Buy stores.
BMW shifts production to lightweight carbon fiber ahead of competitors to give its electric cars a performance advantage.
Google launches a new computer operating system and attacks Microsoft.
BASF challenges Monsanto's dominance in the global seed market.

Although these headlines may not have reached a crisis stage for those organizations under attack, they nevertheless did call for the defending firms to develop action plans.

Each of the above competitive situations, therefore, took on its own unique character. Companies began restructuring to respond rapidly with actions to gain an advantageous position, disrupt a competitor, or reverse declining sales by using a variety of thrusts, such as introducing cutting-edge technology, offering enhanced services, launching new products, or initiating low prices.

THE AGE OF THE DIGITAL ORGANIZATION

The above historical review of how organizations evolved, the thought processes of the noteworthy leaders and writers of that period, and the changing practices of management illustrate and contrast the differences over the decades with the organizational needs of today's digital world. Yet a finite connection does exist with the past. Some perceptive leaders recognized the power of economic, environmental, and behavioral changes, and thereby the value of becoming more responsive to the marketplace. These forces prompted them to revamp their organizations with a customer-centric orientation, rather than stick to their heritage as a production-centered organization.

As for the new workers, they are portrayed as positive, creative, authentic, expressive, and spontaneous—and described by some as independent, insubordinate, and less awed by the perceived wisdom of experts or even the dictates of common sense. Thus, with the emphasis now on big data, algorithms, and analytics as essential tools for competitive advantage, these talented workers are considered key differentiators in a digital world of competitive encounters. As such, they need to be nurtured and trained.

In the course of one year, 2016, AT&T delivered 50,000 big data–related training courses, from one-week boot camps to advanced PhD-level data science courses. As important, employees were taught to interact within an organizational structure that strives for collaboration among all corporate functions. That means influencing the two primary zones of activity that shape a dynamic marketplace: first, making certain that the organization's products and services meet customers' needs, and second, strengthening the firm's ability to defend its markets against the inroad of aggressive competitors. Both zones, in turn, contribute to a balanced organization that is flexible enough to protect what it has gained. Yet it has the internal capability to expand according to the objectives of its strategic business plan.

Thus, to achieve such collaboration, an operational structure is needed that is supported by five forces to provide stability, openness, resilience, and responsiveness to the enterprise. These are contained in Exhibit 9.1 as digital technology, competitive strategy, corporate culture, organizational structure, and strategic business planning.

The Five Forces of Leadership Shaped by the Digital Age

- Digital technology
- Competitive strategy
- Corporate culture
- Organizational structure
- Strategic business planning

EXHIBIT 9.1

For an organization operating in the digital age, the five-force structure provides an all-inclusive framework to deal with aggressive competitive inroads, as it maintains a strong interface with customers.

10

Activate an Agile Organization

Complex and centralized bureaucracies are obsolete. Change requires new business models ... leaner, faster, more decentralized.

Jeff Immelt
Chairman and CEO, General Electric Co.
(from Murray, 2016)

What is the thinking behind the above quote, and what are the underlying issues contained in "complex and centralized bureaucracies are obsolete"? Based on the theme of this chapter, activating an agile organization means that your company culture is flexible enough and your corporate systems and personnel are adaptable enough to meet the new and uncertain conditions from within and outside your industry.

It also means your firm can handle the huge inflow of data, sort out the meaningful information, and systematically convert it into probabilities and possibilities for new opportunities. Then, you are able to see where the potential areas of disruptions might come from. At that point, you can prioritize objectives and strategies into actions. This entire process is typically housed in a business plan. (See Section V, "Strategic Business Planning.")

Where planning is ingrained as part of your operation, you can view how you want the future of your organization or business unit to evolve. Your aim, then, is to develop offensive and defensive initiatives that would permeate the organization and emerge as tactical business unit plans.

Agility, then, entails maneuver, speed, and the ability to concentrate at decisive points—areas covered in previous chapters. Spearheading it all are applications of technology and new product development for the digital age. Thus, within an agile organization, the use of big data and planning has a twofold purpose: First, reach and satisfy the consumer, or as

Peter Drucker stated, "Create a customer." Second, neutralize the competitors' efforts to interfere with your plans.

The clear implication to these points is that your company cannot remain idle. Even if you have no immediate threat from a competitor, without doubt, rivals will eventually seek you out, especially if your firm has made some breakthrough with a new product, service, or technology. And even if you enjoyed peaceful coexistence with a rival, you cannot be assured of continuous live-and-let-live harmonious relationships.

Then, there are the potential threats from outside your industry that can cause major disruptions. Such was the case in the automotive industry with the rise of autonomous cars and the accelerating trend in ride-sharing firms. General Motors, for instance, felt that long term its business model would be upended with the rapid movement by organizations outside the automotive industry that were actively immersed in driverless cars and shared mobility services. Worse yet, industry forecasts indicated that U.S. auto sales could fall 40% within 25 years. That spiraling threat had Detroit-headquartered GM executives sprinting to Silicon Valley to seek alliances with the prime innovators.

At stake for GM was the clear need to defend its market position, not only by speeding up its own mobility programs, but also by forming relationships with ride-sharing outfits that were involved with driverless car software. GM subsequently invested heavily in self-driving cars and struck an agreement with the number two ride-hailing firm, Lyft.

GM also made a $1 billion investment in Cruise Automation, a self-driving software maker company. Clearly, GM followed the defensive–offensive strategy of attempting to protect its basic business by going on the offensive. "We can wait to be disrupted, or we can take an active role to disrupt," stated a GM executive.

Other companies in the automotive industry also heard the call to action—or be left behind. Fiat Chrysler Automobiles looked to partner with Apple to make cars. And Ford scanned for alliance possibilities, prompted by the notion that in the foreseeable future, Google and Apple would be its key rivals.

AGILITY LINKS TO PREPAREDNESS

If you suspect your competitor's intentions are to disrupt your existing mode of operations, there is no safer course of action than to prepare contingency plans for ready use. That is somewhat axiomatic. Yet if you look at preparedness from another vantage point, it would take on a more precise course of action. That is, if you desire some measure of marketplace peace, you must organize for confrontation.

Preparations made in times of peaceful coexistence give a greater chance for success in times of competitive challenges. Competitors do not easily take action against a company that is ready to actively resist. By contrast, peaceful and complacent companies are vulnerable unless they activate contingency plans in time and in a way that becomes a visible threat to active rivals.

Of particular importance, these plans must take into account the rapid advances in data, modeling, and automated analysis that allow for greater precision in targeting and measuring the effects of competitive campaigns. As part of that effort, analytics offers powerful clues about why consumers behave as they do.

The essential point regarding preparedness is "to make what is desirable first possible and then actual," according to Peter Drucker, which requires an organizational design that establishes seamless relationships with marketing, production, logistics, finance, product development, and other basic activities.

Organizationally, then, you need an integrated planning function and active cross-functional teams with the authority and responsibility to develop offensive and defensive strategy plans that reach, satisfy, and perpetuate your firm's position in an evolving marketplace. This is where preparedness through an agile organization can accommodate to that tempo by developing new opportunities. "The days of cycling global ideas through a central headquarters are over. Globalization requires pushing capability to local teams who are empowered to take risks without second guessing," declared Jeff Immelt.

Whereas the physical structure of an organization varies with individual tastes, the design must permit the digital linkages to enhance relationships. Specifically, then, it is digitization that forms the underpinnings of the organization's configuration that connects customers with the internal operations of your firm.

Given those attributes and conditions, how would you describe your firm? Exhibit 10.1 is a worksheet that will assist you in determining your firm's profile, as well as provide clues as to what you believe would be the optimum profile for your firm. Based on McKinsey & Company's Organizational Health Index, results showed that companies with speed

	Strong		

Start-up — Total

- Start-up
- Chaotic
- Creative
- Frenetic
- "Free-for-all"
- Ad hoc
- Reinventing the wheel
- No boundaries
- Constantly shifting focus
- Unpredictable

Agile — Total

- Quick to mobilize
- Nimble
- Collaborative
- Easy to get things done
- Responsive
- Free flow of information
- Quick decision making
- Empowered to act
- Resilient
- Learning from failures

Trapped — Total

- Uncoordinated
- Struck
- Empire building
- Fighting fires
- Local tribes
- Finger pointing
- Under attack
- Rigid
- Politics
- Protecting "turf"

Bureaucracy — Total

- Risk-averse
- Efficient
- Slow
- Bureaucratic
- Standard ways of working
- Siloed
- Decision escalation
- Reliable
- Centralized
- Established

Dynamic capability (vertical axis)

Weak — Stable backbone — Strong

EXHIBIT 10.1

Worksheet: where does your organization fall today? Place a check mark by every word that describes how it currently feels to work at your company. Total the number checked in each quadrant to see where your company falls. (From "Agility: It Rhymes with Stability," *McKinsey Quarterly*, December 2015. Copyright © 2015 McKinsey & Company. All rights reserved. Reprinted by permission.)

and stability have a 70% chance of being ranked in the top quartile by organizational health. That is a far higher proportion than McKinsey found among companies focused only on one or the other.

McKinsey's work also highlighted three core areas where balancing between stability and flexibility is critical: "organizational structure, which defines how resources are distributed; governance, which dictates how decisions are made; and processes, which determine how things get done, including the management of performance."

AGILITY LEADS TO EFFECTIVE PERFORMANCE

The attributes listed in Exhibit 10.1 under "Agile" serve as guidelines for activating an organization suitable for the digital age. As McKinsey's research points out, however, attributes from other quadrants may need to provide a "stable backbone." The following explanations refer only to "Agile."

Quick to Mobilize

Speed of mobilization means removing barriers that prevent reacting rapidly to changing marketplace conditions. Barriers appear in various forms, such as sluggishness among staff, which is often due to a lack of understanding about the urgency of a threat, or not completely internalizing a sudden opportunity.

Such was the above case of General Motors. Executives in the C-suite finally saw the danger of their almost century-old business model coming apart. Then, in relatively quick moves, they proactively reached out to Silicon Valley to negotiate with organizations that presumably had no history in making cars. Yet that is exactly what those nonautomotive companies were doing with their autonomous test cars: racking up hundreds of thousands of miles.

Then, there is the issue of executives creating their own barriers to speed. In some instances, it is due to a leader's basic personality that requires him or her to check, recheck, and quantify every detail beyond reasonable limits as time ticks away without a decision. Or it is the case of sheer procrastination, whereby the overly cautious leader simply will not move, even if prodded with quality data.

This behavior may be due to an innate fear of making an error, so that the feeling of insecurity about what lies ahead is unreasonably magnified. And should that person realize the urgency of speed, the more he lingers with the potential dangers, and the more doubtful and indecisive he becomes.

Beyond personality, there is another dynamic at work whereby a manager rises in the organization to a leadership position, primarily due to a dedicated specialty. However, when thrust into a situation that relies on a broader knowledge of markets, strategies, and maneuvers, the experience and training needed for effective decision making are lacking.

Nimble

Somewhat similar to the above, this attribute suggests flexibility, dexterity, and an outstanding ability to adapt to changing situations. This factor is difficult to quantify, since each situation creates its own criteria of what makes up nimbleness. This point is illustrated by the actions of Apple.

With its smartphone shipments experiencing continuous declines, iPad sales slowing, phone upgrades slackening, and the Apple Watch not living up to sales expectations, in 2016 Apple moved rapidly to cut a momentous deal with Chinese ride-sharing service Didi. At the time, Didi handled more than 11 million rides a day and served about 300 million users across China. That timely maneuver expanded Apple's presence in China, the world's largest mobile arena, with its entire product line, including Apple's CarPlay and Apple Wallet.

Nimbleness, as a corporate attribute, is exceedingly valuable in many of today's markets where establishing a first-in market position often provides a distinct competitive advantage. It is valuable, too, where forming joint ventures to accelerate a company's growth, especially where few viable relationships are available, as was the case with Apple and Didi.

Collaborative

Collaboration has been mentioned numerous times in previous chapters. It is the hallmark characteristic of the digital corporation. The issue, then, is what can get in the way of effective collaboration?

The inhibiting element is *friction*. It takes on many forms and can affect a firm's ability to mobilize rapidly and stay nimble. Friction tends to penetrate the behavior of staff members, often among team members who challenge others to claims of status, power, or authority.

Another place where friction resides is in the adversarial relationships that commonly exist among diverse functions, such as marketing versus finance, product design versus manufacturing, sales versus logistics, and the like. Then, there are the opposing personalities of individuals clashing from a variety of natural or contrived circumstances.

One significant source of friction that should be anticipated comes about from expending excessive physical effort. Exhaustion is one of the characteristics that wears away at individuals' energies and consequently has an adverse effect on job performance. This is especially critical where extra levels of stamina and clear judgment are needed during an active market campaign.

Such signs are noticeable among those individuals who spend extensive periods of time in travel beyond their normal schedules. Or it could be through excessive amounts of overtime and weekend work over long periods that show up as mental and physical wear and tear. They all can have an adverse effect on the delicate balance of work, family, and personal life.

Thus, from a leader's point of view, expending physical energy for an extended period of time should be a major concern. What matters most is the effect of fatigue on staff morale, which could negatively affect the outcome of a campaign. It is the singular issue that makes a critical difference between success and failure in implementing the business plan, especially where attitudes tend to be fragile and mood swings can deepen into depression.

Friction, then, is a powerful force that can stall any plan and create organizational turmoil that reflects in missed opportunities and disorganization. On the surface, the organization and everything related to it seems clear-cut and appears manageable. Yet each business unit is composed of individuals, and everyone has the potential for creating friction.

That is why discipline, training, effective communication, high morale, and adherence to a well-developed plan can contribute to welding the staff together for a collaborative effort. Consequently, the leader must be an individual of tested capabilities, so that the workings of the system move with a minimum of friction.

In sum, understanding the foundation concepts and underlying nuances associated with friction should be taken with the utmost seriousness for collaboration to flourish. That means making every effort to internalize the full scope of friction's capacity for irreparably damaging the organization.

Easy to Get Things Done

Reducing the level of friction is one sure way of lifting barriers and permitting things to get done easily. Another is removing layers within the organization. Organizational layers, long chains of command, and cumbersome committees prolong deliberation and foster procrastination.

The essential ingredient for an efficient enterprise is simplifying the system of control, and in particular, shortening the organizational layers from the field to top-level executives. "Sometimes everyone agrees with an idea you've helped formulate, and then, instead of being sent through seven different management layers for approval, it's put into action the next week," according to one management consultant.

In a small organization, the chief executive officer or president is at the helm. He or she is in a unique position to control both policy making and execution. Because decisions do not have to be channeled through others, they are unlikely to be misinterpreted, delayed, or contested. Plans can be implemented with consistency and speed.

In the larger multiproduct firms with more people, products, and additional levels of authority, results may fall victim to a cumbersome, inflexible operation. Individuals in the field often feel that there are obstructions in the decision-making process for moving into new markets. Missed opportunities are common, and "go" decisions get stuck for reasons other than the competition.

Even field managers think that there are too many people at the staff level or not enough on the job with revenue divisions. The large office staffs and the shortage of line personnel are sources of constant complaint. Much of that condition is handled by downsizing and reducing staff to an efficient "lean and mean" level.

Your own experience may well support the obvious inference that an organization with many levels in its decision-making process cannot operate efficiently. Notwithstanding advanced mobile technology, this situation exists because each link in the managerial chain carries four drawbacks:

1. Loss of time in getting information back from the field
2. Loss of time in sending orders forward
3. Lack of full knowledge of the situation by senior management
4. Reduction of the top executive's personal involvement in key issues that affect the availability of resources

Therefore, for ease of getting things done, reduce the chain of command. The fewer the decision-making levels, the more dynamic the operation. The result is improved speed and increased flexibility to adjust to varying circumstances. You can thereby concentrate at the decisive point before competitors have a chance to respond.

Responsive

Responsiveness is a presence of mind. It permits you to deal with a range of business transactions, competitive confrontations, and unexpected market interventions during times when timely and accurate decisions are required. Within that climate, four elements make up the competitive marketplace: risk, physical exertion, uncertainty, and chance. And where deep deliberation and extensive research are needed, the marketplace says, *act now.*

Where responsiveness is not present, it shows up in the complacent attitudes of some executives who feel protected by their company's longevity in the market and by a strong public image. Yet many of those once-proud enterprises were left in shambles. Or they were forced to exit their primary markets and go in entirely new directions, as in the case of the reorganized, downsized, and redirected Eastman Kodak Co. (described in Chapter 3).

Free Flow of Information

Embedded in this factor is the need for a receptive audience that willingly accepts and uses the flow of data. Yet there are instances where you may face cynical groups. Very likely, they are the millennials who have experienced tough economic times. They have seen, and perhaps have been part of, layoffs. They experienced unfilled promises, although not intentional, but due to the dynamics of a competitive marketplace. And, increasingly, they may avoid the emotional attachments of previous decades of "feeling corporate."

In any event, the necessary information must still get through to the various groups within the organization, even to those who may seem emotionally detached. For best results, information should attempt to foster a positive mindset among individuals. Thus, you will have to decide how to communicate bad news and when to announce the good happenings. Undoubtedly, it takes some level of communications skill to place a positive spin on bad news, where the central aim is to motivate the staff to action.

Fortunately, there are more effective tools to call into use, including mobile connectivity and social media, that can get the staff more involved. For instance, modern digital communications make it easier to personalize messages to the needs of business units, teams, and individuals. Using two-way communications, such as online polling software, permits rapid feedback to address sensitive issues or provide further details about a proposed program. The essential point is that the personalized messages from the CEO or other senior executives go directly to frontline employees without getting transposed or misinterpreted through a filtering system of middle management.

To expedite the free flow of information and eliminate points of interference, it is also useful to identify key individuals within the firm who enjoy a high level of influence over specific groups. These individuals can be likened to the familiar consumer hierarchy of influencers who can sway others. For instance, innovators can guide the thinking of early adopters. They, in turn, influence the early majority, followed by the late majority and laggards. These individuals, then, are the ones you should enlist to assist in positively influencing the mindsets of others.

Finally, where the organization establishes the free flow of information, it helps individuals internalize the goals and priorities of the organization. It also provides them with a pathway for individual career growth through further training and active participation.

Quick Decision Making

In a competitive situation, your object is to place your rival in a static situation where it cannot harm you. That means taking some action to weaken or totally neutralize the competitor. Such action, however, does not take place in one decisive campaign. Instead, it occurs in an ongoing series of market encounters; some are major, as with the introduction of a new technology, and some are minor, as in the announcement of a new promotion. However small the resources employed, or however limited the objectives of the campaign, once an effort is underway, actions cannot be interrupted. Each campaign, therefore, is subject to time and urgency.

Considering that you would be involved in an ongoing series of campaigns, the rival manager would dictate to you as much as you dictate to him. Thus, in your attempt to overcome your rival, you must match your effort against his power of resistance. Doing so is an outcome of two inseparable factors: first, the total resources at the disposal of your competitor, and second, the strength of his will.

The extent of the rival's resources can be estimated with a fair degree of accuracy. However, the strength of his resolve is far more difficult to determine. Based on examining a known competitor's typical operating pattern, it is possible that algorithms can lead to some substantive conclusions. Assuming you arrive at a reasonably accurate estimate of his power of resistance, you still need to make an appropriate decision.

And should more data trickle in, there may be little time to review the situation or even think it through thoroughly. In any case, whatever your decision, expect that the competing manager will respond. Thus, the decision-making cycle repeats.

Empowered to Act

This attribute allies with quick decision making. Yet there is one additional component to empowerment: the courage to act. Without courage, empowerment is a dormant issue. Courage is of two kinds: first, courage to face the pressures associated with taking risks, and second, courage to accept responsibility for committing company resources and being accountable. The first kind of courage may be an inbred character trait, where adventure and risk are part of an individual's psychological makeup. The second would reflect an individual's personal ambitions, feelings, and emotions, which tend not to be changeable.

Both kinds of courage involve dealing in the realm of the unknown, which could be speculative and take on the effect of a gamble. Notwithstanding that you may be relying on reliable data, chance is ever present. The outcome could affect individuals' careers and an organization's present state and future position.

With either kind of courage and in the context of the agile organization, empowerment is a potent force that must be encouraged, especially when dealing with today's intelligent staff. With evolving campaigns requiring immediate action, a leader is often governed by emotions rather than by logical thought. That is where the intellect needs to arouse the quality of courage, which then supports and sustains it in action.

One more trait needs to be added to empowerment: *determination*. Some individuals may command the keenest mind and may even possess the courage to accept serious responsibilities. But when faced with a difficult situation, they still find themselves unable to reach a decision. The required determination is aroused by the intellect and by a specific state of mind. "A dream doesn't become reality through magic; it takes sweat, determination, and hard work," stated General Colin Powell. And "the truest wisdom is a resolute determination," declared Napoleon Bonaparte.

Resilient

An agile organization permits individuals to operate with a resilience that glows by means of an inner light, which often leads to innovative outcomes. It is a quality embedded in most individuals: intuition. To some people, intuition suggests a fragile quality that cannot be pinned down when it comes to developing actionable strategies or reducing the dire effects of unfavorable situations.

Yet there is sufficient scientific evidence to rely on this innate quality to confidently take action without being immobilized by doubt. This is especially so where rational thinking and incomplete data do not produce trustworthy solutions.

If you and your staff are able to experience intuitive assistance, then all can benefit from multiple impressions expressed as instinct, insight, hunch, or gut-feel. That includes receiving sensations through such forms as vision, hearing, and perception. Intuition tends to be personal and takes on an individual's inborn personality, as the mind goes to work on a problem.

Thus, resilience is an essential organizational attribute where market events are hidden in a fog of uncertainty. That is where the interplay of possibilities, probabilities, good luck, and bad luck weaves its way to an eventual outcome.

Therefore, the weightiest decisions are often made on inexact premises, with always the element of chance hovering over all events, even with the input of data. Yet it would be totally false to assume that success is a matter of sheer luck. It is not luck in the ordinary sense that brings achievement. In the long run, so-called chance favors the courageous, intelligent, and intuitive individuals.

Learning from Failures

For the agile organization, failure functions as a learning experience. It is recognized as a temporary condition from which cause-and-effect reviews are pored over and fresh solutions emerge for the next campaign. This ability to continue with energy and purpose means that the above attributes are in place and working.

Thus, the firm is quick to mobilize. It is nimble and things get done easily without a cumbersome and excessively layered structure. The notion that the firm is responsive to opportunities means there is a free flow of data and analytics to permit quick decision making. The implication, too, is that individuals are empowered and the firm enjoys a resilience that can create and respond to opportunities.

Given the above attributes of an agile organization suitable for the digital age, what type of behavior should you reasonably expect from your staff? There are four areas that represent reasonable expectations.

Active participation. Considering the relative freedom of intellectual thought that exists today in the majority of organizations, and with the variety of communication tools readily available and familiar to most individuals, you should expect ongoing dialogue that leads to tangible solutions related to the changing dynamics of the marketplace. Thus, the active participation and information exchange should capture the insights, knowledge, and observations of your staff.

Momentum. Losing momentum is dangerous. For the alert competitor—and you have to assume there is one or more—signs of complacency represent an opportunity for the rival to introduce a new service, snare a key customer, or attack the vulnerable segment of your market. Further, any loss of momentum should alert you to organizational flaws that indicate a loss of agility.

Specifically, expect your staff to keep up momentum in the following ways:

- Search for revenue expansion opportunities, as well as cost reduction opportunities.
- Report on new systems and disruptive technologies that could create a sustainable competitive advantage, and possibly neutralize the competitor's capabilities.
- Reduce the rival's effectiveness by reinforcing your market position, so that the competitor is likely to dissipate its strength without achieving its objectives.
- Initiate plans that identify emerging or neglected markets. The aim is to expand by avoiding a direct, head-on confrontation against a stronger rival.
- Create a differentiated product, or value-added service, that is not easily cloned.
- Integrate data analytics into tactical plans, so that you can take fast action to benefit from new market opportunities, as well as react rapidly to competitors' actions.
- Form constructive relationships with customers that lock out competitors for an extended sales cycle.

Innovative thinking. As already mentioned in numerous scenarios, this expectation is quite realistic with today's (mostly) educated workforce and in an agile organization. At Google, for instance, innovative thinking is valued, essential, and required. It is embedded in the core culture of the organization. As such, its management creates a working climate that attempts to tap the innovative thinking of the staff in all aspects of their jobs.

For instance, Google management gives all engineers one day a week to develop their individual pet projects, no matter how far from the company's central mission. If work deadlines get in the way of those free days for as much as a few weeks, they accumulate. Also, the system is so pervasive that anyone at Google can post thoughts about new technologies or businesses on an ideas mailing list, available company-wide for inspection and input.

At Amazon, CEO Jeff Bezos instituted the Just Do It Award. It is an acknowledgment of an employee who did something notable on his own initiative, typically outside his primary job responsibilities. Even if the action turned out to be a mistake, an employee could still earn the prize as long as he or she had taken risks and shown resourcefulness in the process.

What are the leadership traits that support such expectations? First, it means recognizing and appreciating the inherent worth of people. And even where some individuals' ideas will not succeed, their efforts are recognized and respected. This is especially relevant working with culturally diverse personnel with a wide range of ethnic and religious backgrounds.

Second, at each level, leaders stand aside and let subordinates do their jobs. They empower their people, give them tasks, delegate the necessary authority, and let them do their work. The fundamental leadership issue here is that in the process of fostering innovative thinking, the staff is actively encouraged to grow professionally and personally.

Alertness. Staying alert relates to many of the topics already discussed, such as responsiveness, quick decision making, and urgency, as well as the strong emphasis throughout the previous chapters on competitive threats and aggressive actions. Thus, a reasonable and necessary expectation is for your staff to internalize the importance of staying alert. That means, in part, unraveling market events and then recommending strategies supported by market data.

Unless you actively play a part, however, alertness can be a vague and illusive expectation. Recapping some of the techniques previously mentioned, you can participate by broadening your staff's view of the competitive world by tailoring the following guidelines to your organization's needs:

- Keep your staff informed about meaningful market and competitor events.
- Motivate them by providing a venue to exchange ideas and insights.
- Tap into their diversity, thought patterns, experiences, and collective knowledge, thereby integrating individuals and their functions.
- Develop an electronic-based forum to share ideas and viewpoints and stimulate conversations.

As you encourage a healthy interaction among your employees, you also sensitize yourself to their moods, temperaments, and increasingly, the nuances of their thoughts. Doing so assists in sustaining their psychological well-being and unifying the group. By taking such constructive action to shape positive relationships, you acknowledge that your people are a major influence in market performance. And, as important, they can serve as key competitive differentiators.

As long as their mindsets tune to fresh opportunities, it is reasonable to expect that your staff will be alert to possibilities that every day and each event has to offer, providing, that is, they understand how their actions contribute to the overall company's fortunes.

Also, they will act positively if they believe it is personally beneficial for them to play an active role in the organization. You must be sure, however, that your employees see the opportunities, agree with them, and are of the same opinion. As a result, you should see tangible improvements in performance, innovation, and employee harmony.

Much of this chapter focused on the benefits of an agile organization to meet the high-speed, flexible, responsive operating needs of a digital environment. As illustrated with the automotive industry in Chapter 9, business models evolved with the creative geniuses of Henry Ford and Alfred P. Sloan, as each shaped an industry that had never before existed.

Both leaders pioneered new technologies and methods of manufacturing. They created markets to absorb the enormous output of products never before available to mass audiences. Ford and Sloan structured their respective organizations around the availability of a workforce and an innovative assembly-line structure. Much of this progress was based on the ambition, courage, tenacity, and individual management styles of those company leaders at a time when there was no viable precedent.

Across the decades, organizations meandered through continuous transitions, from a manufacturing focus, to a marketing orientation, to an information technology period, to a transformative digital and technology future. Now, the corporate world calls for an organizational design to meet a highly competitive global environment where talented, highly educated groups of individuals use evolving technologies to develop not only world-class products for the masses, but also customized products for individual usage. Algorithms, big data, and analytics are the foundation tools for those everyday operations.

Yet within such an organizational framework, there is one all-encompassing component that you have to highlight to convey uniqueness and stability to the otherwise freewheeling spirit of agility: *corporate culture.*

Culture reflects your organization's values, visions, norms, working language, systems, symbols, beliefs, habits, and history. In effect, it makes the organization a living, working entity. Culture shapes the behavior of personnel and reflects their feelings and actions. You will want to make certain it is aligned with your company's digital future.*

---

* Chapter 7 provides a detailed discussion of corporate culture.

The Five Forces of Leadership Shaped by the Digital Age

- Digital technology
- Competitive strategy
- Corporate culture
- Organizational structure
- Strategic business planning

Section V

Strategic Business Planning

The plan is nothing; planning is everything.

Dwight D. Eisenhower

11

Leadership and the Strategic Business Plan

There are compelling reasons for highlighting strategic business planning as a leadership force, especially during this digital age where massive quantities of data flow into the operation.

First, the planning process helps you sort through the incoming data and allows for more insightful interpretations over the long term. It is especially useful if placed within a framework of a clearly defined strategic direction about where your organization or business unit is headed, over at least a three- to five-year period.

Planning helps you *think like a strategist* as you prioritize objectives, develop competitive strategies, and drive future product development. From a tactical position, planning allows for developing the numerous details to reach customers in geographically and culturally dispersed markets, using the seemingly limitless potential of algorithms, big data, and analytics.

Second, with reference to Eisenhower's opening quote, transposing his comment into a pragmatic application, planning is a mental process that provides clarity of purpose to your thinking and serves as a reliable interactive network to improve collaboration among your staff. The overall intent is to give a human face to your leadership with the endpoint of galvanizing your staff to react to a changing competitive and fast-moving environment that is driven by new opportunities gleaned from big data.

When completed, the plan is perhaps one of the most comprehensive and useful people-to-people communications vehicles of all. It reduces the possibility of vaguely transmitted directions that can be easily misinterpreted, particularly where there is controversy among decision makers. And it generally decreases the level of confusing conclusions up and down the organizational chart.

Thus, the plan, when viewed against a backdrop of long-term strategic goals and strategies, lessens the intensity of miscommunications and mis-understandings. With that view in mind, the plan is a "living" document that is pliable and subject to modification when documented with new data to provide clarity.

Consequently, embracing the strategic planning process as a component of your leadership will enhance your capabilities with a higher level of competence, as you manage the increasing complexity being thrust upon you. As part of the process, you will more accurately assess the strengths and weaknesses of your organization or business unit. You can then install systems and controls to monitor results and thereby form rational judgments about trends and opportunities to pursue, as well as assessments of individuals and resources needed to do the job.

What follows is implementing the plan. The quality, and thereby the effectiveness, of the plan depends on your personal commitment to planning, the level of tangible support within the C-suite, and the skill of individuals delivering on the plan. As important to the planning process is the willingness and courage to move beyond the pressing problems of today and take a thoughtful look into the foreseeable future, where fresh opportunities prevail, new markets materialize, trends surface, and breakthrough technologies offer enticing new possibilities.

While the erratic behavior of a marketplace offers no guarantees of success, even where your plans and strategies are diligently implemented, all that you can reasonably expect from your best efforts is to build a competitive edge that goes in your favor in an environment of possibilities and probabilities. And even where some objectives and strategies lack total accuracy, consider the opportunistic effect if your competitor has done little planning.

Consequently, your rival would likely react to every news headline and piece of data and scatter resources without an overall strategic direction. Certainly, under those circumstances the competitive edge would be on your side. Thus, the advantage goes to those managers who avoid sustained and careless expenditures of resources; instead, they achieve their objectives by seeking a more strategic viewpoint.

The following list summarizes the positive outcomes of immersing yourself, and those with whom you interact, in the planning process. Acquiring the skills to develop resourceful plans will enhance your leadership to

- Make more accurate market decisions from data analytics and thereby allocate resources with greater accuracy
- Identify the patterns of your competitor's strategies and counter them more effectively before they materialize
- Resolve internal conflicts before they arise by referencing agreed-upon objectives
- Recognize customers' needs and buying behavior, and then translate the data analytics into new market and product opportunities
- Create strategies and tactics that result in a sustainable competitive advantage
- Concentrate your strength against a competitor's weaknesses at decisive points
- Manage personnel performance with greater efficiency
- Assess your company's and employees' states of readiness
- Select the markets in which to concentrate your resources
- Make strategic decisions with greater precision
- Energize your group or organization to take advantage of the immense global opportunities

In all, developing competence in planning helps you to *win* through effective leadership—to win markets and customers, to win a profitable and sustainable market position, and to win over competitors.

COMPONENTS OF A STRATEGIC BUSINESS PLAN

We look for game changers; areas which Fuji can win at. Controlling microenvironments? We know that.

Fujifilm Holdings executive

"We look for game changers." What is behind that statement from Fujifilm? What challenges are embedded in those words, and how do they impact strategic business planning and its interface with leadership?

Fujifilm's management awoke over a decade ago to see the beginning of a sharp drop in sales of its familiar green photo-film boxes. The reason: There was a distinct trend that its customers were latching onto digital photography, followed by the pervasive use of smartphones. It was at that point that Fujifilm began serious efforts at turning around the company from its photo-film roots and exploring new science and technology markets. In contrast, rival Eastman Kodak faced the same trend, but waited too long to plan a transition and eventually filed for bankruptcy.

Fujifilm began by examining its core competencies and searching for ways to apply the primary technologies used in producing its core film products. That led to one of its first ventures: a beauty line called Astalift, which uses the expertise it developed researching photographic applications. Other extensions of its technology and know-how paved the way to move the company into Ebola drugs, antiaging lotions, and stem cell research.

How does strategic business planning fit the Fujifilm scenario? Let us look at the overall structure of the strategic business plan model for answers. The plan involves a two-level structure:

Level 1: *Strategic.* Consists of a strategic direction or vision, objectives, strategies, and a portfolio of products and services.
Level 2: *Tactical.* Consists of a situation analysis, market opportunities, objectives, tactics, financial controls, and budgets.

LEVEL 1: STRATEGIC

Strategic Direction or Vision

Developing a strategic direction permits you to take the long-term view of your business. By using the output of data analytics, you can focus your attention on specific market and industry trends, forms of customer behavior, and other major forces affecting your business.

This is where Fujifilm* looked at its big picture, which clearly displayed a deteriorating business of its legacy film products. Company personnel

---

* This author has no inside knowledge of Fujifilm's actual planning procedure. The discussion reflects information reported in the business press from which these extrapolations are made to demonstrate key parts of the planning process.

then looked at its internal processes, overall competencies, and specific areas of scientific expertise honed over decades in search of product applications and corresponding new markets.

Doing so meant venturing into unfamiliar territory, such as health care, which then led them to regenerative medicine for the repair of damaged tissues or organs. In turn, that extended into stem cells, capable of morphing into any body part, and to skin products for use on burn victims and other patients.

Thus, the process incorporated algorithms and data analytics and was driven by a spirited leadership that motivated personnel to expand its intuitive insight into new businesses. All the exploring formed the basis for expressing Fujifilm's strategic direction over the long term.

For your purposes, developing a strategic direction from trend data can fashion your efforts over the long term. Your strategies would affect such areas as engaging competitors, determining the level of risk your company will incur, and selecting offensive or defensive efforts to protect your market positons.

The following questions provide a framework for taking a collaborative approach to developing your strategic direction. Your introspective answers will help shape a clear vision of what your company, business unit, or product or service will look like over the long-term planning period.

Implicit in these questions are issues you should first clarify with senior management, such as how big to grow, how fast to expand, what people skills are required, and particularly, the availability of financial, material, technology, and other resources.

Let us examine each of the questions in detail:[*]

1. *What are our organization's distinctive areas of expertise?* This question takes some soul searching to understand the DNA that makes your firm different and unique. It will also take some pragmatic examination to see how your firm stacks up against a variety of factors, from management strength and employee morale to technology and financial resources. For instance, Fujifilm found that the same precision manufacturing techniques it used to make photo film could be used on other products that require the meticulous

---

[*] You can fine-tune the questions to fit the primary issues relevant to your company and industry. Also, where time and resources permit, use a cross-functional team to conduct an extensive strengths, weaknesses, opportunities, threats (SWOT) analysis.

handling of small molecules. In turn, that steered Fujifilm to think of other new businesses, including pharmaceuticals.

2. *What business(es) should we be in over the next five years?* This requires looking out beyond your existing business to examine, and reimagine, what is on the horizon in new technologies, industry trends, competitive moves, and evolving market needs. The implications are that if your business is too narrow in scope, the resulting product and market mix will be generally narrow and possibly too confining for growth.

On the other hand, defining your business too broadly can result in spreading capital, people, and other resources beyond the capabilities of the organization and your ability to defend against aggressive competitors. Therefore, as part of the process of defining what business you should be in, you have to take into account the culture, skills, and resources of your organization. It also means considering such factors as customer needs, business functions to be enhanced or added, and types of new technologies you need to compete successfully.

For Fujifilm, the broad outlook led to controlling microenvironments. Its chairman, Shigetaka Komori, set the dimension of change by declaring that the company would shift focus from its photo-film roots toward new science and technology markets.

3. *What segments or categories of customers will we serve?* Customers exist at various levels in the supply chain and in different segments of the market. The end of the chain consists of end-use consumers with whom you may or may not come in direct contact.

For Fujifilm, the new markets did entail entering new segments, as well as a supply chain with unaccustomed characteristics. To deal with those unfamiliar issues, the company acquired firms that had access to dedicated segments, such as Toyama Chemical, the producer of an antiviral medicine used by some Ebola patients in West Africa. Another acquisition was U.S.-based Cellular Dynamics International, a producer of various types of stem cells, which permitted Fujifilm to move into regenerative medicine with its focus on repairing damaged tissue or organs.

4. *What additional functions are we likely to perform for customers as we see the market evolve?* As competitive intensity increases worldwide, each intermediary customer along the supply chain is pressured to maintain an advantage. This guideline question asks you to

determine what functions or capabilities are needed to solve customers' problems.

More precisely, you are looking beyond your immediate customers and reaching out further along the supply chain to identify those functions that would solve your customers' *customers'* problems. Such functions might include providing specialized proprietary data, utilizing the Internet of things to enhance quality control programs, financial assistance, or rapid delivery. As experience is absorbed and data usage is analyzed, additional services can be identified, which would likely be of a tactical nature.

5. *What new technologies will we require to satisfy future customer needs and meet and exceed those used by competitors?* Within the framework of the previous question and the practices of your industry, examine the impact of technologies on customer retention. Look at where your company ranks with the various technologies and types of software used for product design, manufacturing, and logistics. That means truly making a commitment to tracking, analyzing, and interpreting customer behavior and attitudes.

Look, too, at the continuing changes in information technology and business intelligence with their disruptive effects on product innovation and market competitiveness. Also appraise such technologies as the above-mentioned Internet of things to provide expert diagnostic systems for problem solving. Then, there are the rapidly changing communications systems to manage and protect an increasingly mobile enterprise, as well as for dealing with the threats of damaging cyber-attacks.

6. *What changes are taking place in markets, consumer behavior, competition, legal and environmental, and economic issues (global and local) that will impact our company?* This form of external analysis permits you to sensitize yourself to those critical issues that relate to markets, the industry, and existing and emerging competitors. This broad-based question is open ended and can cover the changes that are most likely to affect your long-term view of the marketplace. They can be as narrow as local economic conditions and as broad as pending governmental regulations.

Specifically, for competition, the analysis considers the likelihood of confrontations with the rival's entire company or with its individual business units and product lines. Therefore, as part of the analysis, also look at the managerial issues that affect employees' ability to react to competitive conflict, such as discipline, training, leadership, communications, and the underlying culture of the organization.

Using these six questions as a discussion guide with your team allows you to make a long-term visionary inquiry that forms your strategic direction. In turn, it guides your decision making when faced with a competitive conflict.

Objectives

Objectives give tangible form to the strategic direction and vision of the plan. There are two primary guidelines that should have your attention when setting objectives: first, objectives should indicate what outcomes you want to achieve, and second, they should address the issues or events that initially set the plan in motion. For Fujifilm, it was the digital trend that threatened its traditional product line of film, which was on a downward slope, and there was an urgent need to reinvent the company if it was to survive and grow.

The quantitative objectives should indicate performance metrics such as sales growth, market share, return on investment, profit, and any other quantitative objectives required by your management. For Fujifilm, it set a revenue objective for its health care operations of $8 billion by 2018, up from $3.2 billion in fiscal year 2015.

Nonquantitative objectives would span such diverse areas as initiating organizational changes, reorienting corporate culture, upgrading relationships within the supply chain, consolidating a segment position, establishing strategy teams, building specialty products to penetrate new markets, improving competitive intelligence systems, rallying staff morale, upgrading technology, and any other issues that are pertinent to the business (see Table 11.1).

For Fujifilm, the areas in Table 11.1 that outweighed other categories were "Markets" and "Products and Services." Although the other categories were not insignificant, they had to be ranked according to priority. Yet, in the process, reorienting people to the new strategic direction and reorganizing Fujifilm to develop its R&D function certainly had to place high among the priority issues. A sampling of Fujifilm's nonquantitative objectives might look like the following:

TABLE 11.1

Sources for Developing Objectives and Strategies

Markets	Products and Services	Price	Communications	Supply Chain	Personnel	Organization
• Market segments ranked as emerging, neglected, or poorly served • Markets designated by reputation, level of market penetration, and availability • Level of commitment to long-term development; level of investments in people, research, and technology	Attributes that outperform by • Quality • Features • Reliability • Packaging • After-sales services • Warranties • Returns policy • Level of technology • Scope of applications • Brand name recognition • Stage in product sales cycle	Market position established as • Price leader or price follower • Level of discounts, allowances, credit, and financing terms	Comparative advantages in • Advertising commitments by business to business and business to consumer • Sales force (selling skills, training, sales aids, incentives, compensation, motivation, market coverage) • Sales promotion (trade shows, webinars, contests, premiums, coupons)	Capabilities related to • Sales force directed at end-use customers or intermediaries along the supply chain • Market coverage related to gaps in market reach • Inventory control systems • Physical transportation • Support systems along supply chain	Orientation as • Customer-driven vs. product-driven mindset • Morale, group unity, collaboration displayed by competitive spirit and motivation • Market and competitor awareness and ability to foresee trends • Capabilities to deal with threats	Advantages related to • Company culture • Type of work environment and management support • Extent of internal communications • Managers' ability to react to market opportunities and threats

(Continued)

TABLE 11.1 (CONTINUED)

Sources for Developing Objectives and Strategies

Markets	Products and Services	Price	Communications	Supply Chain	Personnel	Organization
• Ability to sustain long-term customer relationships	• Frequency of new product introductions		• Telemarketing and mobile communications • Internet by usage and application • Publicity • Data analytics		• Experience, skills, and training by job level • Experience and knowledge of the business or industry • Capabilities related to strategy and tactics and ability to apply techniques to market opportunities and competitive threats	• Managers' competence in planning and developing competitive strategies • Commitment to ongoing training and development of personnel • Financial resources and ability to sustain operations

- Secure a position as a leading innovator in controlling microenvironments through advanced scientific applications of its legacy manufacturing expertise.
- Aggressively enter cosmetics and pharmaceuticals markets through acquisitions.
- Reorganize the organization to permit engineers and executives to collaborate on developing products that require the precise handling of small molecules.

Note, too, how these objectives have long-term strategic implications. Where possible, you can add quantitative information for each objective. However, it is not always necessary in this strategic section, as long as there is noticeable movement through such actionable terms as *investigating*, *testing*, *examining*, and *exploring*.

Quantitative details can be added later in the plan, usually in the growth strategy section and certainly at the tactical one-year portion of the plan, where details are given, dates specified, and responsibilities assigned. The essential point is that this planning format permits flexibility to accommodate to the practices of the entire organization, as well as to their individual business units and product lines.

Thus, the aim of the strategic direction is to provide a "vision" of what the future of the organization or group can look like; the objectives delineate the precise outcomes, and strategies indicate the actions.

Strategies

A major component of the plan, which covers significant portions of the previous chapters, focuses on strategies. These are action elements that set the plan in motion. This section, then, outlines the means by which you achieve your objectives.

Whereas the emphasis of this book is at the strategic level with a time frame of three to five years, you may find that an urgent need persists to take immediate action, particularly in a situation where timing is the pressing issue and artificial structures of timelines fade away in favor of survival.

Your thinking about strategies generally emphasizes the following issues:

- Identifying decisive points in which to concentrate resources against a market segment

- Specifying actions to neutralize the competitor's advantages
- Selecting market segments that are best suited for regaining the offensive
- Pinpointing areas that would represent competitive advantages for defending existing markets from aggressive rivals
- Utilizing data analytics to identify the root causes of declining market share
- Reinvigorating a dispirited group to drive next-generation products and services
- Incorporating data analytics to improve audience targeting and segmentation
- Identifying hidden relationships, patterns, and trends within data, based on individual or group behavior

As indicated in Chapter 4, think of strategies as actions to achieve your longer-term objectives, and tactics as actions to achieve shorter-term objectives. In a broader sense, strategy is the art of coordinating the means (money, human resources, and materials) to achieve the ends (profit, customer satisfaction, and company growth) as defined by the organization's strategic direction, policies, and objectives. Further, strategy consists of *actions* to achieve *objectives* at three distinct levels: corporate strategy, midlevel strategy, and tactics.

Tactics cover such areas as social media, applications of big data, sales force deployment, supply chain methods, customer relationship programs, training, product branding, value-added services, and the selection of market segments to launch a product or dislodge a competitor.*

Techniques and formats for indicating strategies can vary. Whereas some objectives tend to be longer term and broader based, you may need to develop multiple strategies for each objective. For instance, you can use general strategy statements and then follow by restating the specific objective along with the related strategies. Look again at Table 11.2.

Portfolio of Products and Services

The business portfolio includes listings of *existing* products and markets, as well as *new* products and markets. Following a logical progression, it is

---

* Details about short-term tactics go beyond the scope of this book. Those topics are adequately handled by the specialized books and articles on those subjects.

TABLE 11.2

Comparative View of Strategies and Tactics

Strategies	Tactics
Covers broader issues, which impact a longer time period, and is more closely aligned with the strategic direction and objectives	Covers shorter-time durations and is subordinate to longer-term objectives and strategies

Strategies:
- Develop initiatives that would better align the corporate culture with strategies and tactics.
- Introduce product or service projects that lead to longer-term customer retention, profitability, and defensible market positions.
- Initiate systems and programs to solidify long-term relationships within the supply chain or with end-use customers.
- Update existing production capabilities to improve service to markets with high growth potential.
- Acquire appropriate technologies to sustain a competitive advantage through proprietary software, or the challenges promised by such advances as three-dimensional printers.
- Optimize the performance of the sales force—includes such areas as incentives, training, acquisition of competitor intelligence, and deploying individuals to support long-term opportunities identified from data analytics.
- Find sources to build financial strength to carry out long-term commitments.
- Pinpoint R&D and other product development initiatives that address both existing and all-new products.
- Assess levels of customer or technical services required by each market served.
- Initiate training programs that develop employees' unique skills and are compatible with the strategic goals of the organization.
- Organize corporate systems and functions that support the long-term strategic plan.
- Develop plans to guard the organization against the growing threats from cyber-warfare.

Tactics:
- Initiate actions that create a competitive advantage, with the specific aim of neutralizing a competitor's ability to react quickly and decisively at a particular time and location.
- Develop marketing plans that (1) introduce differentiated products and new applications, (2) launch creative applications that utilize social media, or (3) test promotional themes that embrace such movements as "going green."
- Probe into new, poorly served, or unserved market segments for further development.
- Select decisive points for market entry or defense.
- Test product or package offerings, including introduction of new value-added services to preempt and blunt a competitor's entry strategies.
- Change promotions, incentives, prices, discounts, or services that could positively affect supply chain agreements.
- Identify internal changes in the operating systems that would speed up communications from the field to the home office, and alert management to take rapid counteractions against damaging threats from aggressive competitors.

based on the strategic direction, objectives and goals, and growth strategies outlined in the previous parts of the plan.

In particular, your portfolio should mirror your long-term vision. That is, the broader the scope of your strategic direction, the more expansive the range of products, services, and markets in the portfolio. Conversely, the narrower the dimension of your strategic direction, the more limited the content of products and markets.

Use the following format to develop your own business portfolio:

Market penetration: Existing products in existing markets. List those *existing* products and services you currently offer to *existing* customers. In an appendix of the plan, you can document sales, profits, market share data, and other pertinent facts related to growth potential or competitive issues. You can then determine if your level of penetration is adequate and if possibilities exist for further growth.

Product development: New products in existing markets. List potential *new* products or services you can offer to *existing* markets. Again, recall the guideline that the broader the dimension of your strategic direction, the broader the possibilities for the content of your portfolio. Also, continue thinking in a time frame of three to five years.

Market development: Existing products in new markets. List your existing products that could sell into *new* markets. Explore possibilities for market development by identifying emerging, neglected, or poorly served segments in which existing products can be utilized.

Diversification: New product in new markets. This portion of the business portfolio is somewhat visionary, since it involves developing *new* products for *new* and yet untapped markets identified from data analytics. Consider new technologies, global markets, the green trend, and potential alliances.

Once again, interpret your strategic direction in its broadest context. Do not seek diversification for its own sake. Rather, the whole purpose of the exercise is for you to develop an organized framework for meaningful expansion. After identifying new opportunities, it may be necessary for you to revisit your growth strategies and list actions you would take to implement the opportunities.

The business portfolio completes the strategic portion of your plan. By reviewing the Fujifilm example, you can see where at least three of these sections—product development, market development, and diversification—would be filled with products and markets to match the company's new direction. What follows is the structure of the one-year tactical plan.

LEVEL 2: TACTICAL

The tactical section encompasses two stages. The first one is creating concrete actions to carry out longer-term objectives. In Fujifilm's case, that meant dealing with such details as absorbing the wave of acquisitions and integrating them into the company's core operating systems.

Then, there were the myriad factors associated with implementing the other strategic objectives and strategies associated with regenerative medicine and skin care. As one Fujifilm executive explained, "We have decades of technology and know-how backing us, and now that we've opened up these possibilities, expect much more to come."

The second stage is preparing for campaigns related to two zones of activities: launching campaigns to enter new markets and introduce the Astalift beauty products, and campaigns that deal with the inroads of aggressive competitors attempting to block Fujifilm from achieving its objectives. From a leader's viewpoint, Fujifilm is likely to face several of these campaigns and thereby needs to be ready with action plans.

The essential point: When viewing types of campaigns, they should be considered from the standpoint of the strategic direction of your firm over a defined planning period. For instance, what new markets are worth entering—and fighting for? What additional product and service categories will be needed to secure a profitable market position, and which would provide room for sustained growth and expansion? What might those products and service offerings look like? What form of delivery systems will be needed? What new technologies will be required to satisfy future customer and market needs?

The following components make up the tactical level of the plan: situation analysis, market opportunities, objectives, tactics, and financial controls and budgets.

Situation Analysis

To provide some perspective and a logical starting point, a situation analysis views the past and current situations of your business by using a three-part lens:

1. Historic performance
2. Competitor analysis
3. Market background

Historic Performance

The purpose of the situation analysis is to define your business in a factual and objective manner. Compile historical data for a period of at least three years. Doing so provides an excellent perspective about where your company has been, where it is now, and where you want it to go as defined in your strategic direction.

For instance, you will want to address such key issues as performance of your product or service by sales history, profitability, share of market, level of technology, and any other required data to give an accurate picture of the situation. You will also examine the history of pricing strategies for each market segment and describe its impact on the product's market position.

Next is an analysis of the makeup of your supply chain. Identify the functions performed at each stage within the network (distributor, direct, and e-commerce). Indicate levels of performance, expressed in sales volume, profitability, and market share. Where appropriate, also analyze your physical distribution system, such as warehouse locations, inventory systems, transportation, or just-in-time delivery procedures.

Then, there is a review of all forms of communication. The evaluation is directed at each market segment or distribution channel based on the following: expenditures, creative strategy, social media, types of promotion, Internet, advertising, sales promotion, publicity, and other forms of communications unique to your industry.

Competitor Analysis*

Make your competitor analysis as comprehensive as possible. The more competitor intelligence you gather and use, the more strategy options you have open to you. For instance, list all your competitors in descending size order, along with their sales and market shares, if applicable.

Identify each competitor's strengths and weaknesses related to such factors as product development, distribution, pricing, promotion, management leadership, caliber of employees, and financial condition. (Refer to Table 11.1 for a more comprehensive list of criteria.)

Indicate any significant trends that would signal unsettling market situations, such as aggressive moves by a competitor to grow market share or to solidify its market position—mostly at your expense. Identify those competitors firmly entrenched in low-price segments of the market, those at the high end of the market, and competitors that are lodged in dedicated niches.

Specify by means of predictive analytics significant trends in specific market segments. Further, identify where each competitor is making a major commitment and where it may be relinquishing control by product and segment.

Market Background

This last part of the situation analysis focuses on the demographic and behavioral factors of your market. Here is where you determine market size and customer preferences—both business to business and business to consumer.

This information also highlights any gaps in knowledge about markets and customers, which helps you determine what additional market intelligence is needed to make effective decisions. Included are geographic, demographic, psychographic (lifestyle), and other relevant characteristics of your customers. That includes buyers' purchase patterns and any distinctive types of behavior, as well as attitudes toward your company's products, services, quality, and image.

Further, there needs to be a review of segment trends, which should be provided by industry forecasts and information from your data analytics.

---

* Within this section, or as part of objectives and strategies, incorporate approaches to neutralizing your competitor. See Chapter 3 for details to weaken the rival, prepare successive campaigns, reduce the competitor's effectiveness, make the conflict costlier for the rival, and wear down the competitor.

From a highly pragmatic viewpoint, a segment should be considered if it is accessible, measurable, and potentially profitable and has long-term growth potential.

Then, there should be a means to identify emerging, neglected, or poorly served markets that can catapult you to further sales growth. You can also consider segments as part of a defensive strategy to prevent inroads of a potential competitor through an unattended market niche at a decisive point.

Market Opportunities

Your approach here is to look for opportunities by assessing strengths, weaknesses, and options, and by considering a full range of alternatives offered through data analytics.

As you go through the assessment, try to avoid restrictive thinking. Take your time and brainstorm. Using a collaborative approach, dig for opportunities with other members of your planning team. Ideally, if the team includes individuals from different functional areas of the business, you will gain a diverse range of viewpoints.

Consider, too, possibilities for expanding existing market coverage and laying the groundwork for entering new markets by reviewing the portfolio section of the plan. Also consider opportunities related to out-thinking and outmaneuvering your competition with indirect strategies. For instance, offensively, which competitors can you displace from which market segments? Defensively, which competitors can you deny entry into your market space?

As you go through this section, revisit your strategic issues. Then refer to the situation analysis, specifically the competitor analysis, which would reveal voids or weaknesses that could turn into opportunities.

Use the following screening process to identify your major opportunities and challenges. Once you identify and prioritize the opportunities, convert them into objectives and tactics, which form the action topics for the next two sections of the plan.

Present Markets

Identify the best opportunities for expanding present markets by

- Cultivating an additional revenue stream through new users
- Neutralizing competition

- Increasing product usage or services by present customers
- Redefining market segments
- Reformulating or repackaging the product
- Identifying new applications for the product
- Repositioning the product to create a more favorable perception by consumers, which would turn into a competitive advantage over rival products
- Expanding into emerging, neglected, or poorly served market niches

Targets of Opportunity

List any areas outside your current market segment or product line, not included in the above categories, that you would like to explore. Be innovative and entrepreneurial in your thinking. (This is an area in which Fujifilm spent a great deal of creative time and expenditure.)

Objectives

Now list the short-term objectives you want to achieve during the current planning cycle—generally defined as a 12-month period to correspond with annual budgeting procedures. You also want to be certain that they relate to your long-range strategic direction, objectives, strategies, and business portfolio.

Tactical objectives consist of three parts:

- *Assumptions*: Projections about future conditions and trends
- *Primary objectives*: Metrics related to what you want to accomplish, including targets of opportunity
- *Functional objectives*: Operational and functional goals representing various parts of the business

Assumptions

- For objectives to be realistic and achievable, you must first generate assumptions and projections about future conditions and trends. These should be based on as much data as you can assemble. Then list only those major assumptions that will affect your business for the planning period.

- Economic assumptions: Comment on the overall economy, local market economies, consumer expenditures, and changes in customer buying patterns. Also document any impact on market size, growth or decline rates, costs, and trends in your market segments.
- Technological assumptions: Include the likelihood of technological breakthroughs and digital applications that would impact your business.
- Sociopolitical assumptions: Indicate positive and restrictive legislation, political tensions, tax outlook, population patterns, and educational factors. Also list changes in customer habits linked to social media, green issues, and e-commerce.
- Competitive assumptions: Identify activities among existing competitors and inroads of new competitors, with particular attention to surging global competitors.

Primary Objectives

Focus on the primary financial objectives that your organization requires. Also include targets of opportunity that you initially identified as innovative and entrepreneurial in the previous section.

Where there are multiple objectives, you may find it helpful to rank them in priority order. Be sure to use metrics to quantify expected results where possible. You can separate your objectives into the following categories:

- Primary objectives: Current and projected sales, profits, market share, return on investment, and other metrics
- Targets of opportunity objectives

Functional Objectives

State the functional objectives relating to both product and nonproduct issues in each of the following categories. Should any of the categories not apply to your current business situation, consider applications for the future, and then move on.

- *Product objectives*
  - Quality: List quality objectives that could achieve a competitive advantage.

- Development: Set objectives to obtain new technology by exploring internal R&D, licensing, or joint ventures.
- Modification: Describe major or minor product changes through reformulation, redesign, or reengineering.
- Differentiation: Identify objectives to differentiate the product by delivering new applications to reach new customer groups within existing markets, or by expanding into additional geographic areas. (Here, again, Fujifilm focused its objectives on this category and the following.)
- Diversification: Indicate technology transfer objectives to drive new product development.
- Deletion: List products to be removed from the line due to unsatisfactory performance, and those to be kept in the line for strategic reasons, such as presenting your company to the market as a full-line supplier.
- Segmentation: List potential line extensions (adding product varieties) to reach new market niches, or to defend against an incoming competitor in an existing market segment.
- Pricing objectives: Show list prices, volume discounts, and promotional rebates.
- Promotion objectives: Indicate sales force support, sales promotion, webinars, advertising, Internet, social media, and publicity to intermediaries and consumers.
- Supply chain objectives: Identify potential new intermediaries to increase geographic coverage and solidify relationships with the trade; list distributors or dealers to be removed from the chain.
- Physical distribution objectives: Identify logistical factors from order entry to the physical movement of a product through the supply chain, and eventual delivery to the end user.
- Packaging objectives: List functional design or decorative considerations for brand identification.
- Service objectives: Identify a broader range of services, from providing customers access to key personnel in your firm to providing on-site technical assistance.
- Other objectives: Indicate other objectives as suggested in targets of opportunity.
- *Nonproduct objectives.* Although most activities eventually relate to the product or service, some are support functions that you

should consider. (Obtain input from personnel in other functions, as needed.)

- Key accounts: Indicate those customers with whom you can develop special relationships through customized products, distribution, value-added services, or participation in quality improvement programs.
- Manufacturing: Identify special activities that would provide a competitive advantage, such as offering small production runs to accommodate the changing needs of customers and reduce inventory levels. Another activity would include implementing the Internet of things, as discussed in the introduction with General Electric, IBM, and Caterpillar.
- Marketing research: Cite any industry studies, customer surveys, and other input from big data that reveal opportunities for new revenue streams.
- Credit: Include any programs that use credit and finance as a value-added service, such as providing financial assistance to customers in specific situations.
- Technical sales activities: Include any support activities, such as 24/7 hotline assistance or on-site consultation to solve customers' problems.
- R&D: Indicate internal research and development projects, as well as joint ventures that would complement the strategic direction.
- Human resource development and training: Identify specialized training and development programs to upgrade the skills of those individuals who are responsible for implementing the plan.
- Other: Include any activities that would contribute to your organization's uniqueness, and thereby provide an indirect strategy to achieve a competitive advantage.

Strategies and Tactics

In this section, tactics are identified and put into action. Responsibilities are assigned, schedules set, budgets established, and checkpoints determined. Make sure that individuals involved with developing and implementing the plan actively participate in this section.

Restate the functional product and nonproduct objectives and link them to the strategies and tactics you will use to reach each objective. One of the reasons for restating the objectives is to clarify the frequent misunderstanding between objectives and strategies. Objectives are *what* you want to accomplish; strategies are actions that specify *how* you intend to achieve your objectives.

Note: If you state an objective and do not have a related strategy, you may not have an objective. Instead, the statement may be an action for some other objective.

Summarize the basic strategies for achieving your primary objectives. Include alternative and contingency plans should you come up against unexpected situations that prevent you from reaching your objectives. You may choose to repeat this information as an *executive summary* in the beginning of the plan.

As you develop your final strategy statement, use the following checklist to determine its completeness. Does your plan include content related to the following?

- Changes to the product or package, including differentiation and value-added services
- Developments in digital technology, including such areas as artificial intelligence and the Internet of things
- Strategies that create a competitive advantage, along with contingency plans to block competitors' aggressive moves
- Changes to price, discounts, or long-term contracts that impact your market share
- Changes to marketing strategy, such as the selection of features and benefits, or copy themes to special groups
- Strategies that utilize data analytics to identify and reach new, poorly served, or unserved market segments—along with indications of decisive points for entry and defense
- Promotion strategies aimed at dealer or distributor, consumer, and sales force
- Internal changes in the operating systems, as well as initiatives that would better align the corporate culture with your strategies

Financial Controls and Budgets

Having completed the strategy phase, you must decide how you will monitor its execution. Therefore, before implementing it, develop procedures for both control and review, or follow established procedures set by your firm.

Included below are examples of additional reports or data sheets for you to consider. They are designed to monitor progress at key checkpoints of the plan and to permit either major shifts in strategies or simple mid-course corrections.

- Forecast models related to the industry, environment, competition, and any other areas that are applicable to your company and plan
- Sales by channel of distribution, including
  - Inventory or out-of-stock reports
  - Average selling price (including discounts, rebates, or allowances) along the supply chain and by customer outlet
- Profit and loss statements by product
- Direct product budgets
- R&D budget
- Administrative budget
- Spending by quarter

As an overall guideline—regardless of the planning forms you use—make certain that the system serves as a reliable feedback mechanism, and that it is fortified with the input of big data.

Your interest is in maintaining explicit and timely control so you can react swiftly to impending problems. Further, it should serve as a procedure for reviewing schedules and strategies.

The only other section is an appendix. It should include the following items:

- Relevant industry and market data that provides information on technology trends, product usage, market share, and the like
- Data on competitors' strategies, including supporting information on their products, pricing, promotions, distribution, and market position, as well as profiles of management leadership (if available)
- Details about your new product features and benefits

In addition, various computer databases, as well as a wide variety of customized or off-the-shelf software programs, are available to assist in monitoring and strengthening your plan.

After completing your plan, take a thoughtful look at its key parts. For instance, review the breadth of your strategic direction and be sure it impacts the objectives, strategies, and portfolio sections that follow. Finally, implementing the plan takes leadership and your ability to reach the hearts and minds of the individuals who are going to make it all happen.

12

Using Segmentation to Engage Customers and Neutralize Competitors

It's really about focusing on something we already have in our DNA since the very beginning of Tiffany.

Nicola Andreatta
Vice president, Tiffany & Co.
(from Wahba, 2015)

The above quote relates to Tiffany reentering the watch segment of the market with the strategic aim of winning a bigger piece of the $28 billion (2015 estimate) global luxury-timepiece market. After almost two decades of letting that category languish to the point that it generated a mere 1% sales, Tiffany decided to rebuild its watch business from almost zero.

The effort began with developing a strategic business plan that clarified a strategic direction, which eventually led to the quantifiable objective of achieving 10% of sales from watches in a decade. (Defining a clear long-term outlook in a changing market was somewhat similar to the approach used by Fujifilm, cited in Chapter 11.)

To implement the plan, Tiffany's leadership used data to precisely target markets according to types of consumer behavior. In turn, that analysis led to opportunities for singling out real-time personalization with customers across several channels and touch points. It was all part of a strategy to engage consumers with individualized programs, which tended to strengthen long-term customer loyalty. Relying on such secure customer relationships, Tiffany considered it a pathway to capitalize on one-on-one, cross-selling, and upselling opportunities.

As part of the targeting, Tiffany had to find a point of entry, or decisive point, for concentrated effort. It began by selecting a watch design that would project a distinctive image. To that end, designers selected a timepiece inspired by a watch given to President Franklin D. Roosevelt in 1945. "It has a strength and clarity to it that is very American," declared a Tiffany vice president describing the watch design.

Next was a decision to establish a position that did not go too high end and thereby compete head-on with the likes of Rolex and Patek Philippe. Here, again, managers relied on data analytics to assist in targeting through websites, blogs, YouTube, social media, and mobile.

Other factors for the leaders to consider related to such organizational essentials as ensuring control of manufacturing, availability of parts, and convenience of services to make certain that Tiffany would be fully embedded in the watch business and not just a jeweler that carries a line of watches. Included, too, were issues related to obtaining ongoing market intelligence and data that tracked the operating patterns of their chief competitors.

Thus, two major forces played a role in effectively relaunching the watch business from scratch: first, utilizing the energy of digital marketing to connect producer to consumer, and second, employing the power of segmentation to concentrate all resources at decisive points.

UTILIZING THE ENERGY OF DIGITAL MARKETING

Digital tools add precision to targeting and connecting with customers. Whereas digital marketing requires systems, capabilities, skilled individuals, and technologies, above all, it needs dedicated leadership to effectively bring about balance when operating in the two zones of customers and competitors. In Tiffany's case, that means, first, reentering and expanding into the watch market with a defined sales objective and a product line, and second, establishing a market position that would not clash with strong rival watchmakers.

From a leadership viewpoint, your efforts should focus on understanding customers, applying technology, monitoring systems, and measuring success.

Understand Customers

After decades of listening to lectures, attending seminars, and being repeatedly preached to about focusing on the customer, it may seem unusual to see this area covered once again as if it were fresh information. Yet within the context of digital marketing and the ability to utilize algorithms, big data, and analytics, something is new in that the real fruits of that advice are finally here. And the means for forging a capability to track, analyze, and interpret customer behavior and attitudes through those technologies is readily available.

Organizations such as SAP provide the sophisticated software solutions that would allow you to engage one-to-one with target audiences across digital and traditional channels. Then, there are the numerous web survey providers, such as Qualtrics and SurveyMonkey, that have evolved into full-service business intelligence firms.

Once the analysis comes in, there is the juncture where your leadership comes into play. It begins with the strategic plan as an overall guiding beacon, and then utilizes a cross-functional team to provide interpretive insights and tactical plans. You thereby can make more precise judgments and finalize decisions using the full impact of predictive analysis.

If done correctly, you can deliver an outstanding customer experience, which was one of Tiffany's much sought-after goals of gaining customer loyalty and securing a competitive advantage. You also benefit by establishing two-way communications, so that information is captured about the buying experience and you can make adjustments in your mix of product offerings, promotions, pricing, delivery, after-sales service, and the like. Conversely, if done imperfectly, you face negative customer experiences, which can result in relinquishing control in the supply chain and suffering the effect of nonreturning customers.

Apply Technology

For many organizations, acquiring technology comes down to the classic make-or-buy decision. In turn, that takes in a variety of considerations based on available talent to run such operations, including such titles as data scientist and chief digital officer. And, then, there is the initial outlay of funds to obtain up-to-date technology. On the other hand, by outsourcing the necessary technology to qualified vendors, you benefit from the continual updating to state-of-the-art systems.

Again, whichever choice you make, your interest is to be in the forefront of offering technology-based solutions that can deliver meaningful buying experiences for customers, while maintaining a competitive lead over rivals. Part of that choice is considering how well the technology integrates with existing systems, procedures, and yes, the culture of your organization.

Other considerations include the level of sophistication of the software being imposed on existing systems, the need to change the system to accommodate the technology, and the effect of employing a hybrid system of legacy platforms.

Monitor Systems

Responsibility for monitoring the digital systems, procedures, and people lies squarely with you as a leader to ensure technology does what it is supposed to do. Not only does it require making sure the system works; as important is that the data is shared in a meaningful form, on time, and to the correct individuals across the organization.

In turn, a feedback loop is needed to find out from various individuals what actions result from the data. The objective is to prevent redundant efforts, as well as to trigger new areas of inquiry. Candid feedback also helps you determine if the data consists of nice-to-know information or is in reality breakthrough intelligence that can create new revenue streams and forecast evolving segment opportunities.

You can then make more qualified decisions with a greater level of confidence, as you reduce some of the uncertainty that may cause you to hesitate in making financial and personnel commitments. Consequently, more than at any other time, you will be functioning as a tech company.

Measure Success

There is an endpoint, a moment of truth when you must ask, did the move of people, procedures, and resources to digital technology work? Was it worth the investment? The partial answer is that today's metrics are more complex than those traditionally used to track major initiatives, such as market share, customer acquisition and retention, product usage, and various financial criteria.

Metrics in the digital age go beyond the above and focus with greater depth and precision on customer activity and behavior throughout the buying journey. That capability includes quantifying how rapidly data can be integrated into legacy systems and how quickly changes in strategies and tactics can be made to take advantage of deviations that, for instance, can single out an emerging or poorly served customer segment.

Expressed another way, metrics need to detail the hallmarks of the customer's buying experience and deliver key data for decision-making individuals to take action along the various touch points of the buying process. Organizationally, at the field level, that means salespeople would have increasingly more authority and responsibility to take on the role of general manager of their respective territories to think like strategists. Yet tactically they would be able to make on-the-spot decisions in as close to real time as possible.*

BUYER BEHAVIOR

In the above sections, numerous references were made to customer behavior, connecting with customers, building customer loyalty, and the like. What, then, from a leader's viewpoint, are the core issues with which you need to be concerned? What are the patterns of buyer behavior when operating and competing in the digital age? More specifically, are you equipped to intercept your prospects and customers along their decision-making journey with personalized information and offers?

That means devising a system to obtain usable answers, which may not be realistic for some organizations. Yet knowing what is ideal provides you with a strategic working map of what the system looks like. The mapping methodology is known. And the digital tools, systems, and services that incorporate big data, analytics, and algorithms are available from numerous highly competent vendors.

These sophisticated tools and systems are advancing rapidly to connect with individuals through image, voice, eye movement, and even thought. Forging these abundant components into a viable network takes leadership that can pull together the managerial resolve, investment, and organizational structure to function within a digital-minded culture.

An important organizational element that is key to making the system work is the cross-functional team, which includes the active involvement

---

* An organization known to this author has trained its salespeople in strategic business planning and competitive strategy to conceptually assume the role of a general manager in charge of a sales territory.

of individuals with expertise in analytics and information technologies. They would be the ones to comprehend, transpose, and clearly communicate the nuances of customer behavior over various cycles. That includes any signals embedded in customers' mobile or social media data.

Again, the object is to utilize the data to engage your customers on their buying-decision journey in a manner that will have a long-term, positive impact toward a confident buying experience. Whereas such a team would contribute to strategic and tactical considerations, there are likely to be specific outcomes related to segment growth, cost reduction, and opportunities for driving new product development.

The following is an example of a cross-channel decision journey.

An individual is preparing to furnish a home office. Along with an associate, he looks at several company websites, which include an office supply store, such as Staples, and various furniture stores that carry office furniture. They narrow the search to three styles of furniture, which leads them to one particular retail outlet to see the actual furnishings.

Upon arrival at the store, a transmitter mounted at the retailer's entrance identifies the two individuals and sends an alert to their cell phones welcoming them and providing them with updated information and recommendations based on their search history at the website. The information provides updated prices and current discounts, data about special features, types of wood finishes, measurements, and availability. Also, with an app that is linked to the store's systems, they obtain outside consumer reviews and price comparison information.

Further on in their journey, a link with the store's automated designer service graphically displays various designs of how the specific furniture can be set up in the prospect's room—which includes displays of additional pieces of furniture, wall hangings, and other accessories for purchase. Once the buy decision is made, the payment and delivery information are finalized over the buyer's cell phone. Then, at the point of delivery, the buyer is notified electronically with information about additional services for purchase.

Across the entire customer journey, numerous opportunities permit engaging the prospect, closing on the sale, and extending sales opportunities into additional cycles. Thus, using available business process software and services, marketing has the potential to function with the highest level of precision by targeting prospects and customers in real time with personalized approaches that can potentially make an individual a stand-alone segment of one.

EMPLOYING THE POWER OF SEGMENTATION

With the first force described above as utilizing the energy of digital marketing to connect producer to consumer, the second force is employing the power of segmentation to concentrate resources at decisive points.

The generally accepted understanding of segmentation is splitting the overall market into smaller submarkets or niches where you can enjoy measurable and substantial advantages by providing maximum benefits to customers, as well as for neutralizing the efforts of a competitor to interfere with your efforts. That approach is in contrast with spreading resources over numerous areas and thereby being strong nowhere and weak everywhere, or as suggested above, making a segment as finite as targeting a single individual through the precision of digital marketing.

The core strategic concept underlying segmentation can be found in the writings throughout history where strategy is applied. In particular, it is found in the classic works of Carl von Clausewitz, who stated, "The best strategy is always to be very strong: first in general, and then at the decisive point. There is no higher and simpler law of strategy than that of keeping one's forces concentrated."*

Focusing on decisive points or segments incorporates a four-step process:

1. Employ data analytics to define customer segments.
2. Use a comparative analysis to identify one or more decisive points within segments that would represent opportunities to (a) provide an outstanding buying experience within a defined segment and (b) expose competitors' weaknesses that can be exploited.
3. Pinpoint a segment for initial entry in which to concentrate; once secured, systematically roll out into additional market segments— still using comparative analysis, data analytics, and market intelligence to determine a defensible position.
4. Customize products and services to those segments with unique and definable benefits based on data of customer interests and behavior.

---

* Clausewitz is regarded by soldiers, statesmen, historians, and intellectuals around the world as one of the greatest Western military thinkers on strategy. His wisdom on the subject has been transposed to business applications in Norton Paley's book *Clausewitz Talks Business*, Taylor & Francis, Boca Raton, FL, 2015.

What Does a Decisive Point or Segment Look Like?

First, from a broad market perspective, China is a prime example of several spheres or segments. For instance, take its enormous population of 1.3 billion, speaking more than 100 dialects. That alone makes China about as diversified as any single country can be from a marketing perspective.

It is with such immense diversity that segmentation plays a central role in developing a viable portfolio of opportunities. In turn, gateways open to what people eat, wear, and drive—from north to south, east to west, rich to poor, young to old, city to countryside. From a manager's position, then, China stands out as a superb example of the potential opportunities when using decisive points to penetrate a market.

The following broad guidelines can assist in screening a potential segment:

- *Measurable.* Can you quantify the segment with whatever metrics are required by your organization? (Also see the "Monitor Systems" and "Measure Success" sections above.)
- *Accessible.* Do you have access to a supply chain that gives you entry through a dedicated sales force, distributors or dealers, transportation, or e-commerce?
- *Substantial.* Is the segment of adequate size to warrant your attention as a viable segment? Is the segment declining, maturing, or growing?
- *Profitable.* Does concentrating on the segment provide sufficient profitability to make it worthwhile? Use your organization's standard measurements for profitability, such as return on investment, gross margin, and profits.
- *Comparative goals with competition.* To what extent do your major competitors have an interest in the segment? Is it of active interest or of negligible concern to your competitors?
- *Effectiveness.* Do your people have acceptable skills and resources, especially digital ones, to serve the segment effectively?
- *Defendable.* Does your firm have the capabilities to defend itself against the attack of a major competitor?

Answering those questions will provide an initial screen to help you decide on a market segment with enough potential for concentrating your resources. A more refined approach would then be used with input of additional qualitative and quantitative data required by your organization.

ADVANCED TECHNIQUES FOR SELECTING A MARKET SEGMENT

The most common ways to segment a market are demographic, geographic, psychographic (behavioral and lifestyle), and product attribute factors. Each of these approaches can be subdivided into additional niches. Or they can be used in various combinations to create unique segment permutations.

Even with those traditional techniques, today's complex marketplace calls for more specialized approaches that take into consideration the intense competition that comes not only from the lower-cost regions of the world, but also from the huge impact of disruptive technologies. And organizations are responding in a variety of ways: Alcoa has split in two, separating its business of making aluminum from that of developing value-added parts specifically for the airline, auto, and other industry segments.

Then, there is Hewlett-Packard separating its printer and personal computer business from its server and data business. The justification is that the separated organizations can do a better job of concentrating on their respective business segments. Google, in turn, approached segmentation in its broadest context by creating an entirely new company, Alphabet, which allows it to run dissimilar businesses, each independent of the other, yet under an overall supervision.

Whereas the above examples are primarily strategic, segmentation is particularly important at the tactical level, where there are everyday dangers of competitors upending your plans. Thus, the techniques go beyond those listed above and are classified in a more finite approach as *natural, leading edge, key, linked, central, challenging, difficult,* and *encircled.*

By using these eight categories as a guide, it is assumed that you are attempting to engage the customer with an outstanding buying experience. Similarly, it is assumed that your competitor is attempting to achieve the same result. Thus, a great emphasis in this segmentation approach is to counter the effects of any competitor interfering with your efforts.

You also have the advantage of looking with a more critical eye at what challenges you will face. Then you will be better able to assess the risks and potential rewards when selecting your strategies. As you examine the characteristics for each market category, you may find some overlapping. That is acceptable since there are inherent commonalities among the various markets.

Natural Markets

In this type of marketplace, you operate in the familiar setting of your established segments. The implication is that within such customary surroundings, your personnel tend to be at ease and may not be motivated to venture out of their comfort zone. Yet, to expand, you have to motivate them to move beyond the confines of existing markets. That means looking at your organization's culture. That is, what is your organization's attitude toward risk taking and venturing out of familiar territory?

This point is illustrated in the contrasting performance of Fujifilm versus Kodak. Where Fujifilm saw the indisputable trends of a falling market for its traditional film products, it was transformed by a strategic thinking leadership into an organization with a growing trajectory by making use of its technologies to enter new industries and markets. Kodak delayed and fell into bankruptcy.

On the other hand, where there is a robust market outlook for your natural market, you and your rivals generally learn to adopt a live-and-let-live policy. That is, to ruin it through constant price battles and damaging claims is an unacceptable approach. Of course, that condition exists only as long as each company sticks to its own dedicated segment. Generally, outright aggressive confrontations are seldom used.

The primary reason for this uncharacteristic display of togetherness in a highly competitive world is that you and your rivals share a common interest in furthering the long-term growth and prosperity of the market. On the other hand, if any one competitor chooses to move forward and gain a meaningful benefit, here is where you have to decide on your goals. If your aim is to block the expansion of the competitor, then you have to look for your possible comparative advantage. How aggressive you choose to be entails looking at your strategic viewpoint about maintaining stability in the marketplace.

There is one additional dimension that characterizes this category, which you should actively keep in the forefront of your thinking: industries, markets, and products go through successive life cycle stages—introduction, growth, maturity, decline, and phase-out. Much of the movement through those stages is driven by the adoption rate of technology, which can affect changes in consumer behavior. Again, this was quite apparent in the Fujifilm example.

There are also variations triggered by legislative issues and the current trends about the environment. Unless there is an industry-wide movement to deal with such concerns, these are generally out of your ability to control. Therefore, your best course of action to sustain growth is to take the lead in searching for new niches in which to concentrate.

Leading-Edge Markets

Leading edge means exploring market segments by making minor penetrations into a competitor's territory. The intent is to investigate the possibility of opening another revenue stream.

Therefore, you want data analytics to sort out the following types of intelligence:

- The feasibility of the market to generate a revenue stream over the long term and, if possible, to expand into additional niches
- The resources needed to enter and gain a foothold in a market and then develop it into a secure and profitable segment
- A time frame for payback and eventual profitability
- An assessment of competitors: their market positions, strengths, and areas of vulnerabilities

Apple's and Amazon's venture into the television market with their smart TVs represents their versions of entering a leading-edge market. Amazon with its Fire TV and Apple TV with its built-in applications let users quickly access content from software included in the television. The smart TV market is not new and is becoming more crowded with technology-rich companies such as Google, Samsung, Sony, and LG ready to match any intruder feature for feature. Thus, to enter a leading-edge market, even if it is exploratory, would mean Apple and Amazon would have to make a substantial investment, backed up with outstanding market and competitor analysis, to sustain a foothold.

Key Markets

Key means that you and many of your competitors seem evenly matched. The general behavior is that you would not openly oppose an equally strong rival.

However, you may find that a competitor is attempting to dislodge you from a long-held position with the clear aim of taking away customers or disrupting your supply chain relationships. Then you may be forced to launch a countereffort by concentrating as many resources as possible to blunt the effort. Such actions are appropriate, if they fit your overall strategic objectives.

Therefore, keep the big picture in mind: if you expend excessive resources in hawkish-style actions such as price wars, then you may be left with a restricted budget to defend your market position. In any event, you want to make sure that any confrontational action you take is the true decisive point.

Linked Markets

In this category, you and your competitors are linked with easy access to markets. Your best strategy is to construct barriers around those niches (decisive points) that you value most, and from which you can best defend your position.

Barriers you can create include

- Above-average quality
- Feature-loaded products
- First-class customer service
- Superior technical support
- Competitive pricing
- On-time delivery
- Generous warranties
- Patent protection
- Outstanding buying journey (see above example)

Not only do you build barriers against competitors' incursions, but you also benefit by solidifying customer relationships. In particular, customer loyalty gives you a long-lasting, profit-generating advantage that is difficult for a competitor to overcome.

It is the one area that makes a meaningful addition to your growth. As one management analyst put it, "If you currently retain 70% of your customers and you start a program to improve that to 80%, you'll add an additional 10% to your growth rate."

CVS Health took a broad-based strategic approach to building barriers. First, the company set a long-term direction to transform its drugstore chain into a health care force in the market. It began by discontinuing the sale of tobacco products and replacing the traditional junk food snacks at the checkout counter with products considered "healthy" snacks.

Keeping with the aim to create an image of a health-oriented company, CVS continued to build itself into the country's biggest specialty pharmacy, which included focusing on the mail-order drug segment. It also built the second-biggest pharmacy processing prescription drug programs for large companies and health insurers. Altogether, CVS created substantial barriers.

Central Markets

Central means that you face powerful forces that threaten your market position. These forces are as diverse as watching competitors eat away at your position through aggressive pricing, or by offering dazzling feature-laden products, or through technology-rich applications overlaid with value-added services.

To counter such threats, look for joint ventures so that the cumulative effects yield greater market advantages and offer more strategy options than you can achieve independently. The merger and acquisition (M&A) route and other types of joint ventures have proven the strategy of choice for companies such as Microsoft, Facebook, and Google.

Challenging Markets

If you enter a market segment dominated by a strong and aggressive competitor, be watchful. You could place your company at excessively high risk.

If, however, your long-term objectives strongly support maintaining a presence in a challenging market, and if the expenditures of financial, material, and human resources are consistent with your overall strategy, then find a secure position, again, at the decisive point. It could be one of your single best chances for lessening the risk and achieving a solid measure of success.

Dell Computer is a prime example of employing excellent supply chain management. From its beginnings, the company's strategy relied on activating its manufacturing process and supply chain only when an order was received from a customer. For many years, that strategy worked at eliminating the cost of storing excessive inventory.

Dell benefited by shipping just the right amount of components to its factories, thereby avoiding investing in expensive warehousing. For instance, in one facility, what used to be done in more than two buildings was accomplished in one by applying the techniques of supply chain management. In more recent times (2015), Dell entered the challenging storage segment of the market through an acquisition of EMC.

Difficult Markets

This type of market segment is characterized as one where progress is erratic and highly competitive. If attempting to make any meaningful market penetration, secure key accounts, or maintain reasonable levels of logistical support, you are likely to be blocked by asset-draining barriers.

Also, if a competitor takes you off guard, and you subsequently lose your market situation, it is difficult to retrieve it. In effect, you are entrapped in an untenable condition and your entire business strategy could be in jeopardy. Your best course of action is to look for a segment on which you can concentrate and then use it as a platform to go forward. That means looking back at your strategic plan, which may entail developing a turn-around plan that redirects its strategic direction and long-term strategic objectives—as with Dell's shift to data storage and its connection with EMC.

Encircled Markets

Encircled segments foretell a potentially risky situation, that is, a market condition in which you control limited resources, and any aggressive action by a stronger, well-positioned competitor can force you to consider pulling out of a market.

Under those threatening conditions, your best approach is to look to big data for clues about which segments provide the greatest opportunities to break out of an encircled market. As part of the process, conducting a meaningful comparative analysis would open opportunities by exposing your opponent's vulnerabilities so that you can single out a decisive point of entry.

What follows is developing a strategy, which would include various options, such as initiating a series of product enhancements on a phasing-in schedule, and launching value-added services that favor your strengths and highlight your rival's weaknesses. Or it could include preempting your competitor's promotional programs and neutralizing your competitor's ability to maintain a profitable market position.

The essential aim, of course, is to discourage your opponent from making a monumental effort to push you out. By taking a bold approach, you may even stall or completely discourage your competitor from pursuing an aggressive action against you. If your strategies are well positioned, you may even place your competitor in his own encircled position!

SUMMARY

The primary purpose of detailing these segmentation categories is to show that segmentation is not a mechanical progress for dividing your markets. Rather, its purpose is to describe the dynamic interactions of customers and competitors under a variety of real-world market conditions. The eight categories of segments are summarized in Table 12.1.

TABLE 12.1

Advanced Techniques for Selecting a Segment

Category	Characteristics
Natural market	You and your rivals can operate harmoniously as long as each company sticks to its own dedicated segment.
Leading-edge market	Market entry means a minor penetration into a competitor's territory to determine the feasibility for generating a long-term revenue stream.
Key market	Competitors appear evenly matched within key market segments. The general strategy is that you would not openly oppose an equally strong rival. If the competitor attacks your position, then you are forced to launch a countereffort by concentrating as many resources as you can to attack the competitor's plans.
Linked market	You and your competitors are linked with easy access to markets. Your best strategy is to construct strong barriers around those niches from which you can best defend your position.
Central market	You face powerful competitors that threaten your market position. Counter such threats by joint venturing with other firms. You thereby gain greater market advantages and strategy options than you can accomplish independently.
Challenging market	An aggressive competitor dominates the market and thereby could place your company at excessively high risk. If your long-term objective strongly supports maintaining a presence in the market, then find a secure position by locating your competitor's decisive points of weakness.
Difficult market	Competition is pervasive and market behavior is erratic. Gaining and maintaining market penetration is difficult. Overall, your best course of action is to go forward by conducting a comparative analysis to identify your areas of strengths, and data analytics for pinpointing market niches and areas of competitors' weaknesses.
Encircled market	This market is risky, where any aggressive action by a stronger, well-positioned competitor can force you out of the market. Maintain ongoing competitive intelligence to accurately assess the vulnerabilities of your opponent. If you lack a capability to mount a meaningful competitive response, then exiting the market is a prudent strategy.

And what about those dynamic interactions of customers and competitors? They are the key ingredients for engaging customers, neutralizing competitors, and defining the boundaries of a segment. To that end, the operating systems, software, and procedures for gathering and utilizing big data and analytical applications are available.

What is needed is a leader's resolve to instill that need into the culture of your organization. "We want to treat analytics like it is as core to the company over the next 20 years as material science has been over the past 50 years," declared General Electric CEO Jeffrey Immelt. He went on to say that his company needs to act more like Oracle and Microsoft, and that all companies should look at themselves as being in the information business.

As noted above, one highly successful approach is to begin by installing or elevating the use of the cross-functional team, with its intrinsic capabilities to unite dissimilar functions of the organization. It thereby serves as a vital communications network to disseminate data, news, and stories that foster grassroots collaboration.

13

Leadership at the Culminating Point of a Competitive Campaign

Handsets are commoditized. They've gone from being technological devices to fast-moving consumer products. It's like Coke and Pepsi now. That's the war these companies are fighting. It's not a sexy business anymore.

Kirt McMaster
CEO, Cyanogen Inc.

The above quote refers to the evolving competitive conditions facing the makers of smartphones. That massive market is global, contentious, volatile, and highly uneven. Of the top 10 brands, 2 dominated the field in 2016: Apple and Samsung. Together, they accounted for more than a third of all smartphones sold, with Apple reaping more than 90% of the profits. Some of the other contenders, such as LG, Sony, HTC, and Lenovo, still advanced, but did so in more selected market segments.

Yet there is another reality in the competitive world that dictates a scenario whereby expansion does not move in a straight, predictable path. That is, the continuous forward-marching movements do not always play out according to plan. Rather, they signal a time where executives in those companies face a *culminating point* in which their campaigns turn from advance into defense.

No longer are they able to implement their original business plans. Often, unexpected competitive pressures force a few companies to pull their product lines out of the market. And there are instances where one company's advanced technology makes a rival's product line obsolete. Still others may decide to remain in an unprofitable position just to keep a presence in the marketplace to protect other interests.

There is another scenario where a campaign achieves its sales and market share objective. What then? Would further expansion be the best approach? Or would additional expenditures of human, material, and financial resources be better served by consolidating positions and vigorously defending what was achieved?

Thus, each manager has to decide if the cost of gaining an extra point of market share would be worth the expenditures. Stated another way, would continuing the advance risk the entire campaign and result in exhausting company resources? These are some of the issues that define the culminating point.

As for Apple and Samsung, even as market leaders, they will likely face a time when smartphones lose their uniqueness and become, as predicted above, commoditized. At that culminating point, market battles would be fought around such tactical areas as product features, price, convenience, warranties, and service contracts. Although there would likely be ongoing introductions of new model designs and software enhancements, all activities would be concentrated within the most profitable market segments.

What typically follows is that consumers will become enchanted with a new wave of wonder products as the smartphone category continues to lose its spark. As of 2016, however, Apple and Samsung enjoyed advantages in that their smartphones were prioritized as key profit centers in their respective organizations. Accordingly, major commitments were given by each company to develop products designed for advanced power-efficient chips, along with new innovative software.

As for the remaining smartphone brands in the top 10, their strategies entailed avoiding head-on clashes with the two market leaders. HTC, for instance, incorporated its high-tech features into cheaper models that aimed for the high-volume, low-margin segments of the market, mostly in the emerging parts of the world.

Yet they all faced two challenging forces that represented culminating points: First, in time emerging markets would become saturated. Second, local start-ups would attempt to undercut their efforts with lower prices. "We will see under $35 phones in sub-Saharan Africa," according to one industry analyst.

It was also a period where some astute managers began thinking strategically and pragmatically of a time of transition whereby their offensive campaigns would revert to the defensive. That eventuality meant looking into possibilities for realigning their respective companies and moving in an entirely new direction, as previously described with Fujifilm.* That, too, turned out to be a point where strategic business planning became an ongoing process as a way of maintaining a continuous pattern of strategic thinking. The practice was supported by the reliability, acceptance, and utility of big data and predictive analytics to help add greater precision to planning, and specifically to strategy development.

HTC, for instance, recognized the powerful undercurrents of competitive volatility and formed a partnership with Under Armour to build mobile technology into that company's sportswear. The defense, thereby, turned into an offense—but in a new direction with new applications.

Consequently, determining the culminating point should be of vital interest to you and requires your insightful judgment. That is also why it is the justification for relying on analytics to monitor market and customer behavior; it thereby provides the qualitative and quantitative foundations for making your decisions.

This is especially important if you are responsible for shaping strategies and committing your organization's resources to such campaigns as entering new markets against entrenched competitors, and holding a market position against aggressive rivals intent on preventing you from expanding further—or dislodging you completely.

CULMINATING POINT: APPLICATIONS

The culminating point utilizes a combination of strategies that impact a variety of market campaigns. They apply where an offensive campaign ends and a defensive campaign begins. The culminating point also applies where it is necessary to terminate an existing business and move onto an entirely new path. (Refer once again to the Fujifilm case in Chapter 11.)

The culminating point applies to the following types of campaigns. And for each campaign, the common theme is that the organization with superior market and competitor intelligence, supported by outstanding predictive analytics, is more likely to win an encounter.

1. *Campaigns to reclaim a former market position.* To reclaim a market position means finding out what caused the organization to either voluntarily quit the market or exit the market because of failure to

---

* See Fujifilm case details in Chapter 11.

keep up with technology, an inability to provide technical and customer service, and the like. Regaining a market foothold, however, requires careful analysis to find the optimum point of reentry.

2. *Campaigns to retain a share of market in a key region.* These efforts tie into what LG, HTC, and Lenovo would undertake. Collectively, the leaders of those companies needed to undertake a highly segmented approach, with each company carving its own target position. Further, the leaders had to prepare for swings from offensive actions to expand market share, followed by defensive moves to consolidate their new positions.

3. *Preemptive campaigns against a competitor to blunt his actions.* Speed is the essential requirement for successfully implementing a preemptive campaign. As such, it needs outstanding competitor intelligence to detect the driving force supporting the competitor's strategy. Then it is up to the defending organization to develop counterstrategies to rapidly neutralize the advancing company's efforts. Implicit in this effort is a flexible organization with superior up-and-down communications that permit decision-making authority at the tactical field level.

4. *Campaigns to probe and exploit a competitor's weaknesses.* Probing a competitor's weaknesses consists of two parts: First is a search of the physical areas, such as product and service performance, levels of technology, and functioning of the supply chain. The second is observing broad psychological areas that include corporate culture, leadership, morale, and employee collaboration (see Table 13.1).

5. *Campaigns tied to obligatory commitments made under joint-venture agreements.* If a joint venture combines the efforts of two weaker organizations to defend against a dominant competitor, the leaders of each company have to judge its long-term strategic implications, versus one of narrower scope, and possibly a more limited time and resource commitment.

   If the joint venture is between organizations that compete in nonconflicting segments, but within the same industry, both could benefit from sharing algorithms and big data for common usage. Thus, each agreement would have to be judged on its own objectives. In turn, these would be anchored to each organization's strategic plan.

6. *Campaigns that expand into additional market niches.* Here, market research and data analytics play a big part in defining competitors'

TABLE 13.1

Comparative Advantage of Physical and Psychological Strengths

Physical Strength	Psychological Strength
Product	• High-performing corporate culture
• Quality	• Positive morale and competitive spirit
• Features	• Customer-driven orientation
• Reliability	• Group unity
• Packaging	• Market diligence supported by predictive analytics
• After-sales services	• Superior awareness and confidence to deal with competitive threats
• Warranties	• Disciplined workforce supported by ongoing training
• Returns policy	• High-level experience and knowledge of the business or industry
• Commitment to technology and innovation	• Skill in developing business plans, strategies, and tactics
• Range of applications	• Collaborative work environment
• Brand name awareness	• Ethical behaviour
Logistics	• Strong leadership and a demonstrated ability to think strategically
• Inventory control systems	
• Physical transportation	
• Support systems along the supply chain	
Financial	
• Commitment of financial resources to sustain operations	
Organization	
• Organizational design that permits rapid communications of internal and external events	
• Organizational structure and systems	
Marketing and sales	
• Digital age capabilities	

Note: The items included here are adapted from Table 11.1. You may wish to weight each in level of importance, as well as add other key factors that would be unique to your industry or organization.

strengths and weaknesses, patterns of customer behavior, and segments that are emerging or poorly served. The process also permits more accurate budgeting as the expansion goes forward.

However, the leader has to recognize that there is a crossover point—a culminating point—where the advance turns into a defense. If the leader is not consciously aware of that crossover, a strong possibility exists for overshooting the mark in a zealous effort to make headline-worthy wins. Instead, it would threaten what was already achieved.

7. *Campaigns to solidify an existing market position and make it more defensible.* These campaigns take continuous monitoring. Whereas the effort is ostensibly defense, there are distinct periods of surges of offensive actions. Thus, the objective is to conduct an active defense. These include some of the campaigns described above, such as developing preemptive campaigns and probing the weaknesses of challenging competitors. As with all efforts to create a defensible position, ongoing input from market research and data analytics is essential.

8. *Campaigns to establish a foothold into new markets or new businesses.* The central issue here is to avoid replicating the strategies used by companies firmly entrenched in the market. Where they have deep-seated relationships with customers and those within the supply chain, such barriers are difficult to penetrate using me-too approaches. Rather, any success would result from innovative strategies that have enough power to move customers in a new direction.

   In its extreme, wielding such power takes a special breed of organization with the business model, technical expertise, and spirit of the likes of Uber and Airbnb to upend entire industries in an amazingly short period of time. Others have to plod along a more traditional path of monitoring market behavior and seeking out the early adopters, and then follow the path of reaching the early-majority and late-majority sectors of the market over a period of time.

9. *Exploratory campaigns initiated by senior management or from the upward pressure of junior-level managers.* These campaigns can be problematic at a few levels. They could be knee-jerk responses to some enticing Monday morning headlines. As such, they are impulsive actions that are speculative and can eat away at time and resources, unless firmly supported by documented evidence of market trends.

   On the other hand, exploratory campaigns can be the result of alert executives recognizing that a market has matured and the existing industry is fast reaching a culminating point (as forecasted for the smartphone market). The issue then becomes which firm organizes an effort to first explore, validate, and establish a new market position.

   Such campaigns may become challenges to the culture of an organization, to some executives in the C-suite, and to those managers running dedicated operations. In some instances, it is not unnatural to find junior-level managers disheartened by the lack of courage displayed by senior-level executives. And it is not unusual for executives to distrust what they perceive as rash and impulsive actions at the junior level.

The disconnect signals a huge corporate and cultural problem and calls for open communications and a forum that delivers messages about the long-term strategic direction of the firm. The intent is not to seek consensus; rather, the aim is to communicate a direction, provide a platform of criteria to approve or disapprove campaigns, and maintain a sense of unity at all levels.

10. *Campaigns against moves of an aggressive competitor attempting to weaken a defender's resistance.* In this campaign, a rival would try to increase market share at the expense of another firm serving the same market. In an attempt to change the equilibrium of the market, the attacker would likely focus on one or more decisive areas, such as dramatically increasing product performance or introducing new-wave technology.

    In turn, the defender's initial response would be to quickly discover the driving force behind the action and, if possible, match it. However, in situations where the defender cannot duplicate the strategy, an alternative would be to employ a segmentation approach. This strategy is not unlike that used by the majority of smartphone makers.

11. *Campaigns intended to make the competitive encounter costlier for the rival to continue operations.* This is another case of locating the rival's weaknesses and initiating actions to neutralize the rival's strategies. Such actions can be as dramatic as tying up sources of critical supplies through long-term contracts, thereby denying such sources to the rival. Or it could take the form of introducing numerous short-term promotions that tend to affect pricing and create profit-draining problems for the competitor.

12. *Limited-term campaigns versus mobilizing resources for longer-term decisive campaigns.* Sound management practice dictates that limited-term campaigns should be undertaken if they fulfill long-term objectives that link to an organization's strategic business plan. Here, too, practicality intervenes if there are dramatic changes, such as in consumer buying behavior, unexpected expansion moves by competitors, or new disruptive technologies. Then,

there could be numerous game changers related to robotics, artificial intelligence, and the Internet of things that rock the market and force companies to change course or fight the kinds of campaigns described above.

In the above competitive encounters where one side gains over the other, there is one additional matter a leader must keep in mind. Success chiefly comes about with the winning side using superior strategies built around comparative advantages. Such strategies derive from a diverse number of physical and psychological strengths, shown in Table 13.1.

But these references come with a qualifier: even in instances of a clear advantage, it is rare that a rival can be completely overwhelmed. And should a leader believe that complete success was achieved, in all too many cases there is a tendency to slacken off and cause the organization to get into an unwelcome state of complacency, which is often threatened by an inability to reverse a decline.

And where an opposing company has shifted to the defense, it is vitally important for the leader to show his or her people that any perception of a failed campaign should be considered only a temporary condition. As such, it should be treated as only a pause to regroup, develop new counter-strategies, and go back to the offensive. Thus, these inevitable swings from offense to defense should be taken into account when preparing a business plan and briefing the staff.

Consequently, as a competitive campaign unfolds between two rivals, regardless of type of campaign, a reduction in strength on one side can be considered an increase on the other. These alternating conditions of strengths and weaknesses are intrinsic parts of offensive and defensive campaigns—and natural characteristics of the culminating point.

As a leader, therefore, your aim is to examine the underlying causes of changing conditions among those listed in Table 13.1, or from any unique situation that your organization currently faces. An example of changing conditions hit Procter & Gamble as it attempted to transition from decades of continuous expansion to a strategy of consolidation and defense in areas where it retained brand and market share strength for decades.*

In this instance, P&G faced a range of external conditions: recession in key markets, cheaper competing brands, and changing buying patterns.

---

* See details about the Procter & Gamble case in Chapter 1.

In effect, the company reached a culminating point whereby its expansion moves switched to consolidating its existing positions. For P&G management, the primary consideration was to understand that consolidating and defending are only pauses to correct problems, find effective solutions, or redirect efforts in a new direction. Expressed another way, staying put and stagnating cannot be a successful course of action.

There is still another major consideration that deserves your attention as you make your assessment of strengths and weaknesses. It occurs at the time of changeover where strategies and tactics alternate from offensive to defensive, or vice versa. The issue takes the form of a powerful human dynamic: *employee morale.*

Reorienting your people during the regrouping and switching from one mode of operation to another can have an unsettling psychological effect on your personnel. Some individuals can handle change. A few may falter, become discouraged, and infect the attitudes of others. The essential point from a leadership viewpoint is that you must maintain a high level of morale among those you manage, as well as with others who are only remotely involved with the campaign.

The importance of morale is meaningfully expressed by an individual from another field of endeavor who was intimately involved with volatile campaigns and their effect on the performance of personnel.

> The final deciding factor of all engagements … is morale. Better weapons, better food, and superiority in numbers will influence morale, but it is a sheer determination to win, by whomever or whatever inspired, that counts in the end. Study men and their morale always.
>
> **Field Marshal Archibald Wavell**

Thus, with morale as the centerpiece for leading your personnel through the subtle swings from advance to defense or reverse, the topic requires more attention.

BUILDING MORALE

The process of building morale begins with establishing trust among your people. That includes using the most fundamental practices of offering words of encouragement and projecting your image of reliability and competence. These positive expressions should be supported by means of inclusiveness and nourished through ongoing communications. That means providing details of the ongoing campaign and preparing staff on what to expect during the transition from one level of strategy to another.

Specifically, it means briefing them on the topic discussed here: that every forward-moving effort will reach a culminating point, either self-imposed or created by marketplace forces, that will cause forward-moving actions to slow or come to a complete halt. At that point, there will be a shift in strategy to defending what was previously achieved.

During that changeover, it is likely that festering in the minds of some individuals is a refusal to buy into your well-intentioned explanations. Still others may not fully internalize the nuances of the new strategy and tend to become anxious and restless. Thus, the situation exposes another vital personnel issue: Do your people have enough confidence in your judgment to assess the situation accurately and make a correct decision?

The purpose of gaining your people's trust is to overcome the negative feelings among those who, for a variety of life experiences, harbor mistrust and doubt. Some have valid reasons due to having been misinformed and misled in the past by their leaders. Nonetheless, it is your challenge to create trust and convince them that you have their best interests at heart.

The following diverse examples illustrate the positive and negative aspects of establishing trust: When Air France's leaders announced in 2016 a plan to cut 2,900 jobs, 3% of the total, they knew the move would be disliked. They just did not realize its full impact. One the same day of the announcement, dozens of workers stormed a company conference room and ripped the shirts off top executives, some of whom desperately climbed over a fence to escape the raging mob.

In contrast, during the same time at Twitter, CEO Jack Dorsey announced he would have to cut 335 jobs, 8% of the total. He also stated he was giving one-third of his own Twitter stock, worth $200 million at that time, to the employee equity pool. No riots occurred and the news slowly faded away.

In another instance, Whole Foods co-founder and co-CEO John Mackey paid himself $1 a year to compensate for poor performance resulting from poor decisions. It was his way of showing employees that he would share in any suffering.

Whatever the causes, it is still your leadership responsibility to take command and look for success from the situation and not place the complete burden on your people. Stated another way, trust means inclusion, teamwork, and collaboration. They are not just the slogans of the day; they are essential in order to obtain the best thinking from an involved and dedicated staff. In the end, however, the decision is yours. As Airbnb CEO Brian Chesky expresses the idea, "Usually in a crisis you have to go left or right, and everyone wants to go to the middle. And the middle is the storm."

What your staff must know without a doubt, however, is that you and they have the support at the highest levels of the organization. Also, they must see and feel your physical presence, which would provide the psychological comfort to sustain their morale and motivate them to keep trying, even under crisis conditions.

Taken together, your intention is to strive for unity of effort. It is not isolated actions that make high-performing employees. Rather, it is the collective efforts of individuals within teams interacting among themselves that cultivate unity.

For that reason, it is your essential role to continue encouraging interaction. Once again, this is one of the chief purposes of a team. In the end, it is the leader who knows his or her people best and understands the reasons behind such highly charged displays of behavior as anguish and fear, or courage and dogged determination.

Therefore, you cannot be a stranger to your employees. It is your influence and physical presence that affect morale. If they feel themselves no longer supported, it creates an untenable situation for you. Unity also requires trust that you sustain confidence in your personal ability to lead. If, on the other hand, you are habitually gripped by fear, then you should have second thoughts about leading your group.

Morale is also nurtured by a cohesive corporate culture, which is reinforced by an ethical climate built around core values. A healthy culture fortifies your leadership role and helps guide your organization or business unit's strategy (see Table 13.2). Consequently, leaders seek to shape their companies' or business units' cultures to support their visions, articulate their goals, and improve their overall performances through high morale.

Morale Interfaces with Innovation

Innovation can be a prime differentiator during the transition, for instance, from defense to offense, as well as when launching new technology-advanced products. Therefore, when some significant innovation results from employees' creativity, express appreciation publicly for jobs well done. Your approach should be evenhanded, sincere, and fair-minded.

TABLE 13.2

Morale and Its Impact on Business Strategy

- Morale suffers and defeats become competitive debacles without reliable communications with staff during the culminating point transition.
- Morale fades when there is no inspiring goal to fight for.
- Morale weakens when employees work in a state of uncertainty.
- Ineffectual training affects morale with a corresponding serious effect on implementing strategies.
- Lack of C-suite commitment to a competitive strategy affects morale.
- Unethical corporate behavior impacts morale.
- A leader's inability to create a long-term vision and develop attainable objectives influences morale.
- Undisciplined behavior that readily gives in to fear sways morale.
- A leader who procrastinates and visibly displays an inability to handle responsibility weighs heavily on morale.
- A leader who stifles employees' input has a negative influence on morale.
- A leader's inability to accurately assess a competitive situation shapes morale.
- A leader who does not know how to reach the heart, mind, and spirit of a group, and instead shows more interest in his or her personal agenda, greatly impacts morale.

And as important, stand by them should an idea fail. Or else you shut them down—along with creativity.

Further, in all initiatives associated with innovation, communicate to your staff a vision of growth that goes beyond their view of the markets they serve. For instance, one unique approach is used by 3M. The company enlists old-time employees to recount company history and hand down stories of 3M's long traditions for innovation to new engineers. After a while, every new employee is able to recite the foundation precepts that are the underpinnings of the organization.

To develop criteria for evaluating innovation, you will need to let the staff know how they will be measured. The frequently used metrics for innovation include the following:

- Overall revenue growth resulting from employee innovations
- Changes in customer satisfaction ratings
- Improvements in market share
- Comparisons of innovations measured against chief competitors by product category
- Number of new products or services launched
- Ratio of new product successes to losers
- Other criteria required by your company

Relationship of Morale with Digital Technology

Much has been said about diminishing human intervention with the remarkable advances in digital technology, artificial intelligence, and robotics. Should that view persist, it is likely to have a serious impact on employee morale and an organization's overall performance. The essential point: Individuals are still the most significant element in conducting business. People, not things, are decisive to achieving a favorable outcome. To that end, it is worth repeating Google chairman Eric Schmidt's comment:

> There's no algorithm or formula that says technology will do X, so Y is sure to happen. Technology doesn't work on its own. It's just a tool. You are the ones who harness its power.

Even with disruptive technologies and formidable strategies, a plan could languish if employees are not personally motivated with the spirit and will to succeed. Understood another way, new technologies have limited value in the hands of disheartened employees. Here, too, it is essential to work at developing their morale. Doing so can open an infinite range of possibilities for rousing individuals to greater efforts in offensive or defensive actions.

As for Apple and Samsung, they will likely continue to grow with frequent improvements in their products and with the morale-boosting momentum associated with being on the advance. Then, almost unperceptively, events could change. Even as their advance continues, there will be more obstacles that will trigger culminating points.

These stumbling blocks can be the result of unintentional outcomes. A new model change does not take off with the public, a start-up makes a sudden hit with a wildcat innovation, or a production snafu causes a supply chain problem. These may be so debilitating as to easily cancel out all previously gained advantages. And as the advances continue, the risks they represent will progressively increase.

Then, there are the obligations associated with an extended supply chain and expanded customer services, all of which stretch their resources and weigh down their total efforts. These would tend to challenge the spirit and morale of their employees and negatively impact their internal capabilities. The sum of these consequences can result in dire effects for Apple and Samsung if left unattended.

As for you, with every advancing step you take, similar obstacles can place excessive burdens on your organization. Unless you started with exceptional superiority, you will notice your freedom of action dwindling and your offensive power progressively reduced. In the end, you could feel unsure and unsteady about your company's or product line's future.

Therefore, if you take an objective and fact-based view of these barriers, you may draw a logical conclusion that continuing an offensive campaign could exhaust your superiority and jeopardize your competitiveness. At this point, you could legitimately ask, If all this is true, why persist in staying on the offensive and risk so much? Can such a move still be called a prudent decision? Would you be better off at some culminating point calling a halt before losing the upper hand?

One pragmatic answer is that superior strength is not the end, but only the means. The end is to neutralize the rival and its ability to interfere with you reaching your objectives. The main point behind this thinking is that you are not looking to just improve your current market position. Rather, the end aims to improve your overall prospects for long-term success.

And there is still another relevant factor to consider: remaining in a permanent defensive positon is not the natural aim of a campaign. Rather, it is a natural characteristic of an offensive effort. This reasoning is based on the principle that every major attempt at launching a new product or entering a new market is made up of a series of campaigns; each has a number of culminating points. In turn, each culminating point contains elements of offense and defense, which provide fresh opportunities to regroup and develop new strategies.

As for neutralizing your competitor's advantage, you have to face up to the reality of unexpectedly diverting resources to defuse or preempt its efforts. That means maintaining a high level of competitive data so that you are able to rapidly match or exceed a rival's technical services, undertake major and unbudgeted marketing efforts, and if necessary, do the unthinkable, get enmeshed in price wars—all of which can weaken your own superiority and prevent you from moving forward to your main objective.

Nonetheless, in many instances human nature will likely rule and staying on the offensive with all the potential honors and rewards will prevail. The rationalized attitude would dictate moving forward and dealing with any blatant problems at a later date. You just have to keep top of mind that there is a point of vulnerability at which the offensive can overshoot the target and instead of gaining new advantages, you forfeit success.

Thus, the culminating point is bound to recur in every competitive encounter, so that the natural ingredient of all campaign plans is the crossover or turning point at which attack becomes defense. If you were to go beyond that point, it would end up as a useless effort, which could not add to success. In fact, it would be a damaging one.

To eliminate any misinterpretation, the above principle rests on the assumption that as long as you remain on the offensive and it is progressing according to your plan, and there is no sign of meaningful competitive resistance that you cannot confidently overcome, superiority will remain on your side. Thus, you are not in much danger of unexpectedly becoming the weaker side.

Yet there are instances where campaigns might end up as a draw because the side that should take the initiative lacks determination, which could be attributable to such factors as falling morale or faltering leadership. It is certainly not uncommon for leaders to lose their nerve and hesitate during the critical period, where the human factor can make the decisive difference in the outcome. For either company, it could be an opportunity to take advantage of the opposing manager's fear and lack of confidence through aggressive tactical moves.

Far from idle theory, consider that as the action of a campaign continues, there is a line when one side crosses the threshold of equilibrium—the culminating point—without knowing it. It is even possible that the offensive-moving company, reinforced by the uplifting psychological forces normal to attack and despite exhaustion, continues to go on rather than stop.

It is therefore essential to calculate this point correctly when planning the campaign. An advancing company may otherwise take on more than it can manage and incur excessive debt. As for the defender, it must recognize such an error and exploit it to the fullest. That is where such tools as predictive analytics play a key part in the calculation.

In reviewing the whole array of factors a leader must weigh before making a decision, remember to gauge the value of the most important ones by considering numerous possibilities—some immediate, some strategic. Others are speculative or subject to whatever criteria executives use to make judgments. For instance, Sony Betamax and its VCR format peaked in 1984, presumably at its culminating point. Yet Sony surprisingly kept making players and recorders until 2002. And the company finally stopped shipping cassettes in 2016.

Then, there is IBM that continues selling mainframe computers, which seemingly had their prime-time and culminating point in the 1960s. Notwithstanding, IBM felt confident about maintaining the offensive as it invested heavily to reverse the downward trend. The company went on to introduce its brand-new line in 2015, the z13, "built for the mobile era."

Thus, calculating the culminating point entails a range of factors, some fact based, supported by algorithms and big data. Others could relate to an executive's personal agenda or to a surge of interest in maintaining a legacy of the company's historic contributions to the industry. These and much more require reflection and discreet judgment.

Therefore, it is no small task for the human mind to deal with, considering the thousands of wrong turns running in all directions that tempt perception and judgment. And if the range and complexity of the issues are not enough to overwhelm any leader, the hazards associated with taking on the associated responsibilities may.

This is why the great majority of leaders will prefer to stop well short of their objective rather than risk approaching it too closely. And that is why those with high courage and an enterprising spirit will often overshoot it and so fail to attain their purpose. Only the leader who can achieve great results with limited means and still keep an eye on the culminating point has really hit the mark.

SUMMARY

The following summarizes the key principles of the culminating point:

- The diminishing force of the offensive is one of the leader's main concerns with excessive expenditures that go beyond what can be replaced during a reasonable time period.
- The natural goal of all campaign plans is the turning point at which attack becomes defense. If one were to go beyond that point, it would tend to be a useless effort with meager returns on the investment of resources.
- The object of the offensive is to make inroads into the rival's primary market territory.
- Relaxation of efforts due to dragged-out attempts drains resources and morale.
- Defections of key customers or others along the supply chain can signal a turning point in a campaign.
- As soon as the objective has been attained, the attack ends and the defense takes over.

- The diminishing force of staying on the offensive is one of the leader's main concerns.
- What matters is to detect the culminating point of actions with discriminative judgment.
- If an offensive lacks superior physical resources, it must have psychological superiority to make up for those material weaknesses.
- Prudence and judgment are the true spirit of defensive campaigns; courage and confidence are the true spirit of offensive campaigns.
- Every leader has to ask how he or she will exploit success after the encounter.
- An important factor besides the morale of personnel is the outward confidence of the C-suite.

In absolute terms, therefore, you have to take into account that every offensive campaign has defense as its natural component.* And once you turn to the defense, your role is to actively defend your market gains and totally avoid getting into a state of complacency, so that defense should be considered only a pause before once again resuming the advance. The direction of the advance could remain in your traditional markets or, depending on circumstances, take on an entirely new direction and even a new business. In both cases, the directions would be a product of your strategic business plan supported by the digital tools to provide as much accuracy as possible.

---

* See Chapter 8 for a detailed discussion.

Appendix: A Model Program for an Internal Communications Network

At any given time some aspect of a business is always in start-up. New products and services are introduced, functions come online and change in priority as the business grows. That means making certain that employees stay mentally fit throughout all phases of growth, beyond start-up. All things considered, managers still have to keep encouraging them to work steadily toward quarterly and annual targets.

Throughout the growth phase of a company, managers need to be able to keep changing gears, sometimes from one hour to the next. It is also my experience that the managers who learn to enjoy those gear changes are the managers who thrive.

Paul Lee
Former CEO, BBC America

"Making certain that employees stay mentally fit" is a major purpose for establishing a comprehensive internal communications network that enables leaders to connect with employees at all levels of the organization. Such a network is rooted to the following six realities that define today's digital environment:

1. Rigorous business principles do exist and need to be followed regardless of the type of business. (Many of these foundation principles are discussed within the chapters of this book.)
2. Utilizing data analytics about markets, consumers, and competitors is the essential prerequisite before committing any amount of resources.
3. Implementing even the most basic competitive strategies requires talented, informed, and trained individuals who can think like strategists, as well as advancing a core group of managers with superior abilities to motivate and retain skilled employees.

4. A customer-driven culture with core values that are unique to the firm provides the essential underpinnings if you are to expect winning performances from employees.
5. Finding fresh opportunities requires individuals who can see openings as if by looking through a wide-vision lens. As geographic distances dissolve, cultural differences emerge as the more important possibilities for growth.
6. Winning in the marketplace and neutralizing competitors require aligning strategies with the organization's culture.

Thus, the structure for an internal communications network is founded on the rock-solid principle that properly trained and motivated employees can turn the tide and decide the success of an enterprise. Such a network provides a platform to (1) empower personnel with the skills and tools to grow the business and, where needed, to recast the strategic business plan's objectives and strategies, and (2) inspire them to actively use the new digital tools to pursue opportunities for growth.

NETWORK OBJECTIVES

With the proliferation of mobile devices, more than at any other time you are better able to reach out to your staff with creative forms of programming to achieve the following:

Unite employees to a common purpose through ongoing communications. This is the opportunity to restate and reinforce your organization's strategic direction and long-term objectives, thereby keeping personnel informed and committed.

Ongoing communications also permit clarifying misconceptions, misinformation, or rumors before they solidify and do unnecessary damage. Such information includes explaining the organization's competitive situation and informing personnel of plans to deal with serious threats. Leaders can thereby get out in front of the company grapevine, rather than needing to sweep up behind it.

Lift employee morale through positive messaging. Healthy employee relationships start with consistent messages delivered with regularity. These include highlighting noteworthy achievements of the company, a group, or an individual, as well as announcements of new products, technologies, or business alliances.

An internal communications network provides a virtual platform where executives from key functions of the organization can influence staff's behavior, reinforce those cultural values that make the company unique, reenergize sagging confidence, and cultivate an entrepreneurial mindset.

Equip employees with strategy skills. An internal network supports self-development of the staff, as well as augments formal training programs. By feeding in current data, especially in the use of analytics, the system is continuously refreshed and better able to assist the staff to shape new expansion strategies, suggest innovative techniques to pursue additional revenue streams, and prepare contingency plans to defend against competitive threats.

NETWORK CONTENT

A model for an internal communications network would include the following components: First, personalized audio and video messages would permit executives to engage employees by way of motivational talks that speak about the organization's current plans, provide details about a particular group's achievements, or initiate internal dialogue about applications of digital technology. These messages can influence positive employee behavior, strengthen a collaborative team culture, revitalize morale, and cultivate an entrepreneurial mindset.

Second, skill-building content for employee self-development would be provided through the following three-part format:

Case studies. Using company examples from within and outside the organization's industry, employees would learn about techniques to solve specific problems. This approach is meant to stoke the minds of individuals and get them to develop their own creative applications.

Further, the case study format is valuable for showing ideas, techniques, and methodologies of how organizations formulate strategies to deal with issues related to the digital age.

Strategy applications. This section would feature different executives who would lead discussions and demonstrate a variety of business-building strategy techniques, with emphasis on matching them to the overall strategic objectives of the organization, such as embracing digital technology. The intent is to open their minds to think like strategists.

Tool box. This part provides approaches to sharpen and deepen employees' abilities to analyze situations and make better decisions. Such moves would include assessment tools to evaluate the effectiveness of specific strategies (see Table A.1). A sample format of an assessment tool is shown in Table A.1.

BENEFITS OF AN INTERNAL COMMUNICATIONS NETWORK BY CORPORATE SIZE

Large Organizations with Multiple Divisions

Where business units may be dispersed, or where there is a vacuum in effective communications, a unifying message to personnel on a regular basis that updates, informs, and educates connects individuals and improves collaboration.

Here is where vice presidents and general managers of divisions in large organizations would aim to

- Reduce internal friction that causes low morale, fear, and uncertainty; also, calm feelings of defeatism, particularly where there is a dispersed workforce
- Reinforce the core beliefs that drive the organization's culture
- Reenergize the staff; get them to shift to the offensive and support the current business strategy
- Motivate employees with purpose, confidence, and a willingness to overcome the inevitable competitive obstacles
- Curb excessive caution, which tends to immobilize individuals and results in a loss of momentum

Small and Midsize Companies

As part of personnel development, leaders in these organizations can inspire employees with positive messages. The executives' supportive words, when joined with skill-building content, open employees' minds to new ideas and innovative thinking.

TABLE A.1

Strategy Assessment Tool

This sample format of an assessment tool relates to Section II, "Competitive Strategy," which includes content from Chapters 4 through 6.

Each of the following strategy guidelines consists of three parts:[a]

- Part 1: Indications the guideline is functioning *effectively* in your organization
- Part 2: Symptoms the guideline is functioning *ineffectively* in your organization
- Part 3: Remedial actions based on Parts 1 and 2

Strategy Guideline: Concentration
(Based on Chapter 4, Apply Analytics to Concentrate at Decisive Points)

Concept: Strategies that concentrate resources at decisive points are more likely to gain market superiority in targeted segments. That includes focusing on a competitor's specific weakness or a general area of vulnerability.

Part 1: Indications the Strategy Functions Effectively

1. We deliberately use a strategy of concentrating at a decisive point to challenge larger competitors.

   1_____10
   Rarely   Occasionally   Frequently

2. We feel confident about concentrating our resources to gain a superior position in a selected market segment, even if it creates some exposure elsewhere.

   1_____10
   Rarely   Occasionally   Frequently

3. We use data analytics to pinpoint a segment for initial market entry.

   1_____10
   Rarely   Occasionally   Frequently

4. We are adept at reaching beyond traditional demographic and geographic segmentation approaches by employing advanced analytics to identify new or underserved segments.

   1_____10
   Rarely   Occasionally   Frequently

5. We are flexible about pulling out of underperforming segments and concentrating on faster-growing ones.

   1_____10
   Rarely   Occasionally   Frequently

6. We are capable of concentrating our resources against competitors' weaknesses.

   1_____10
   Rarely   Occasionally   Frequently

7. Marketing and sales personnel are sufficiently tuned in to changing buying trends and are skilled at recommending new products and services.

   1_____10
   Rarely   Occasionally   Frequently

(*Continued*)

TABLE A.1 (CONTINUED)

Strategy Assessment Tool

8. Our organization is skilled at uncovering market gaps and allocating resources to efficiently exploit a rival's limitations.

1_____10
Rarely　　　　Occasionally　　　　Frequently

Part 2: Symptoms the Strategy Functions Ineffectively

1. We fail to use data analytics to select market segments that offer long-term growth.

1_____10
Frequently　　　　Occasionally　　　　Rarely

2. We dissipate resources across too many segments.

1_____10
Frequently　　　　Occasionally　　　　Rarely

3. Our company's product launches disappoint in the absence of a strategy focused on sufficient market data.

1_____10
Frequently　　　　Occasionally　　　　Rarely

4. Our people have not internalized the principle that achieving a competitive edge means employing a strategy of concentration, even if it exposes our vulnerabilities.

1_____10
Frequently　　　　Occasionally　　　　Rarely

Part 3: Remedial Actions Based on Parts 1 and 2

Parts 1 and 2 provide qualitative assessments of your ability to use a *strategy of concentration*. Based on your team's evaluation, the following remedies can apply corrective actions:

- Install an ongoing data-gathering system to identify a competitor's weaknesses.
- Concentrate on emerging markets or those that are poorly served in order to get a foothold into additional segments.
- Secure our position with dedicated services and customized products that would create barriers to competitors' entry.
- Within customer segments, tailor products and services built around product differentiation, value-added services, and business solutions that exceed those of competitors.
- Conduct internal strategy training sessions, especially for those individuals who do not understand the value of finding a decisive point and resist adopting a strategy of concentration.

Strategy Guideline: Speed
(Based on Chapter 5, Initiate Speed to Maintain a Digital Advantage)

Concept: There are few cases of prolonged operations that have been successful. Drawn-out efforts often divert interest, diminish enthusiasm, and damage employee morale. Nothing drains resources like an overlong campaign.

(Continued)

TABLE A.1 (CONTINUED)
Strategy Assessment Tool

Part 1: Indications the Strategy Functions Effectively

1. We realize that dragged-out campaigns have rarely been successful. We work to avoid them in our team and organization before they divert interest, depress morale, and deplete resources.

   1_____10
   Rarely   Occasionally   Frequently

2. We recognize that speed is an essential component to securing a competitive lead. This impacts market share, product positioning, and ultimately customer relationships.

   1_____10
   Rarely   Occasionally   Frequently

3. Our staff understands that even minor delays can result in a loss of momentum and could signal a vigilant competitor to move in and fill the void.

   1_____10
   Rarely   Occasionally   Frequently

4. We know that a plan that integrates speed with technology puts us in an excellent position to secure a competitive lead.

   1_____10
   Rarely   Occasionally   Frequently

5. We acknowledge that speed adds vitality to a company's operations and becomes a catalyst for growth.

   1_____10
   Rarely   Occasionally   Frequently

6. We have internalized the idea that acting defensively to protect a market position is but a preliminary step to moving rapidly to the offensive against a competitor.

   1_____10
   Rarely   Occasionally   Frequently

Part 2: Symptoms the Strategy Functions Ineffectively

1. We fail to fully understand that excessive delay acting on time-sensitive market conditions can result in losses in market share and competitive position.

   1_____10
   Frequently   Occasionally   Rarely

2. A general malaise exists in the organization, which results in missed opportunities.

   1_____10
   Frequently   Occasionally   Rarely

3. Personnel lack initiative in implementing business plans with speed.

   1_____10
   Frequently   Occasionally   Rarely

(Continued)

TABLE A.1 (CONTINUED)

Strategy Assessment Tool

4. We are slow in preventing a product from reaching a commodity status, which frequently results in price wars.

1_____10

Frequently   Occasionally   Rarely

5. Inadequately trained and inexperienced staff have slowed us down and prevented us from taking advantage of opportunities.

1_____10

Frequently   Occasionally   Rarely

6. Despite correct market data, we are unable to act boldly and rapidly.

1_____10

Frequently   Occasionally   Rarely

7. We have failed to secure a competitive lead due to sluggishness in integrating technology into the marketing mix.

1_____10

Frequently   Occasionally   Rarely

8. Organizational layers prolong deliberation and delay decisions, creating a trickle-down corporate culture of procrastination.

1_____10

Frequently   Occasionally   Rarely

9. There is a persistent lack of urgency in employing predictive analytics to develop new products.

1_____10

Frequently   Occasionally   Rarely

Part 3: Remedial Actions Based on Parts 1 and 2

Parts 1 and 2 provide qualitative assessments of our ability to *act with speed*. Based on our team's evaluation, the following remedies can apply corrective actions:

- Reduce organizational obstacles that prevent us from increasing the speed of internal communication and decision making.
- Require selected individuals on our staff to submit timely proposals with the prime objective of creating additional revenue streams through product innovations, through new technology applications, and by using big data to identify new, unserved, or poorly served market segments.
- Actively seek input from managers and field personnel to pinpoint competitors' weaknesses and areas of vulnerability.
- Conduct training to break down internal barriers and areas of friction to speed.

(Continued)

TABLE A.1 (CONTINUED)

Strategy Assessment Tool

**Strategy Guideline: Maneuver by Indirect Strategy
(Based on Chapter 6, Active Indirect Maneuver to Create Surprise)**

Concept: An indirect strategy applies strength against a competitor's weakness. The aim is to resolve customer problems with offerings that outperform those of your competitors, and to achieve a psychological advantage by creating an unbalancing effect in the mind of your rival manager.

Part 1: Indications the Strategy Functions Effectively

1. You intentionally integrate indirect strategies into your business plans, thereby increasing the success rate of your efforts. You also engage in open dialogues with colleagues and staff about new approaches to indirect strategies, along with their implementation.

   1_____10
   Rarely   Occasionally   Frequently

2. You act with the understanding that acquiring the skills to implement indirect strategies opens your mind to fresh ideas. You thereby reduce the risks of going after market leaders, even where limited resources are available.

   1_____10
   Rarely   Occasionally   Frequently

3. You deliberately employ indirect approaches that distract the competing manager into making false moves and costly mistakes.

   1_____10
   Rarely   Occasionally   Frequently

4. You intentionally avoid getting entangled in direct confrontations with competitors, which would result in the unnecessary draining of resources.

   1_____10
   Rarely   Occasionally   Frequently

Part 2: Symptoms the Strategy Functions Ineffectively

1. You fail to develop indirect strategies that outthink, outmaneuver, and outperform competitors.

   1_____10
   Frequently   Occasionally   Rarely

2. You neglect to probe for unserved market niches where there is minimal resistance from competitors—and where opportunities exist to establish a foothold and expand into a mainstream market.

   1_____10
   Frequently   Occasionally   Rarely

3. Personnel do not rely on competitor intelligence to formulate an indirect strategy.

   1_____10
   Frequently   Occasionally   Rarely

(Continued)

TABLE A.1 (CONTINUED)
Strategy Assessment Tool

---

4. You lack a benchmarking system to periodically evaluate strengths, weaknesses, or best practices, which can then be used to develop indirect strategies.

1_____10

Frequently   Occasionally   Rarely

5. You do not use an organized approach to utilize big data to develop indirect approaches to enter markets or defend against an aggressive competitor.

1_____10

Frequently   Occasionally   Rarely

Part 3: Remedial Actions Based on Parts 1 and 2

Parts 1 and 2 provide qualitative assessments of your ability to maneuver by indirect strategy. Based on your team's evaluation, use the following remedies to apply corrective actions:

- Use a strengths, weaknesses, opportunities, threats (SWOT) examination, or other comparative analysis tool, to help you determine which indirect strategies to employ.
- Institute checkpoints to confirm that your indirect strategies are moving you from your current competitive position toward your new objective. Make shifts quickly and assertively according to your findings.
- Use all available data to interpret your market position. Such input provides additional clues to the development of your indirect strategies and to the determination of a culminating point for your campaign.
- Find an unattended, poorly served, or emerging market segment as a decisive target in which to implement an indirect strategy for market expansion.

---

[a] For best results, each member of the team or group would initially score the statements privately. The individuals would convene and discuss the ratings. Where there is wide divergence of opinions, individuals would again rank the statements privately in a second round. They would reconvene for further discussion until there is consensus. For greater accuracy, each statement can be weighted in terms of importance.

Presidents and senior-level managers of small and midsize firms would seek to

- Motivate their staff to innovate with fresh strategies and not repeat yesterday's actions
- Instill discipline and training so that employees do not cave in against difficult marketplace and competitive conditions, especially against larger rivals
- Foster team solidarity and a winning spirit
- Inform the staff of competitors' aggressive moves and create a sense of urgency to develop countermeasures against potential attacks

All Organizations

Human resource and training managers would aim to reach groups of employees with customized skill development content with the following purposes:

- Strengthen a core training program through blended learning
- Reinforce continuous self-development beyond formal training
- Add a skill-building component to entrepreneurial training programs
- Maintain employee involvement in the ongoing self-improvement process

Then, there are specific applications, such as assisting marketing and sales personnel to bolster positive relationships and interactions with customers by introducing content for the following purposes:

- Reinforce strong relationships with customers
- Prolong the life cycle of a product or service by providing ongoing updates about digital applications, industry trends, and technical data
- Maintain meaningful communications with customers that reduce the chance of customers shifting to a competitor

SUMMARY

An organized and embedded internal communications network is intended to accomplish what Peter Drucker pointed out earlier (Chapter 3) as "fulfilling employees' need for recognition, respect, trust, and growth."

Recognition. Employees need to be recognized for their contribution. Where major changes are made, or an organization shifts direction, employees must be assured that changes are not a result of or reflection on their performance.

Respect. Individuals in the organization must continue to be treated with respect. One way of providing this is to continually communicate why ongoing change is necessary. This is especially important as the transition to the digital age accelerates.

Trust. One way of maintaining trust is to communicate to employees that changes will be consistent with the organization's vision, strategic direction, objectives, and strategy.

Growth. Organizations must continue to provide both managers and employees with an opportunity to learn and grow. Change is intended as a positive opportunity to provide personal learning and growth opportunities.

References

Chambers, J. Interview. http://www.mckinsey.com/industries/high-tech/our-insights/ciscos-john-chambers-on-the-digital-era.

Fortune.com/adsections

Immelt, J. General Electric. http://www.ge.com/about-us/leadership/jeff-immelt.

Lashinsky, A. Becoming Tim Cook. *Fortune*. April 1, 2015.

Murray, A. GE's Immelt Signals End to 7 Decades of Globalization. *Fortune*. May 20, 2016. http://fortune.com/2016/05/20/ge-immelt-globalization/.

Nadella, S. Cloud Platform. Washington, D.C., November 16, 2015.

Wahba, P. Inside Tiffany's Plan to Rebuild Its Luxury Watch Business. *Fortune*. September 12, 2015. http://fortune.com/2015/09/12/tiffany-luxury-watches/.

Wahba, P. The CEO Who's Reinventing J.C. Penney. *Fortune*. March 1, 2016.

Index

Page numbers followed by f and t indicate figures and tables, respectively.

A

Abercrombie & Fitch, 56
Accenture, 46
Action, 18
Active cross-functional teams, 181
Active participation, 191
Additional market, 213, 229, 242
Aeropostale, 88
Agents
  assessment, 29
  broadcasting agents, 31
  competitors' agents, 30
  credible agents, 31–32
  double agents, 30–31
  related questions, 32
  unintentional agents, 29
Aggressive competitor, 245
Aggressively led firm, 134, 136
Agile organization
  and effective performance
    barrier removal, 185–186
    collaboration, 184–185
    decision making, 188–189
    empowerment to act, 189
    failure functions as learning
      experience, 190–194
    mobilization speed, 183–184
    nimbleness, 184
    resilience, 190
    responsiveness, 187–188
  overview, 179–180
  and preparedness, 180–182
Agility
  about, 11
  defined, 179
  loss of, 191
Ahrendts, Angela, 126
Airbnb, 36
Alertness, 192

Algorithms
  behavior of competitors, 7–8
  consumer preferences, 4
Alibaba, 71–73, 77, 79, 80
Alliance, 17
Alphabet, 83
Amazon, 16, 45, 71, 77, 83, 87, 133, 146
Amazon Web Services (AWS), 133
Ambition, 22
American Apparel, 56
American Management Association, 90
American Superconductor, 27
Analytical software, consumer
    preferences, 4
Ann Taylor, 88
Anxiety, 109
Apple Computer, 17, 113, 118, 120, 123,
    125–126
  case study, 184
  data security, 26–27
  innovation, 45
Apple Pay, 125
Apple University, 125
Apple Watch, 125
Applications usage, data, 36–42
  company's performance, 40–42
  competitive problems, 39–40
  competitive strategy, 39
  competitor's performance, 40
  internal planning, 37–38
  organizational procedures
    and processes, 38
The Art of War, 63, 170–171
Assembly line, 167
Assumptions, 215–216; *see also* Tactical
    objectives
AT&T, 177
Attacker, 154–155
Attributes for activation of organization,
    182 (exh)

Authoritarian leadership style, 98, 164
Automotive industry, 180
Awareness, 130–131
AWS, *see* Amazon Web Services (AWS)

B

Bankruptcy, 44, 64–65, 86
Barbie dolls, 50
BASF, 176
Beliefs, 128–129
Bell, Alexander Graham, 76
Bell Lab, 76–77
Belonging needs, 97
Bergh, Chris, 85
Bezos, Jeff, 133
Big data; *see also* Data
    business intelligence, 24
    competition, 7
    consumer preferences, 7
    corporate culture and, 88,
        136–141
    organizational structure, 12
Birdseye, Clarence, 76
Blankfein, Lloyd, 129
Blocking, defensive strategy, 152–153
BMW, 113, 114, 118, 176
Boeing, 132
Boeing/Rockwell, data security,
        27
Boldness, 9
Boston Consulting Group, 169
Bounty, 5
Boyd, John, 104–105
Brennan, Megan, 87
Broadcasting agents, 31
Budgets, 219–221
Burberry, 126
Business intelligence, 24–26
    common issues, 25
    functions, 25
    people part of, 28–32
    questions for employing agents, 32
Business–military connection, 65, 66,
        169–171
Business plan
    developing, 3, 15–16
    guidelines, 16
    strategic, *see* Strategic business plan

Business secrets; *see also* Agents
    college classrooms, 29
    professional meetings, 29, 30
    revealing, 29
    stealing, 26–27
    trade shows, 29, 30
Business unit
    competitive strategy, 1, 9–10
    corporate culture, 1, 10–11
    digital technology, 1, 7–8
    organizational structure, 1, 11–15
    perceptions and attitudes, 14
    strategic business plan, 1, 15–17
    working environment, 15
Buyer behavior, 227–228;
        see also Segmentation
        on customers/competitors

C

Campaign plans, 241–246
Canon, 144
Careerbuilder, 97
Caterpillar, 148
Central markets, 235
Challenging market, 235, 237t
Chambers, John, T., 16–17, 52, 60, 126, 159
Character, 21–22
Chevrolet, 168
Chicago Mercantile Exchange, 27
Chinese consumers, 71–72
Chip manufacturing operations, 17
Chrysler, 167
Cisco Systems, 16–17, 24, 52, 60, 126, 159
Cloud renting system, 133
Coaching, 3
Coca-Cola, 143
Cognizant, 46
Coke, 143–144, 152
Collaboration, 21, 134, 184–185;
        see also Agile organization
College classrooms, business secrets and,
        29
Commitment, 242
Communications
    defensive/offensive strategies, 152
    digitization and, 8
    exchanges of information, 131
    review, 212

skills, 187
speed and, 89, 99–100, 116
Company's performance, 40–42
Comparative analysis, 69, 229
Competitive assumptions, 216
Competitive campaigns, 43, 46, 246
   defensive, *see* Defensive strategies
   destabilizing effect, 116–119
   failed, causes, 107–108
   increasing competitor's expenditure,
      54
   offensive, *see* Offensive strategies
   preparing successive campaigns, 51–52
   primary elements, 147–149
   types of, 119
Competitive encounters, 245, 246
Competitive marketplace, 187
Competitive problems, 39–40
Competitive strategy, 1, 9–10, 39;
        see also Digital age
   applications, 68
   bold action and shifting
      to the offensive, 9
   concentration at a decisive point, 9,
      63–81
   corporate strategy, 67–68
   lower-level strategy/tactics, 68
   maneuver by indirect approach, 9
   midlevel strategy, 68
   military strategy, 65–67
   origins of, 64–68
   positioning, *see* Positioning
   for small and midsize organizations,
      73–81
   speed, *see* Speed
   terminology, strategy, 64
Competitor analysis, 213
Competitors, 34–35
   agents, 30
   aggressive, 138
   agile organization and, 180, 181, 188
   decision-making capabilities, 105
   destabilizing, 116–121
   effectiveness, reducing, 52–54
   expenditure, increasing, 54
   intelligence, 153
   neutralizing, 43, 49–57
   performance, 40
   psychological dimension, 105–106

strength of, 49–50
   weakening, 49–51, 70
   wearing down, 54–57
Competitor's weaknesses, 242
Complacency, 84
Concentration; *see also* Competitive strategy
   at decisive points, 63–81
   developing and monitoring, 70–73
   ineffective application, 71
   neutralization and, 59
   overview, 9
The Concept of the Corporation, 169
Confidence, 13, 93–94
Confidential information, 26–28
Confrontations, 64, 94–95
   head-on, 69–70
Conservative firm, 134
Consumers/customers, 33
   Chinese, 71–72
   loyalty, 85, 111, 113
   need, 53, 88
   preferences, 4
   problem solving, 78
Contingency plans, 14, 181
Cook, Tim, 123, 125–126, 128
Corporate culture, 1, 3, 10–11, 194, 249;
        see also Digital age
   attributes, 128–133
   beliefs, 128–129
   big data and, 88, 136–141
   defensive, *see* Defensive strategies
   defining, 126–127
   employee treatment and expectations,
      129–133
   energizing, 137–141
   Google, 10–11
   offensive, *see* Offensive strategies
   profile, developing, 133–136
   speed and, 95
   values, 128–129
Corporate strategy, 67–68;
        see also Competitive strategy
Cost, of competitor, 54; *see also*
      Neutralization, competitors
Costco, 6, 72
Courage, 157, 189
Creativity, 137
Credible agents, 31–32
Credit, 218

Crest, 5
Critical thinking, 115
Cross-functional teams, 78
    duties and responsibilities, 130
C-suite leaders, 19, 89, 94, 129
Culminating point, applications, 241–247;
        see also Leadership at culminating
        point of competitive campaign
Culture, corporate, 194
Customers, 202–203, 224–225
Cybersecurity, 23, 24; *see also* Data security

D

Data
    applications, 36–42;
        see also Applications usage, data
    big, *see* Big data
    management's participation, 38
    reliability, 26
    resides, 33–36; *see also* Operating arena
Data analytics, 229
    business intelligence, 24
    concentration at decisive points, 63–81
    market intelligence, 90
    market vulnerabilities, 8
    organizational structure, 12
    planning process, 38
    proposal submitting, 89
Data security, 26–28; *see also* Business
        intelligence; Business secrets
    broadcasting agents, 31
    competitors' agents, 30
    credible agents, 31–32
    cybersecurity, 23, 24
    double agents, 30–31
    maintaining, 28
    unintentional agents, 29
Decision making, 186, 188–189
Decisive points
    concentration at, 63–81
    selecting, 69
Defender, 245
Defensive strategies, 3, 6, 117;
        see also Offensive strategies
    advantages and disadvantages, 145–147
    applying, 151
    blocking, 152–153
    moving to offensive, 153–155

overview, 143–144
    phases, 149–155
    relationship with offensive, 147–149
    time and, 144
    waiting, 150–152
De Jomini, Baron Antoine-Henri, 65, 157
Deletion, 217
Delivery network, 87
Dell Computer (case study), 120, 133, 235
Deloitte, 46
Denim market, 84–85
Determination, 189
Detroit, 65
Development, 217
Differentiation, 217
Difficult markets, 236, 237t
Digital age
    business intelligence, 24–26
    changes of operating, 3
    competitive strategy, 1, 9–10;
        see also Competitive strategy
    considerations, 4
    corporate culture, 1, 10–11;
        see also Corporate culture
    digital technology, 1, 7–8
    millennials of, 96–101
    organizational structure,
        see Organizational structure
    strategic business plan, 1, 15–17;
        see also Strategic business plan
Digital camera, 44, 118
Digital communications, 187
Digital marketing, energy of, *see* Energy
        of digital marketing
Digital organization, 177–178;
        see also Organization
Digital photography, 44, 86
Digital technology, 1, 7–8; *see also* Digital
        age
    business intelligence, 23–42
    data security, 26–28; *see also* Business
        secrets; Data security
    developing effective leadership,
        see Leadership, effective
    morale with, 251–254
    neutralization, competitors, 49–60
Digitization, 7–8, 12, 181
Dignity, 13
Direct approaches, maneuver, 103–104

Direction, 18
Direct leadership, 18–19;
    see also Leadership, effective
Discipline, 20–21
Disco Corp., 127
Disney, 50–51, 52, 56
Dissatisfaction, factors leading to, 98
Dissatisfiers, 98
Diversification, 46, 210, 217
Dorsey, Jack, 53–54
Double agents, 30–31
Dow AgroSciences, 27
Dow Chemical, 12
  data security, 27
Drucker, Peter, 13, 115, 168–169
DuPont, data security, 27
Dynamic competitive environment,
    137–138

E

Eastman Kodak Co., 44, 86, 118–119
Economic assumptions, 216
Edison, Thomas, 76
Ellison, Marvin, 103, 111–112, 113, 116
Emotions, 107–112
  anxiety, 109
  fear, 110–112
  frustration, 109–110
  negative, 109
  positive, 108–109
  stress, 110
Employee morale, 247; *see also* Morale,
    building
Employee ownership, 140
Employee treatment and expectations,
    129–133
  key listening areas, 132
Empowerment to act, 189; *see also* Agile
    organization
Encircled markets, 236, 237t
Energy of digital marketing;
    see also Segmentation
    on customers/competitors
  monitoring of digital systems, 226
  success measurement, 226–227
  technology application, 225–226
  understanding customers, 224–225
Espionage, 26–28; *see also* Business secrets

Estee Lauder, 71
Esteem needs, 97
Executive summary in plan, 219
Exhaustion, 184
Expenditure, of competitor, 54;
    see also Neutralization,
    competitors
Expertise, 201
Exploratory campaigns, 244

F

Facebook, 83, 132
Failed campaign, 107–108
Failure, as learning experience, 190
Fairlife, 143
Fear, 110–112
Feedback, 140
Feedback loop, 226
Fiat Chrysler Automobiles (case study),
    180
Field managers, 186
Financial controls and budgets, 219–221
Flexible managerial style, 6;
    see also Leadership, effective
Ford (example), 180
Ford, Henry, 76, 166–167
Ford Motor, data security, 27
Forecast models, 220
Foxconn, 154
Frederick the Great, 67, 121
Friction, 184, 185
Frustration, 109–110
Fujifilm (case study), 44, 200–202
Functional objectives, 216–218;
    see also Tactical objectives
FunLab, 51
Fuze, 143

G

Gap, 88
Genentech, 132
General Electric, 18, 19, 45, 89, 93, 137,
    145–146, 151, 169
General Motors, 167–168
  business strategy, 180
  case study, 183
  industry forecasts and, 180

German automakers, 120
Gillette, 5
Globalization, 181
Goldman Sachs, 129
Goldner, Brian, 50
Goodyear Tire & Rubber, data security, 27
Google Inc., 1, 16, 77, 80, 113, 118, 134, 176
    culture, 10–11, 13, 129
    data security, 27
    innovation, 45
GoPayment, 53
Government/environment, 35–36
Growth, 80–81

H

Hackers, 26
Haier Group, 91–92, 93
H&M, 88
Hardworking, 134
Hart, B. H. Liddell, 65, 103, 169, 170
Hasbro, 50–51, 52
Hawthorne effect, 162
Hawthorne Works, 162
Head-on confrontation, 69–70
Henderson, Bruce, 169, 170
Herzberg, Frederick, 97
Herzberg's motivation-hygiene theory, 98
Hewlett-Packard, 134
High-risk culture, 136
Historical review, organization, 171–176;
    see also Organization
    1950s, 171–172
    1960s, 172
    1970s, 172–174
    1980s, 174–175
    1990s, 175–176
    2000s, 176
Honda, 94, 96
Honest Tea, 143
Human nature, 252
Human relations school, 164–165
Human resource development
    and training, 218
Hygiene factors, 98

I

IBM, 45, 46, 77, 120, 133, 146
"Imagination Breakthrough" proposals, 89, 137
Immelt, Jeffrey, 145–146, 151
Impulsive micromanaging, 125
"Incredibly scrappy" (culture), 10
Indirect maneuver, 103–104, 148, 149, 169
    activating, 112–121
Information, free flow of, 187;
    see also Agile organization
Innovation, 45–46, 137
    criteria, 76
    morale interfaces with, 249–250
    sales life of a product and, 87
    sustaining, 75–80
    vision and, 74
Innovative thinking, 192
Innovators, 188
Insecurity, 183
Integration, information, 115
Intel, 77, 86
Intellect, 189
Intelligence, 233
    competitors, 153
    people part of, 28–32; *see also* Business intelligence
Intermediaries, 34
Internal communications network, model, 257–267
Internal planning, 37–38
Internal sources, 36
Internet of things, 203
Intuition, 190
Inward-focused firm, 136
iPhone, 17
iPhone 6, 125
iPhone 6 Plus, 125
Itochu Corp., 127

J

J. Crew, 88
Japanese automakers, 120
JCPenney, 103, 111–112
Jeans, 84
Jobs, Steve, 125
Job satisfaction, 98

John Deere & Co., 24–25
Johnson, Ron, 111
Johnson & Johnson, 21
Joint venture, 242
Joint venture obligations, 117

K

Kalil, Tom, 43
Key accounts, 218
Key markets, 233–234, 237t
Key performance indicators (KPIs), 18, 37
Kohl's, 21, 56
Kotler, Philip, 77, 170
KPI, *see* Key performance indicators (KPIs)
Kroger, 6

L

Lafley, A. G., 5–6
Leadership, 192, 193, 195
Leadership, effective; *see also* Digital age
    ambition, 22
    challenges, 4
    character, 21–22
    characteristics of, 17–22
    communications, 89
    competitive strategy, 1, 9–10
    corporate culture, 1, 10–11
    digital technology, 1, 7–8
    direct leadership, 18–19
    discipline, 20–21
    flexible role, 6
    function as, 5
    key areas, 3
    levels of, 18–22
    Nadella on, 24
    organizational leadership, 19
    organizational structure, 1, 11–15
    as pivotal factor, 4–5
    strategic business plan, 1, 15–17
    strategic leadership, 19–22
Leadership and strategic business
        planning
    components of
        about, 199–200
        financial controls and budgets,
            219–221
        market opportunities, 214–215

    objectives, 204–207, 205t–206t,
        215–218
    portfolio of products and services,
        208, 210–211
    situation analysis, 212–214
    strategic direction or vision,
        200–204
    strategies, 207–208, 209t
    strategies and tactics, 218–219
    overview, 197–199
Leadership at culminating point
        of campaign
    culminating point, applications,
        241–247
    morale, building
        about process, 247–249, 250t
        morale interfaces with innovation,
            249, 250
        morale with digital technology,
            relationship of, 251–254
    overview, 239–241
Leadership role
    Chambers, John, 16–17
    Cook, Tim, 125–126
    Dorsey, Jack, 53–54
    Ellison, Marvin, 111–112
    Ford, Henry, 76, 166–167
    Immelt, Jeffrey, 145–146
    Lafley, A. G., 5–6
    Liveris, Andrew, 12
    Robbins, Chuck, 16–17
    Rockefeller, John D., 166
    Sloan, Alfred P., 167–168
    Welch, Jack, 18–19
Leadership style
    authoritarian, 98, 164
    flexible, 6; *see also* Leadership, effective
    participative approach, 98
Leading-edge markets, 115, 233, 237t
Lee, 84
LEGO Group, 80, 81
Levi Strauss & Co., 84–85
Life cycle, product, 87, 95–96
    shortening, 114
    stages of, 232
Limited-term campaigns, 245
LinkedIn, 97
Linked markets, 234–235, 237t
Live-and-let-live approach, 48, 53

Liveris, Andrew, 12
Liz Claiborne, 113
Lockheed Martin, 21, 27
Lonely Crowd, 162
Longhi, Mario, 91
Long-term strategic objectives, 119
Loss of interest, 48
Loss of morale, 47–48
Loss of physical resources, 47
Lower-level strategy/tactics, 68;
      see also Competitive strategy
Loyalty, 15, 17, 50, 85, 111, 113

M

Ma, Jack, 72
Machiavelli, Niccolò, 65, 66
Mackey, John, 6–7
Macy's, 71
Management seminars, 29
Managerial chain of command, 186
Maneuver
    aim of, 105
    direct *vs.* indirect approaches, 103–104
    emotions, 107–112
    by indirect approach, 9
    indirect maneuver, activating, 112–121
    psychological effect, 104–106
Manufacturing, 218
Market
    background, 213–214
    competitiveness, 203
    development, 210
    extensions, 46
    intelligence, 90
    penetration, 210
    segments, 152
    vulnerabilities, 8, 69
Marketing planning, 175
Marketing research, 218
Marketing Warfare, 170
"Marketing Warfare in the 1980s," 170
Market opportunities; *see also* Leadership
    and strategic business planning
    present markets, 214–215
    targets of, 215
Market position
    building, 138
    competitive campaign and, 147, 149
    lost, 116
    reclaiming, 241
    weakening, 111
Market segment selection, techniques
        for; *see also* Segmentation
        on customers/competitors
    about, 231, 237t
    central markets, 235
    challenging market, 235
    difficult markets, 236
    encircled segments, 236
    key markets, 233–234
    leading-edge markets, 233
    linked markets, 234–235
    natural markets, 232–233
Maslow, Abraham, 97
Maslow's hierarchy of needs, 97
Mass consumption, 167
Mass production, 167
Mattel Inc., 50–51, 52, 56
Mayo, Elton, 164
McGregor, Douglas, 97, 164
McGregor's XY theory, 98–99
Merger and acquisition (M&A), 235
Metrics in digital age, 226
Mickey Mouse Club, 50
Microsoft Corp., 23, 24, 25, 134, 146,
    161
Midlevel strategy, 68, 71;
        see also Competitive strategy
Midsize organizations, strategy
        applications, 73–81
Military–business connection, 65, 66,
    169–171
Military strategy, 65–67
Millennials
    digital age and, 96–101
    overview, 96
Mills, C. Wright, 162
Mizorogi, Hitoshi, 127
Mobilization, speed of, 183
Model T, 167, 168
Modern organization, 161–178;
        see also Organization
    digital organization, 177–178
    evolution, 163–165
    historical review, 171–176
Modification, 45, 217
Momentum, 191

Monitoring, 75, 76
  of digital systems, 226
Monster, 97
Morale, 50, 51, 96, 154
Morale, building; *see also* Leadership
      at culminating point
      of competitive campaign
  about process, 247–249, 250t
  importance of, 247
  morale interfaces with innovation,
      249, 250
  morale with digital technology,
      relationship of, 251–254
Motivation, 18
Motivators, 98
Motorola, 27
My Little Pony, 50

N

Nadella, Satya, 23–24, 32, 36, 161
Napa Valley, 95
Napoleon, 67, 106
Natural markets, 232–233, 237t
Needs
  belonging, 97
  consumer, 53, 88
  esteem, 97
  physiological, 97
  safety, 97
  self-actualization, 97
Negative emotions, 109
Neutralization, competitors, 49–57
  in agile organization, 180, 188, 191
  casual approach, 44
  concentration, 59
  key concepts, 44–45
  making campaign costlier for rival, 54
  morale, 50, 51
  overview, 43–44
  plan, 57–60
  preparing successive campaigns, 51–52
  reducing competitor's effectiveness,
      52–54
  speed, 59–60
  success in, 47–48
  weaken the rival, 49–51
  wearing down, 54–57
Nike, 21

Nimbleness, 184; *see also* Agile
      organization
Nonproduct objectives, 217–218
Nonquantitative objectives, 204
Nooyi, Indra, 111

O

Obligatory commitments, 242
Offensive strategies, 3, 6, 137;
      see also Defensive strategies
  failure, 156–157
  moving to, 153–155
  relationship with defensive, 147–149
Okafuji, Masahiro, 127
On War, 48, 63
"OODA loop," 105
Operating arena
  competitors, 34–35
  customers, 33
  government/environment, 35–36
  intermediaries, 34
  internal sources, 36
Opportunity, 118
Optimum profile for firm, 118, 182f
Oracle, 133, 146
Organic groceries, 6
Organization
  books, 162
  digital, 177–178
  giants of industry, 165–168
  modern, evolution of, 163–165
  panoramic overview, 171–176
  research studies, 162
  thinkings and strategists, 168–171
Organizational Health Index, 181
Organizational layers, 185–186
Organizational leadership, 19;
      see also Leadership, effective
Organizational procedures and processes,
      38
Organizational structure, 1, 3, 11–15;
      see also Digital age
  aim, 11
  defined, 182
  modern organization, 161–178
  physical, 11–13
  psychological, 13–15
Organization Man, 162

P

Packaging objectives, 217
Pampers, 5
Paramount Pictures, 51
Participative approach, 98
PepsiCo, 111
Performance; see also Agile organization
  barrier removal, 185–186
  collaboration, 184–185
  of company, 40–42
  of competitor, 40
  decision making, 188–189
  empowerment to act, 189
  failure functions, 190–194
  historic, 212
  mobilization speed, 183–184
  nimbleness, 184
  resilience, 190
  responsiveness, 187–188
Personality, 183
Physical, organizational structure, 11–13
Physical and psychological strengths, 243t
Physical distribution objectives, 217
Physical energy, 185
Physical exertion, 187
Physical vs. morale losses, 47
Physiological needs, 97
Planning cycle, 175
Planning process, data analytics in,
  see Data analytics
Positioning, 77
  goal of, 79–80
  guidelines, 77–79
Positive emotions, 108–109
Power, of competitors, 49–50
Power of segmentation, 229–230
Predictive analytics, 87
Predix, 146
Preemptive campaigns, 117, 242
Preparedness, 180–182
Present markets, 214–215
Press releases, 30
Pricing, 152
Pricing objectives, 217
Primark, 56–57
Primary financial objectives, 216;
  see also Tactical objectives
Princess dolls, 50

Procter & Gamble (case study), 5, 6, 71, 80,
  81, 246
Product
  development, 210
  idea, 11
  literature, business secrets and, 29, 30
  objectives, 216
  and services, portfolio of, 208,
    210–211
  testing, 5, 6
Product lines
  dropping, 5
  extensions, 45–46
Professional meetings, business secrets
  and, 29
Profile, corporate culture, 133–136
Profitability, 230
Promotion, 140
  objectives, 217
Proposal submitting, 89
Psychological, organizational structure,
  13–15
Psychological effect, maneuver, 104–106
Publix, 140

Q

Qualcomm, 132
Quality objectives, 216
Quantitative objectives, 204

R

Reis, Al, 77, 170
Reliability, data, 26
Remerchandise, 46
Research and development, 218
Resilience, 190; see also Agile organization
Responsibilities, 218
Responsiveness, 187–188; see also Agile
  organization
Ricoh, 144
Riesman, David, 162
Risk, 187
Rival, see Competitors
Robbins, Chuck, 16–17, 24
Rockefeller, John D., 166
Roosevelt, Theodore, 166
Royal Dutch Shell, 95

S

Safety needs, 97
Salary hike, 140
Samsung, 17
Satisfaction, factors leading to, 98
Satisfiers, 98
Schmidt, Eric, 1, 3, 7
Schwab, Klaus, 83
Scrappy culture, 10
Screening, 75, 76
Sears, 8
Secrets, *see* Business secrets
Security, *see* Business intelligence; Data
     security
Segmentation, 217
Segmentation on customers/competitors
    buyer behavior, 227–228
    energy of digital marketing
        monitoring of digital systems,
            226
        success measurement,
            226–227
        technology application,
            225–226
        understanding customers,
            224–225
    market segment selection, techniques for
        about, 231, 237t
        central markets, 235
        challenging market, 235
        difficult markets, 236
        encircled segments, 236
        key markets, 233–234
        leading-edge markets, 233
        linked markets, 234–235
        natural markets, 232–233
    overview, 223–224
    power of segmentation,
        229–230
Selection, 75, 76
Self-actualization needs, 97
Self-confidence, 14, 17–18
Self-motivation, 91
Service objectives, 217
Share of market, retention, 242
Sharp Corp., 127, 144, 153–155
Sherman Antitrust Act, 166
Singh, Ravi, 170

Situation analysis, 212–214;
        see also Leadership and strategic
          business planning
    competitor analysis, 213
    historic performance, 212
    market background, 213–214
Skills, 18
Skype, 161
Skype Translator, 162
Sloan, Alfred P., 167–168
Small organizations, strategy applications,
    73–81
Smartphone shipments, 184
Smith, Jim, 14
Sociopolitical assumptions, 216
Sound management practice, 245
Speed
    barriers to, 91–96
    communications and, 89, 99–100
    complacency and, 84
    corporate culture and, 95
    delivery network, 87
    Herzberg's motivation-hygiene theory,
        98
    implementing, 88–91
    market/corporate conditions, 85–88
    Maslow's hierarchy of needs, 97
    McGregor's XY theory, 98–99
    neutralization and, 59–60
    overview, 9
    for preemptive campaign
        implementation, 242
Square, 53–54
St. John's Bay, 113
Staff and organization, *see* Business unit
Standard Oil, 166
Starbucks, 21
Start-up climate, 12
Strategic business plan, 1, 15–17;
        see also Digital age
    guidelines, 16
    integrating neutralization plan, 58
    1970s, 174
Strategic business planning and
        leadership, *see* Leadership
        and strategic business planning
Strategic direction or vision, 200–204
Strategic leadership, 19–22;
        see also Leadership, effective

Strategic thinking, 112–116
Strategies, 207–208, 209t;
      see also Leadership and strategic
      business planning
  and tactics, 209t, 218–219
Strength, of competitors, 49–50
Stress, 110
Stubbornness, 22
Stumpf, John, 34–35
Success measurement, 226–227
Sun Microsystems, 133
Sun Tzu, 59, 61, 63, 65, 66, 67, 103, 104,
      106, 121, 170–171
Supply chain, 152, 217
Surprise, 147–148
System of control, 186

T

Tactical objectives; *see also* Leadership
      and strategic business planning
  assumptions, 215–216
  functional objectives, 216–218
  primary financial objectives, 216
Tactical section, neutralization plan, 59
Tactics, 208, 209t, 218–219
Tai Jeng Wu, 127
Target, 56
Taylor, Frederick, 163–164, 169
Technical sales activities, 218
Technological assumptions, 216
Technology application, 225–226
Terminology, strategy, 64
Tesla, 45, 113, 118
Testing, product, 5, 6
Theory X, 98, 164
Theory Y, 98, 164
Thinking strategically, 112–116
Thomson Reuters, 14
Thucydides, 67
Tide, 5
Time, defensive strategy and, 144, 145
Top-down structure, 134
Toyada, Akio, 127
Toyota Motor Corp., 127
Toy shopping, 51
Trade shows, business secrets and, 29, 30

Training and orientation, 3, 71, 93, 125
Transformers, 50
Trout, Jack, 77, 170
Trust, 15

U

Uber, 35–36, 45, 114
Ullman, Mike, 111
Unintentional agents, 29
Uniqlo, 88
"Universal car," 167
U.S. International Trade Commission, 44
U.S. Postal Service (USPS), 87

V

Values, 128–129
Vision, 74
von Clausewitz, Carl, 48, 63, 65, 67, 81, 170

W

Waiting, defensive strategy, 150–152
Walmart, 6, 56, 92, 120, 176
Wavell, Archibald, 106
Welch, Jack, 18–19
Wells Fargo, 34
Whirlpool, 44
White Collar Workers, 162
Whole Foods, 6
Whyte, William, 162
Working environment, 15
Wrangler, 84

X

Xerox, 120, 144–145

Y

Yamaha Motor, 95

Z

Zara, 88
Zico, 143

About the Author

Norton Paley has brought his world-class experience and unique approach to business strategy to some of the global community's most respected organizations.

Having launched his career with publishing giants *McGraw-Hill* and *John Wiley & Sons*, Paley founded *Alexander-Norton Inc.*, bringing successful business techniques to clients around the globe including the international training organization *Strategic Management Group*, where he served as a senior consultant.

Throughout his career, Paley has trained business managers and their staff in the areas of planning and strategy development, raising the bar for achievement and forging new approaches to problem solving and competitive edge.

His clients include

- American Express
- IBM
- Detroit Edison
- Chrysler (Parts Division)
- McDonnell-Douglas
- Dow Chemical (Worldwide)
- W.R. Grace
- Cargill (Worldwide)
- Chevron Chemical
- Ralston-Purina
- Johnson & Johnson
- USG
- Celanese
- Hoechst
- Mississippi Power
- Numerous mid-sized and small firms

Paley has lectured in The Republic of China and Mexico and he's presented training seminars throughout the Pacific Rim and Europe for Dow Chemical and Cargill.

As a seminar leader at the American Management Association, he conducted competitive strategy, marketing management, and strategic planning programs for over 20 years.

Published books include

- Developing a Turnaround Business Plan: Leadership Techniques to Achieve Change Strategies, Secure Competitive Advantage, and Preserve Success
- Clausewitz Talks Business: An Executive's Guide to Thinking Like a Strategist
- How to Outthink, Outmaneuver and Outperform Your Competitors: Lessons from the Masters of Strategy
- Mastering the Rules of Competitive Strategy: A Resource Guide for Managers
- The Marketing Strategy Desktop Guide, 2nd Edition
- How to Develop A Strategic Marketing Plan*
- The Managers Guide to Competitive Marketing Strategies, 3rd Edition
- Marketing for the Nonmarketing Executive: An Integrated Management Resource Guide for the 21st Century
- Successful Business Planning: Energizing Your Company's Potential
- Manage to Win†
- Big Ideas for Small Businesses

On the cusp of the interactive movement, Paley developed three computer-based, interactive training systems: *The Marketing Learning Systems; Segmentation, Targeting & Positioning;* and *The Marketing Planning System.*

Paley's books have been translated into Chinese, Russian, Portuguese, and Turkish.

His byline columns have appeared in *The Management Review* and *Sales & Marketing Management* magazines.

---

* "This book is both intellectual and practical...an interesting vehicle for presenting detailed planning concepts...it is clear and well-organized." T.J. Belich, in CHOICE. Also Selected for translation into Chinese and Turkish.
† "A book too forceful to Ignore." Review in *Business Line, Financial Daily for The Hindu Group of Publications.*

The following are excerpts from reviews of books by Norton Paley:

A book too forceful to ignore.

> **Review in** *Business Line, Financial Daily for The Hindu Group of Publications* **about Paley's** *Manage to Win*

This book is both intellectual and practical...an interesting vehicle for presenting detailed planning concepts...it is clear and well-organized.

> **T.J. Belich, in CHOICE about Paley's** *How to Develop a Strategic Marketing Plan*

9781498764148